THE GENTLE CRAFT

Although it was probably conceived as a trilogy, only the first two parts of Thomas Deloney's prose romance were completed, dealing with the origins of the shoemaker's trade and how it succeeded in London. *The Gentle Craft* is best known as the principal source of Thomas Dekker's *The Shoemaker's Holiday*. But Deloney's tale of cobbler Simon Eyre, who founded Leadenhall, the centre of the leather trade, and rose to be Lord Mayor of London, is itself significant for its adaption of euphemistic romances and jestbooks. In this volume Simon Barker offers in modern typography, with explanatory notes and an extensive introduction, an account of the sources and influence of the book, its publication history and what is known of its author. He suggests that Deloney's combination of romance with the practical morality of an emerging social class produced a text that is uniquely important for those interested in late-Elizabethan popular culture.

NON-CANONICAL EARLY MODERN
POPULAR TEXTS

Series Editor
John Simons

In recent years it has become broadly accepted that the central texts of English literature don't provide adequate materials for the critical study of the history of literary production and readership, a subject of growing interest. However, the availability of other texts, particularly from the early modern period, remains very limited. This series is designed to meet the demand for modern editions of non-canonical texts, concentrating on the period c. 1580 – c. 1650.

The Gentle Craft

Ac

1

2

3

4

5

Edited by
SIMON BARKER
University of Gloucestershire, UK

Sel

Ina

Routledge
Taylor & Francis Group
LONDON AND NEW YORK

Acknowledgements

I should like to acknowledge the support of a research leave grant from the Arts and Humanities Research Board in the preparation of this volume and the assistance given by library staff at the Biblioteka Gdańska in Poland, the University of Gloucestershire and the University of Winchester. For various kinds of help I am also in debt to Erika Gaffney, Linda Hutjens, John Simons, Monika Smialkowska, and Beryl Steel. This volume is dedicated to Alex and Jack Barker.

1

Introduction

Thomas Deloney's *The Gentle Craft* has long been regarded as an important prose work from the closing years of the sixteenth century, yet its significance has hitherto been determined almost solely by the status given it as the source for Thomas Dekker's play, *The Shoemaker's Holiday* (1599). More recently, however, prose works and other non-dramatic popular forms (such as the kind of ballad with which Deloney's name is also associated) have attracted considerable critical attention in their own right and not simply for their relationship with the contemporary drama. The present series testifies to the way in which critics and publishers have revisited non-canonical early modern popular texts for their literary merit and generic innovation. In the case of prose works such as *The Gentle Craft* it is possible to discover in them the beginnings of the literary form that is to gestate into the novel – long before the more universally recognized contributions of Daniel Defoe, Henry Fielding and Tobias Smollet.

Moreover, as criticism turned in the last twenty years or so to consider popular (but non-canonical) texts, just as it did, say, to the previously 'marginal' texts by women writers, it had to come to terms with a literary history that had obscured or undervalued such writing.[1] Inherent in the production of any new edition of a text such as *The Gentle Craft* are those questions of aesthetics that often determined a lowly place for such works in the taxonomies established by earlier generations. For these reasons, this introduction begins with an attempt to describe the sheer appeal of *The Gentle Craft* before turning to what we know of the life of its author and to matters of narrative, form, and textual history.

A case can surely be made to the modern reader for a sustained and enjoyable engagement with *The Gentle Craft*. One obvious aspect of its appeal is to do with the way that the text resonates with the substance of everyday life. Here, if anywhere in the writing of the period, is to be found an account, however romanticized, of the precise detail of the way that life was lived for certain groups of Londoners almost half a millennium ago. While

---

1   It might be said that a key component in the development of the novel is Aphra Behn's *Oroonoko* (1688), a popular text which, along with many others produced by women in the early modern period, remained obscure until relatively recently.

The Gentle Craft remains a work of fiction, there is a firm sense of realism that is convincing enough to suggest that this is a fairly authentic encounter with long dead Londoners, working through their aspirations and set-backs, their petty grievances and their huge desires. Part of this effect is due to the strong evocation of place. This is a London now submerged by cultural change and physical redevelopment, yet still traceable to a degree in the streets of the present-day city. Indeed the idea of place is perhaps most clearly defined in *The Gentle Craft* when one reads in the text of certain streets or districts, whose names we recognize, that were often still separated from each other by fields and by distances measured by walking or on horseback. Deloney's London was, of course, perhaps the most important centre in Europe for the publication, printing, distribution and consumption of the written word. It is therefore unsurprising that the city itself is the subject of much of what is being written – and that this writing inspired a theatre that both complements and compliments these other forms. Yet in *The Gentle Craft*, London is captured in a particular period of its evolution that is coming to a close as Deloney is writing. It is not that the text is simply nostalgic about a passing London, and still less is it an evocation of a kind of fading 'Merry England' – as the constant references to warfare and poverty demonstrate. Rather, its style (a version of reportage rather than verisimilitude) seems to be the product of a need somehow to arrest and record places and people – and the stories that unite them – in the face of the accelerating change that characterized the last years of Tudor England.

In order to do this, Deloney employed a narrative technique that further underlines the appeal of the text. It is hard to quantify (and remains of course a question of individual judgement) but an argument in favour of *The Gentle Craft* can surely be made on aesthetic grounds. Along with all its socio-political insight, and its openness to students of class and commerce, gender and geography, this is a text that also invites investigation because of its consistent sense of good humour, constant vitality, and an elaborate celebration of the human spirit. It is worth repeating that this is not an idealized world, but one where the spirit seems to have to remain optimistic since despair, destitution and danger are never far away.

Deloney left the first two parts of what was almost certainly planned as a trilogy. In Part I he outlines the mythical origins of the shoemaker's trade, recounting the legend of Hugh and Winifred, patron saints of shoemaking. He then tells the story of the shoemaking princes Crispianus and Crispine, and lastly, moving from legend to 'history', describes the spectacular rise of Simon Eyre to Lord Mayor of London, including along the way numerous romantic intrigues and subplots set in and around Eyre's expanding household. A significant governing theme is the belief in the essential nobility of the shoemaker. In folklore a shoemaker is likely to be an exiled prince

Catholicism. Gabriel Harvey, in *Pierce's Supererogation* (1593), advised Thomas Nashe to 'boast lesse with Thomas Delone, or to atchieve more with Thomas More', a statement that points to the position occupied by Deloney in the perceived intellectual hierarchy of London. The lost *Ballad on the Want of Corn* mentioned in John Stowe's *A Survey of London* (1598) seems to have got Deloney into trouble, attention being drawn not only to the ballad's seeming encouragement of discontent amongst the people in this year of food shortages, but also to the whole business of the licensing and printing of such material. *Epistle to Martin Mar-Sixtus* (1592) may have applied to Deloney. It laments that 'every red-nosed rimester is an author, every drunken man's dream is a booke, and he whose talent of little wit is hardly worth a farthing, yet layeth about him so outragiously, as if all Helicon had run through his pen, in a word, scarce a cat can look out of a gutter, but starts a halfpenny chronicler and presently A propper new ballet of a strange sight is endited'.

Deloney is best known today for his three extremely popular prose narratives: *The Most Pleasant and Delectable Historie of John Winchcombe, otherwise called Jack of Newberie*; *Thomas of Reading* (both probably written around 1596); and *The Gentle Craft*, likely to have been written and published between 1596 and 1598.[5] William Kemp, writing in *Nine Daies Wonder* (April, 1600), recalled him as a 'great Ballad-maker' and 'Chronicler of the memorable lives of the Six Yeomen of the west, Jack of Newbury, the Gentle Craft, &c., and such like honest men, omitted by Stow, Hollinshed, Grafton, Halle, Froissart, and all the rest of those well deserving writers.' In a poignant but characteristically mischievous note Kemp added that 'I was given to understand, your late general, Thomas, died poorly (as ye all must do) and was honestly buried, which is much to be doubted of some of you.'[6]

Narrative and Genre

The various interweaving stories that comprise *The Gentle Craft* are evidence of the rich mythology and folklore that underpinned the craft of shoemaking. Other trades (and especially weaving) had similar traditions about their origins and values, some of which have survived to the present day as part of the heritage of craftsmen and craftswomen at work in modern manufacturing. In Deloney's time these elements gave each trade an historical resonance, equivalent, say, to the narratives of aristocratic romance, and yet they also had a topical vitality. It might be said that the health and stability of a particular trade could be measured by the credibility of its folklore – and

---

5   *The Most Pleasant and Delectable Historie of John Winchcombe, otherwise called Jack of Newberie* was entered in the Stationers' Register in 1597 and *Thomas of Reading* in 1600. See 'Notes on the Text' for publishing history of *The Gentle Craft*.

6   See *Social England Illustrated (an English Garner)*, Vol. VII, p. 36.

how widely it was understood and transmitted within the community of a particular trade's practitioners.

The Gentle Craft consolidates the mythical stories of early shoemakers (reinforcing a sense that all shoemakers have an essential 'nobility'), but then shows them operating in the 'real' hierarchies of late medieval and early modern England. Just as hard work, business acumen and good fortune can push shoemakers and their extended families up the social ladder, laziness, profligacy and bad luck can pull them down. In the case of shoemaking and *The Gentle Craft*, a firm connection can be observed at work between the social, economic and general historical context of the text's production, and the form in which it was written.

In terms of genre, critics have seen texts such as *The Gentle Craft* as reflecting a largely metropolitan change in taste, readership and appeal that signalled the end of Elizabethan 'late-medieval' romance and pointed ahead to the early novel form of the late seventeenth and early eighteenth centuries. Indeed *The Gentle Craft* is commonly seen as evidence of an expanding readership's weariness with the existing tradition of courtly romance exemplified by the work of writers such as Edmund Spenser, John Lyly and Philip Sidney. Public taste, sometimes described as 'middle class', was switching to pamphlets about London street life or popular culture in general by writers such as Nashe, Greene and Dekker. Deloney combined features of this kind of writing with the earlier romantic tradition so that 'knights' became artisans and their heroic deeds became more realistic. James Ruoff has described this phenomenon thus:

> Deloney retained much of the polyphonic narration and vagarious events and characterizations still attractive about the courtly romances, but he made ingenious improvisations on the old values by glorifying the craft of shoemaker or weaver as thoroughly as Sidney and Spenser had apotheosized true courtesy. Deloney turned the knights and ladies of the courtly romances into fun-loving artisans and lively wenches, and placed them in the familiar environs of Berkshire, Norwich, or London rather than in Fairyland or Mauritania.[7]

Critical debate over this work has for a long time centred on issues of class identity and mobility, as befits a society where these issues were to the fore. Deloney's texts rest upon popular unifying ideological motifs, such as anti-Catholicism and nationalism, and seem on the surface to support an organic view of the social formation in which artisans can mix with royalty and 'get by' (despite social inequalities) by dint of quick-wittedness and hard work. However, there are tensions in the social world of *The Gentle Craft* just as there are in *The Shoemaker's Holiday*. These texts remain a rich source of

---

7   J.E. Ruoff, *Macmillan's Handbook of Elizabethan and Stuart Literature* (London and Basingstoke: Macmillan, 1975), p. 107.

evidence for the social diversity of a society that is rapidly becoming urban and class-conscious. Issues of identity are to the fore in terms of gender, class, and status – and the issue of warfare in these texts is an example of how they tend to foreground discontinuity (and alienation) in the social structure at the same time as they promote social cohesion and consensus.

Three issues emerge in *The Gentle Craft* that are indicative of changing patterns within the social environment from which the text emerged. These are important in terms of the way that Deloney fashions his evocation of the classical/mythical stories of early shoemakers, and, even more important with respect to his 'history' of episodes and characters from the more recent past. The first of these issues is the way that Deloney acknowledges the 'international' social composition of the societies of the stories and therefore, by implication, of the social world of contemporary London. Second is the emphasis given to social standing and mobility – and the recognition that history is altering the status of the retreating aristocracy and facilitating the emergence of new class formations. Third is the presence of war as a backdrop to both the mythical and 'historical' perspectives on shoemaking. War, or the talk of war, had a part to play in conditioning the social milieu of the Londoners and others for whom Deloney produced his work, making the fictional text intelligible in the light of their own experiences and expectations.

It is partly the way that these issues are presented to the reader through a mixture of genres that gives *The Gentle Craft* its curious potential for an unsettling of an idealized or romanticized vision of the past. Most evident is way that the text is characterized by the formal mixing of prose and song. The songs perform a variety of functions in the text and are often very funny. Yet on occasion the humour is juxtaposed with what seem more serious debates on the issues to hand.

An example of this is the bawdy song about marriage in Chapter VII of Part I. Crispine sings of marriage, but only in the context of the loss of his brother, pressed into the wars in Gaul. His song is followed by 'a deep discourse of the matter' (marriage and sexuality) between Crispine and the journey-men which Deloney leaves hanging as 'it appertaines not to our matter'. This invites the reader to consider perhaps that the narrative voice judges the story to be gloomy enough already without subjecting the reader to a discussion of the fact that were it not for marriage the world would be full of 'haplesse bastards, like to the seed of Cain, men fit for all manner of villainy, and as such would leave behind them a race of runnagates, persons that would live as badly as they were lewdly begotten'.

Indeed, a distinctive formal pattern applies to many of the narratives in *The Gentle Craft* overall that can be said to operate by means of the sudden gathering together of the strands of a particular story in a short closing passage. In some respects this pattern has something in common with the style of the joke: a long story is rounded off with a quick 'punchline' marking the end of the particular episode and building an expectation in the reader of something quite different in the next section. Yet the reader is never clear whether the episode will end joyously (or at least hopefully), or in some sudden tragedy.

The pattern is established early on in Part I. The long story of Hugh and Winifred ends in Chapter III with their poignant deaths, where the romantic genre expected in an account of such noble protagonists gives way to a sharp realism in the graphic treatment of their physical remains, leaving only their good names to posterity:

> There with the last draught he finished his life, whose dead carkasse after hanged up where the fowls devoured his flesh, and the young Princesse was contemptuously buried by the Well where she had so long lived. Then had he the title of Saint Hugh given him, and she of Saint Winifred, by which termes they are both so called to this day.

There is something quite shocking in this sudden closure and switch of styles. Yet in both stylistic and thematic terms the next chapter goes some way to resolving the tension of this discontinuity by emphasizing realism and, as a microcosm of the text overall, privileging the crude but more durable culture of the shoemaker. Stealing away Hugh's bones, and characteristically debating their possible function in a series of jokes, the chapter ends with a critical motif of shoemaking culture (the idea of the shoemaker's tools as 'Saint Hugh's Bones') carefully set against the theme of war that is to be central to the new legend narrative of Crispine and Crispianus, and the one that threads through the 'history' narratives that conclude Part I and constitute Part II:

> And it shall be concluded that what Iourney-man soever he be hereafter, that cannot handle the Sword and Buckler, his Long Sword, or a Quarter staffe, sound the Trumpet, or play upon the Flute and beare his part in a three mans Song: and readily reckon up his Toole in Rime; except he have born Colours in the field, being a Lieutenant, a Sergeant or Corporall, shall forfeit and pay a pottle of wine, or be counted for a colt: to which they answered all viva voce Content, content, and then after many merry Songs, they departed. And never after did they travell without these tools on their backs: which ever since were called Saint Hughes bones.

The switches in style and mood in *The Gentle Craft* may not be surprising if we are to see the text as an example of a form that is emerging against (and informing as a source) the attendant dramatic writing of the period. In the theatre an audience would expect comedy within tragedy and *vice versa* – and early prose 'novelists', with their emphasis on social satire, were less inclined towards a mono-generic stance than their counterparts of the nineteenth and twentieth centuries. Deloney, it might be said, had an eye on the romances of an earlier period, but a committed vision of the serious aspects of nation, class and warfare in his own times. He seems to have sought to engage his readers by distilling a wide range of styles, which would appeal through a sense of contrast and counterpoint. For the modern reader this mixture is entertainingly unpredictable and refreshingly original, reflecting the often very unexpected treatment of the principal issues that are at stake in the text.

Nation and Identity

Histories have noted that the uncertainties in the political environment from which *The Gentle Craft* emerged were numerous and complex, ranging from the increasing sense of crisis over the succession to a fear of foreign invasion. Despite the successful repulsion of the Spanish Armada in 1588, England was awash with rumour of renewed incursions, new enemies, foreign spies, Catholic plots, and all manner of potentially destabilizing phenomena. And all this was set against the realization that there was little to defend the relatively new Protestant state, in the form of a standing army or an internal police force, from its internal and external enemies.[8]

Deloney's earlier work seems to cast him as an influential polemicist in this sea of uncertainties, with his broadsides against Catholicism, his invective against the Spanish, and his complaints about foreign workers.[9] He seems to have been something of a campaigner for the dispossessed and those falling victim to the food shortages that were a recurrent feature of

---

8   See especially I. Archer, *The Pursuit of Stability: Social Relations in Elizabethan London* (Cambridge: Cambridge University Press, 1991); C. Breight, *Surveillance, Militarism and Drama in the Elizabethan Era*, (Houndmills and London: Macmillan, 1996); S. Rappaport, *Worlds Within Worlds: Structures of Life in Sixteenth-century London* (New York: Cambridge University Press, 1988); A. Shepard, and P. Withington, *Communities in Early Modern England: Networks, Place, Rhetoric* (Manchester: Manchester University Press, 200); Walter, J. and Wrightson, K., 'Death and the Social Order in Early Modern England', *Past and Present* 71 (May 1976), pp. 22–42.

9   See D. Morrow, 'The Entrepreneurial Spirit and "The Life of the Poore": Social Struggle in the Prose Fictions of Thomas Deloney' in *Textual Practice*, 20.3 (Summer 2006) pp. 395–418 in which he notes that Deloney co-authored 'A Complaint of the Yeoman Weavers Against the Immigrant Weavers', a letter sent to the French and Dutch churches in London and printed for wider distribution. Deloney was jailed in 1595 for his part in this polemic. See also A. Pettegree, *Foreign Protestant Communities in Sixteenth-century London* (Oxford: Clarendon Press, 1986).

both urban and rural life in the last years of Elizabeth's reign. These were mostly the result of failures in the harvest, especially in 1596 when Deloney was probably writing *The Gentle Craft*, but it was claimed in some quarters that their impact was aggravated by an influx of foreigners with additional mouths to feed. Such alarmist thinking was current in the time of Simon Eyre as much as it was in the last decade of the sixteenth century, and thus Deloney, thinking historically or topically, could not have failed to have been sensitive to the presence in London and elsewhere of representatives of foreign societies and cultures. There is a sustained awareness in the text of the 'otherness' of certain newly arrived settlers from abroad, but it is perhaps surprising to find that although there are exceptional moments, *The Gentle Craft* offers more of a celebration of cultural difference rather than an invective against immigration. Foreign figures are often central to the plots of the various stories, and whilst their fortunes are mixed, and their speech and social skills caricatured (notably in the case of Haunce the Dutchman and John the Frenchman in Part I) they are rarely portrayed as being more deserving of such treatment than others in the eclectic mix of figures that inhabits the overall collection of stories.

The worlds of *The Gentle Craft* reveal a sympathetic awareness of the people of other lands and their customs. The reader can find the 'Dutch Maiden' of Part I, Chapter III, or the 'Egyptian Woman' of Part II, Chapter IX, 'that at Black-wall was in travell with child, and had such hard labour, that she was much lamented among all the wives that dwelt thereabout'. The Egyptian woman is an innocent party in Harry Nevell's deception of the unfortunate Doctor Burket, and it is the latter who expresses a prejudice that is cleverly linked in the narrative to his having to pay a forfeit for all manner of personal and professional failings. Explaining how Nevell duped him, he says:

> since I was here, I have at least ridden an hundred miles with an arrant knave that carried me I knew not whether: he rode with me out of Bishops-gate foorth right as far as Ware, and then compassing all Suffolke and Norfolke, he brought me backe againe through Essex, and so conducted me to Black-wall in Middlesex to seeke out my Lady Swinborne, my good Lady and Mistris: at last I saw it was no such matter, but the villaine being disposed to mocke me, brought me to a woman Egiptian, as blacke as the great Divell, who lay in child-bed and was but delivered of a child of her owne colour: to the which in despite of my beard they made me be God-father, where it cost me three crownes, and I was glad I so escaped, and who was the author of all this deceipt but Master Nevell.

Moreover, news of other lands is treated with considerable knowledge and interest, whether it is the Captains Stuteley and Strangwidge's proposed expedition to Florida on behalf of the King in Part II, Chapter V, or Tom Drum's discussion of the length of days in the following chapter:

> Yes (quoth Tom) I can do it as we travell to Russia, for there every day is five and fiftie of our dayes in length: nay Ile tell you further, quoth Tom, in some parts of the world where I have been, it is day for halfe a yeare together, and the other halfe yeare is continually night: and goe no further, quoth he, but into the further part of Scotland, and you shall find one day there (in the month of June) to be foure and twenty houres long, and therefore my Masters while you live, take heed how you contrary a traveller, for therein you shall but bewray your owne ignorance, and make your selves mocking stockes to men of knowledge.

Writing in 1912, F.O. Mann suggested that Deloney's 'name may indicate French ancestry, and this, combined with his strong Anti-Catholicism, perhaps points to a descent from a Protestant silk-weaving family, one of those which took refuge in East Anglia from Continental religious persecution'.[10] Such a biographical supposition, interesting as it may be, does not adequately explain either Deloney's departure from his earlier attitudes towards foreign workers, or the largely sympathetic nature of his portrayal of 'foreign' characters in atmosphere of heightened sensitivity towards these matters in the 1590s.

Clearly, Deloney may have been tolerant towards Protestant migrants since so much of his work is fervently anti-Catholic, an attitude that extends to Part II of *The Gentle Craft*. The funny, if somewhat macabre story about the 'wilde Knight' Sir John Rainsford is a good example of this. The priest who refuses to bury a poor parishioner (Chapter VII) is cast as an embodiment of casuistry and materialism:

> Above all men (quoth Sir John) Priestes should respect the poore, and charitably regard the state of the needy, because they themselves doe teach charity to the people, and perswade men unto works of mercy: and therefore Sir Iohn, seeing good deeds are meritorious, doe you win heaven by this good work, and let the dead possesse their due.
> I, so they shall (said the Priest) so I may not loose my due: for I tell you further, I count it little better then folly, to fill my soule with pleasure by emptying my purse with coine.

Sir John and his men respond by burying the priest alongside the body of the man whose family had been too poor to pay for a funeral. That the incident involves the Diocesan Dean complaining directly to the King, forcing Sir John to flee his home and family, gives the episode considerable weight and moment as an exploration of the old church's power over local issues – and its response to Sir John's rough (but attractive) justice would presumably have struck a chord with Deloney's readership as an example of the inequities of

---

10 Mann, op. cit., p. vii.

pre-Reformation social hierarchies. The episode ends with Sir John pardoned by the King and his name restored, but only after he has taken up with the shoemakers Harry Nevell and Tom Drum, expressed his solidarity with their 'masterlesse and moneylesse' condition, and travelled with them to London to the house of Master Peachey, representing the archetype of the values of the shoemaking fraternity.

In these episodes and others, cultural differences, in the form of national and religious identities, are eventually overridden by the superior values of the community of shoemakers. And the eventual meeting between Peachey and Sir John, who come to see each other as 'fellows', is an example of the way that formerly strict feudal hierarchies are seen to dissolve in *The Gentle Craft* as sixteenth-century economic conditions transform assumptions concerned with social rank.

Rank and Economy

The relationship between shoemaking and social class is a prominent feature of the later 'historical' elements of *The Gentle Craft*. However, the topic is suggested early on in Part I, preparing the way for the more contemporary allusions. In Chapter VI of Part I, for example, Ursula, the Emperor's daughter, falls in love with Crispine, disguised as a shoemaker. Ursula ponders the relationship between appearance, virtue, rank and nature. The noble lover, perforce disguised as something else, is a commonplace of romantic fiction from its earliest forms, to Shakespeare, the fairytale and beyond. In the early sections of *The Gentle Craft* it not only reinforces the particular qualities of those involved with shoemaking, but also rehearses the discussions of social rank that appear later in the text:

> O Ursula take heed what thou dost, stain not thy royalty with such indignity. O that Crispines birth were agreeable to his person! for in mine eye, there is no Prince in the world comparable to him: if then while he is clothed in these rags of servitude, he appear so excellent, what would he be, were he in Princely attire! O Crispine, either thou are not as thou seemest, or else Nature, in disgrace of Kings, hath made the a Shoomaker.

A great deal of critical attention has been given to the representation of social class in *The Gentle Craft* and the usual approach is based upon situating the narrative in a context defined by the rapidly changing economic environment of sixteenth-century England.[11] The assumption is that the text's various

---

    11   See especially W. Davis, *Idea and Act in Elizabethan Fiction* (Princeton: Princeton University Press, 1969); M. Lawlis, *Apology for the Middle Class: the Dramatic Novels of Thomas Deloney* (Bloomington, Indiana: Indiana University Press), 1960; J.H. Kaplan, 'Virtue's Holiday: Thomas Dekker and Simon Eyre',

stories reveal the extent to which a feudal order of undisputed rank and economic certainty is giving way to a proto-capitalist world of endeavour, and the personal accumulation of wealth by new kinds of social groups. The result is the kind of rapid social advancement epitomized by the progress made by Simon Eyre. A further assumption is that it is only through his individual talent (in the face of various hardships and the potential snobbery of more established entrepreneurs), that he is able to maintain his sense of moral integrity. His 'goodwill' and the distribution of some of his wealth, through acts that the modern world would regard as charity, all proceed from the kind of advancement that the new economic systems of the early modern period facilitated.

This is a seductive view of the economic conditions that apply to *The Gentle Craft*. It fits neatly into a traditional vision of authors such as Deloney (and their readers) as the emerging 'middle class' of the period, further defined by their Protestantism and their sceptical view of a retreating aristocracy. Add to this the sort of democratic impulse associated, perhaps, with the real Simon Eyre's founding of Leadenhall, and a smooth historical narrative emerges that ideologically connects Deloney's characters and their activities to the triumphant entrepreneurial spirit of the later twentieth and early twenty-first centuries.

Clearly Deloney was aware of the impact of the economic instability of the times about which he wrote and the time in which he lived. *The Gentle Craft* records facets of economic exchange such as conditions of employment, investment, and mercantile adventure – all of which speak of the advances made by certain elements in the evolving social formation of the 1590s. Set against this, the wanderings of the various dispossessed and masterless figures in the text, however cheerful, seem all too typical of the grim economic realities that many endured. Moreover, when there is talk of war there is a hint of the kind of colonial competition that is to characterize succeeding centuries.[12]

Deloney certainly acknowledges the extraordinary social advance that can result from certain kinds of astute commerce. Yet he is at pains, both in his folk history of shoemaking and his realization of the values attached to

---

Renaissance Drama ns 3 (1969), pp. 103–22; M. McKeon, *Origins of the English Novel, 1600–1740* (Baltimore: Johns Hopkins University Press, 1987); L. Stevenson, *Praise and Paradox: Merchants and Craftsmen in Elizabethan Popular Literature* (Cambridge: Cambridge University Press, 1984).

12 Indeed, when the 'Sea Captaines' Stutely and Strangwidge appear in Part II, Chapter II, they are 'bound to sea on a gallant voyage, wherein the King hath no small venture' during which they 'would be seeking out the Coast of Florida'. Deloney's Stutely is based on Thomas Stukeley (1525–78), an historical figure. See J.E. Tazon, *The Life and Times of Thomas Stukely* (Burlington, Vermont: Ashgate, 2003).

the art of shoemaking in the sixteenth century, to celebrate something more than the potential of the individual and an ideology of enterprise. Time and again in *The Gentle Craft* an emphasis is placed upon tradition rather than change, and continuity rather than innovation. Above all, the narratives show that the shoemakers prosper, and best demonstrate their noble qualities, when they act collectively as part of a specific community. This is not to say that Deloney wants to return to some lost world of medieval values, but merely that he is aware of the tensions between the behaviour of individuals who recognize themselves as part of a community of values and those who step outside that community. David Morrow has noted that:

> Few if any Elizabethan authors have been so commonly identified with a rising entrepreneurial spirit and with the material interests of the bourgeoisie. [...] Concomitantly under-emphasized, overlooked, or treated as merely mystificatory has been Deloney's dependence upon, and celebration of, moral economy, or communal ideology, which, much evidence suggests, made up a key component of the discursive field within which Deloney produced and others consumed his fictions.[13]

Furthermore, Deloney's shoemakers are 'ennobled' (in the sense that they belong to the folk history of shoemaking that denotes the craftsman as 'gentle') by the physicality of the work itself rather than the abstract accumulation of wealth. Indeed, the sense of community is defined to a large degree by a sense of the corporeal fitness of its members, made strong by their work and judged against competing indices of masculinity derived from elsewhere in the wider social formation.

War

The most obvious alternative code of masculinity is that associated with warfare. Deloney wrote against a background of considerable anxiety, expressed in a range of contemporary prose works, about a decline in military awareness and preparedness.[14] At the heart of the discourse was the body, objectified as a moral and political commodity, and problematized by appeals to a clear ideal of discipline and commitment. Writing in 1578 in

---

13 Morrow, op. cit. p. 396.

14 Examples of these texts would be: Thomas Styward, *The Paithwaie to Martiall Discipline* (London, 1588): Geoffrey Gates, *The Defence of Militarie Profession* (London, 1591); Matthew Sutcliffe, *The Practice, Proceedings and Lawes of Armes* (London, 1593); James Achesome, *The Military Garden. Or Instructions For All Young Souldiers* (London, 1629) Richard Bernard, *The Bible-Battels Or The Sacred Art Military: For the Rightly Wageing of Warre According to Holy Writ* (London, 1629).

Allarme to England, foreshewing what perilles are procured when people live without regarde to Martiall Lawe, Barnabe Rich had suggested that the problem for contemporary militarism lay at the court of Elizabeth where 'carping cavaliers' had corrupted an English tradition of militarism and masculinity by:

> growing lazy and greedy, wallowing in vice and wickenesse [and] neglecting those disciplines which had made them honourable and worshipful – whose magnamitie in the times of warre hath made them famous in forreine countries, and whose noblesse and vertues [...] in times of peace doe shine coequal with the best.[15]

Rich's text is a typical example of the kinds of treatise written about war and the nation in the last two decades of the sixteenth century. And from within a general argument over the question of the preparedness of the nation for war, a lament emerged over the decline in standards in various areas of military culture from which a common corporeal focus arose concerning gender identity and difference. This involved arguments ranging in topic from the sheer strength of individual military personnel (defining their masculinity but thought to be waning), to their dress, demeanour, and education, as well as their overall lack of military awareness and discipline. In terms of gender, Rich offered the view that:

> Gentlemen these days give themselves rather to become Battalus Knights (effeminate Men) rather that Martiall Knightes, and have better desire to be practised in the carpet trade than in real virtue. To be shorte, in England, Gentlemen have robbed our women of halfe their minds, and our women have robbed us of half our apparell.[16]

Indeed, such texts helped establish a polarity between military prowess, realized best in overseas campaigns (which had the added benefit of defining nationhood at home), and a non-military quietude exemplified by those men who preferred domesticity. Such 'non-men' were considered weak because of their preference for hearth and home, their preoccupation with their crafts and trades, and their overwhelming desire for the company of women.[17]

Given this context, *The Gentle Craft* can be seen as a text that radically opposes the argument for military discipline and a formal army that was to gather pace over the course of the seventeenth and eighteenth centuries.

---

15 Barnabe Rich, *Allarme to England, foreshewing what perilles are procured when people live without regarde to Martiall Lawe* (London, 1578), sig. Ciii.

16 Ibid,. sig. H.

17 See S. Barker, 'Allarme to England!': Gender and Militarism in Early Modern England in J. Munns and P. Richards, *Gender, Power and Privilege in Early Modern England* (Edinburgh and London: Pearson), 2003, pp. 140 –158.

Since the standing army became a central component of the modern state, this invites modern readers to view Deloney's implied critique of late sixteenth-century militarism as significant indeed. *The Gentle Craft* is full of allusions to war and its consequences. In the story of Crispine, Crispianus and Ursula, Deloney describes the fighting in considerable detail, contrasting its brutality with the tenderness of Ursula's love for Crispine, and comparing the situations and desires of the brother who is pressed into war abroad with the one who pursues love at home. Crispianus makes a fine soldier, of course, but the contrast between the soldier and the lover (and the soldier and the shoemaker) is established as an important theme for *The Gentle Craft* in general.

The war theme returns in Chapter III of Part II at the end of the long story of Richard Casteler, Long Meg and Gillian of the George. The affectionate portrayal of these figures, so firmly rooted in their experiences of London, and with such resonant and persuasive voices, distinguishes this as one of the text's most elaborate and successful narratives. The evocation of place and custom, and the gossip, jokes, trickery and songs, deliver this tale of lost desire and frustrated sexuality at a consistent and measured pace; and yet, as with many of the narratives in *The Gentle Craft*, the denouement is sudden and unexpected. In the value systems of the text overall, Gillian, like the more successful shoemakers, is reconciled to the favoured discourse of domesticity and labour. Meg, on the other hand, is brought down by domesticity's mirror image, and the narrative ends for her with the excesses determined by war:

> Thus Margaret in a melancholy humor went her waies, and in short time after she forsooke Westminster, and attended on the Kings army to Bullen, and while the siege lasted, became a landresse to the Camp, and never after did she set store by her selfe, but became common to the call of every man, till such time as all youthfull delights was banished by old age, and in the end she left her life in Islington, being very penitent for all her former offences.
>
> Gillian in the end was well married, and became a very good house-keeper, living in honest name and fame till her dying day.

Whilst the enlightened modern reader might question Deloney's idealization of Gillian's eventual situation, and query the equations being established between sexual behaviour and moral redemption, it is still the case that war comes into these characters' world as an indiscriminate agent of destruction. So complete and sudden is Meg's fate that its resonance may carry over into the next chapter (IV) in which Robin and his fellows sing before the King of the siege of Bullen. In the song Bullen is seen as a 'Lady of most high renowne' and the King as determined to 'obtaine' her 'Maiden-head'. The fusing of sexual violation with military prowess is not uncommon in early modern discourse: but the contrast between the open but innocent desires of Meg and Gillian's former London life and this formalized metaphor of military success (as rape) is complete. The fact that the account is sung before the King in a public place (to great acclaim and reward) is an early example of how foreign wars can be made into domestic capital. The account of the siege recalls, and possibly demystifies, that of Henry V at Harfleur, and the general sense of myth-making here casts new light on the Tudor use of the story of Agincourt in its prose histories and in the theatre.

The second part of *The Gentle Craft* ends with a more localized form of myth-making as Tom Drum, with his 'old cogging humor' produces a fictional account of his deeds of war:

> An hundred merry feates more did he, which in this place is too much to be set downe. For afterward Tom Drum comming from the winning of Mustleborow, came to dwell with them, where he discoursed all his adventures in the wars: and according to his old cogging humor, attributed other mens deeds to himselfe, for (quoth he) it was I that killed the first Scot in the battell, yet I was content to give the honour thereof to Sir Michaell Musgrave, notwithstanding (quoth he) all men knowes that this hand of mine kild Tom Trotter, that terrible traytor, which in despite of us, kept the Castell so long, and at last as he cowardly forsooke it, and secretly sought to flye, with this blade of mine I broacht him like a roasting pigge. Moreover, Parson Ribble had never made himselfe so famous but by my meanes. These were his daily vaunts, till his lies were so manifest that hee could no longer stand in them.

To an Elizabethan readership attuned to the phenomenon of soldiers (genuine or counterfeit) begging in the streets of London, Deloney's text, with its characteristic mix of humour and social comment, must have seemed very topical in terms of this aspect of the actual consequences of war. The military prose of the period lamented the neglect of soldiers (advocating both sufficient training in readiness for war and their post-battle rehabilitation), but *The Gentle Craft* seems to favour codes of masculinity and domesticity that are morally superior to war in the first place.

Deloney points to this opposition most clearly in the story of Master Peachey in Part II, Chapter V. Having appeared at the Court with his liveried household of shoemakers, Peachey is challenged by the 'gallant Sea Captaines', Stutely and Strangwidge who resent what they perceive as a civilian undermining of the authority they claim as military men. The contest between the community of shoemakers and these two individualist adventurers is about hierarchy, power and privilege. As sea captains, Stutely and Strangwidge are symbolic of the Elizabethans' cultivation of a heroic masculinity represented by Drake, Raleigh and the real Thomas Stukeley.[18] Intruding into the very workplace of the shoemakers, they suffer first rebuff for their arrogance and rudeness, and when the conflict descends into violence, are harried by shoemakers throughout the streets of London. In the end the captains are forced, 'to make sute to the Duke of Suffolk to take up the matter: who most honorably performed their request: and so the grudge ended betwixt them, to the great credit of Master Peachie, and all his men'. The episode throws into relief the idea that military individualism and its masculine codes are superior to the collective authority of the civilian craftsmen who, initially restrained, are seen as more than a match for the ascendant military discourse. Under threat, the shoemakers defend their territory and their alternative vision of community. As Simons has noted, 'the violence of Peachey's world is seen in terms of the group rather than through the individual status that the captains afford themselves. It is the class, not the individual that is the hero'.[19]

Shoemaking

The sense of class solidarity in *The Gentle Craft* is given credibility, and continually reinforced for the reader, by the traditions and values that the text affords the shoemakers in its dramatization of their history and traditions.[20] It is Sir Hugh in Chapter III of the first part who praises the caring shoemakers and sings that:

> *This Trade therefore both great and small,*
> *The Gentle Craft shall ever call.*

---

18 Morrow notes that 'Stukely's celebrity endured beyond his death in 1578, in oral and written forms, including Holinshed, George Peele's *The Battle of Alcazar* [*c.* 1589] and the anonymous *The Famous History of Captain Thomas Stukely*. The picture of Stukely that emerges from these representations is an ambiguous one. He is courageous and adventurous, but also wholly individualistic, a Catholic double agent whose desire in life – as he reportedly told the Queen herself –was to be a king'. Op cit. p.402. Strangwidge was also an historical figure, killed during an attack on the French coast.

19 See Simons, op. cit., p. 18.

20 See L.A. Hutjens, *The Renaissance Cobbler: the Significance of Shoemaker and Cobbler Characters in Elizabethan Drama*, Ph.D thesis (Toronto: University of Toronto, 2004). In a wide-ranging and persuasive discussion of the numerous plays of the period that feature or refer to shoemakers, Hutjens examines the status of the shoemaker and the symbolism of the trade in terms of early modern economics and social class. Of special interest is her insight into the status of St Crispin's Day as a public holiday, and the history of the term 'gentle craft' itself.

The story of Crispine and Crispianus confirms the words of the Persian general Iphicarates to the King of Gaul – that 'a shoemaker's son is a prince born'. Yet the idea of 'the gentle craft' as a term denoting a definite social (or even moral) standing is a late sixteenth-century one used to recast the legends and myths of the early stories. It may have had a significant contemporary resonance for early modern Londoners as a somewhat double-edged term. On the one hand it denotes the 'gentility' of a particular form of artisan, in recognition of skills, education, good manners and the ability to 'get on' in life – and thus perhaps implies a critique of pre-existing forms of social hierarchy. Another way of viewing the term is as shorthand for 'social climbing' – individuals motivated by ambition to move upwards, disturbing a 'natural' sense of social hierarchy. Whatever the case, Deloney ascribes a set of values to shoemakers that define their community, and he is careful to show that although its cohesion gives it strength, it is by no means an exclusive grouping. Indeed, many of the stories involve strangers being welcomed into the trade from the outside and, as long as they fully participate, work hard, and invest in the values of the community, they will enjoy its benefits and protection. The shoemaking communities within the text are often seen demonstrating their values to the wider worlds of the legends and then to the wider society of fifteenth-century London in the near-contemporary stories. The text itself, widely read and republished many times, may have performed a similar function in disseminating a value system that had significant gravity in a period of accelerating economic transformation and political uncertainty. Deloney seems anxious to give as much detail as possible about the lives and labours of his chosen group of workers. The reader learns a great deal about their faith, their language, their consumption of food and drink, their sexual desires, their work practices and their leisure activities. Deloney's sense of the recent history of his own times is credible (the London of *The Gentle Craft* is fixed firmly as a Catholic one), and his knowledge of the way that people worked is very particular. A good example of these aspects of the text comes in Chapter II of the second part where Meg is inviting Richard Casteler to 'the eating of a Posset at night':

> I know that this Summer (and especially against these holy-daies) you will worke till ten, and I promise you by eleven I will have as good a posset for you, as ever you did taste on in your life. My master is an old man, and he commonly goes to bed at nine, and as for my mistris, I know where she will be safe till midnight masse be ended, so that for an houre we may be as merry as pope John: what say you Richard (quoth she), will you come?

The text is a convincing one because its more abstract values are set in the context of this level of historical detail.

The Gentle Craft also rewards the reader interested in Tudor London by the specificity of its geography. The text is full of individuals and groups of people moving from place to place around the city and the reader quickly recognizes the qualities associated with each location. The city is itself often personified, or, in the case of the following example from Chapter VIII of the second part, used in imagery to denote particular elements of a character's personality or visage:

> Too old? (quoth Harry). Why man she is not so old as Charing Crosse for her gate is not crooked, nor her face withered: but were she an hundred yeare old, having so strong a body and so faire a face, she were not in my opinion much to be mislikt; yet in my conscience I thinke, since first her faire eyes beheld the bright sunne, she never tasted the fruites of twenty flourishing Somers: nor scant felt the nipping frostes of nineteene cold winters, and therefore her age need be no hurt to her marriage.

This sense of the fusing of the people with the features of the city they inhabit is an aspect of the text that is also very apparent in the city comedies of the time.[21] The geography of the sections of *The Gentle Craft* that are most directly sources for *The Shoemaker's Holiday* is, however, a great deal less precise. There are fewer than half-a-dozen London place names in Deloney's story of Simon Eyre, and it was thus left to Dekker to give the story a geography in his appropriation of the narratives of *The Gentle Craft*.

The Text as Source

Three elements of *The Shoemaker's Holiday* are derived from *The Gentle Craft*. The first is the general celebration of the craft of shoemaking, including the legend of St Hugh. More directly appropriated are the stories of Crispine and Crispianus – and the central narrative concerning Simon Eyre. The relationship between *The Shoemaker's Holiday* and its source is a subtle and clever one. R.L. Smallwood and Stanley Wells have noted:

> Dekker uses the Eyre story only as the central anchor to which he attaches the two stories of the contrasted pairs of lovers, Lacy and Rose, and Ralph and Jane. The interdependence of these parts is made possible by an amalgamation of the roles of Eyre and his wife with those of the shoemaker and his wife in the Crispine-Crispianus tale, and by the intervention of a rival wooer in both love-

---

21 A good example of this is Ben Jonson's *Epicoene, or The Silent Woman*, first performed in 1609. Tom Otter describes his wife as if 'made' from the elements of the city:

"All her teeth were made i'the Blackfriars, both her eyebrows i'the Strand, and her hair in Silver Street. Every part o'the town owns a piece of her ... She takes herself asunder still when she goes to bed, into some twenty boxes." (IV.ii.84–9).

plots, whose interference keeps the tension alive, thus postponing, and making more welcome, the happy ending.[22]

The act of transferring of the material from *The Gentle Craft* to the stage is an act of transformation: the theatre opens up the subject matter and introduces new kinds of tension. There is also the influence of other plays in the busy, competitive world of the contemporary stage. *The Shoemaker's Holiday* came not long after Shakespeare's *Henry V*, raising questions about who the king is at the end of the play: Henry VI of Eyre's time or the ideologically and symbolically important Henry V.

Dekker's play has a considerable reputation in the theatre and among scholars – and remains a primary object of study for those wishing to investigate the representation of communities of artisans in the early modern period. This does not mean that *The Gentle Craft* is only of value as a context for the play. The text is a rich resource in its own right and in many ways has a depth (in its detail and scope) that the play cannot reproduce, written as it is for a medium with different priorities and levels of engagement with its audience. What the two texts have in common is their potential to attract the modern student into a world that has long disappeared, but remains somehow vital for its celebration of communal humanity.

---

22 Thomas Dekker, *The Shoemaker's Holiday*, edited by R.L. Smallwood and S. Wells (Manchester: Manchester University Press, 1999), p. 18.

A Note on the Text

The Gentle Craft is a prose narrative in two parts, thought to have been written about 1596 and published in 1597 (Part I) and 1598 (Part II) although there is much speculation over the accuracy of these dates. Most modern editions have been based on surviving seventeenth-century versions of the text: a single copy of 1627 (Part I) held by the University of Sheffield and two copies of 1639 (Part II) held in the British Library and the Bodleian Libray in Oxford. The provenance of an earlier edition (dated 1599 and held by the Biblioteka Gadańska in Poland) is uncertain, but it is of immense interest because it includes several additional pages and indicates that the author intended to produce a third part.

Part I of *The Gentle Craft* shows the origins of the shoemaking trade and Part II how it flourished in London. It is thought that Part III would have shown how shoemaking developed across England. According to R. L. Smallwood and Stanley Wells, editors of the *Shoemaker's Holiday*, early editions of *The Gentle Craft* were 'read out of existence by the popular audience to which they were directed' (p. 203) – and this comment hints at the sheer popularity of this kind of writing.

In addition to those mentioned above I have consulted the following extant editions and fragments in the preparation of this volume: THE GENTLE CRAFT A DISCOURSE, …. Shewing what famous men have been SHOOMAKERS … LONDON, printed for *John Stafford* and are to be sold at his house in Saint *Brides* Churchyard 1648 (British Library): the 1652 edition for John Stafford 'to be sold at the sign of the George at Fleet Bridge', 1652 (Bodleian); the c. 1675 edition 'Printed for *H. Rhodes*, at the *Star*, the Corner of *Bride-Lane, Fleet Street*' (British Library); the 1678 edition 'Printed by T.M. for *William Thackerey* in *Duck Lane*, near *West-Smith-field* and the editions of c. 1680, c. 1690, and 1696 in the British and Bodleian Libraries. I am indebted to the work of the twentieth-century scholars F.O. Mann and Merritt E. Lewis for their editions of the text included in *The Works of Thomas Deloney* (Oxford, Oxford University Press, 1912) and *The Novels of Thomas Deloney* (Connecticut, Westpoint Press, 1961) respectively.

Editorial interventions have been made to assist the modern reader. This edition does not attempt to reproduce the typography of early copies of the text. Variations in spelling have been retained except where meaning is unclear and I have followed many of the corrections made by earlier editors.

I have silently emended some typographical errors and adjusted the way that quoted speech is reported in order to clarify which character is speaking. I have also adjusted the layout of some parts of the text to suit the flow of the narrative.

The Gdansk text is of great scholarly importance despite uncertainties about the authenticity of its date. This edition of the first part of *The Gentle Craft* is subtitled: 'A Discourse containing many Matters of Delight, Pleasant to be read, and nothing hurtfull to be regarded: Shewing what famous men have bin shoe-makers in this land, their worthie Deedes, & great Hospitalitie'. The title page (A1r) attributes the text simply to 'T.D.', but the edition contains a dedication (sigs, A2r-v) signed 'Thomas Deloney' (reproduced in this edition as page 2). It also has the date 1599 and although this is no guarantee that the text was printed at that time, it is not unreasonable to suppose that it was. Sigs H2r to H4v is a chapter recounting Simon Eyre's dream about obtaining a ship's cargo and building Leadenhall. Sigs L3r to L4v describe the early life of Richard Casteller. I have appended these additions with a note explaining where they would appear in the substantive text, the sequence and narrative of which I have maintained from the authenticated and corrected editions that followed Deloney's death.

3
THE GENTLE CRAFT

The Gentle Craft.

A
DISCOURSE

Containing many matters of Delight, very
pleasant to be read:

Shewing what famous men have been SHOO-
MAKERS in time past in this Land, with
their worthy deeds and great Hospitality.

Set forth with Pictures, and variety of Wit and Mirth.

Declaring the cause why it is called the GENTLE
CRAFT: and also how the Proverb first grew.

A Shoomakers Son is a Prince born. T. D.

With gentlenesse judge you,
At nothing here grudge you;
    The merry Shoomakers delight in good sport.
What here is presented,
Be therewith contented;
    And as you do like it, so give your report.

Haud curo invidiam.

LONDON, Printed for *John Stafford*, and are to be sold at his
House in Saint *Brides* Church-yard. 1648

TO THE MASTER AND WAR-
DENS, OF THE WORSHIPFUL COM-
Pany of Cordwainers in London

The Romans in ancient time (right Worshipfull) were so carefull to keepe in memorie the rare actions of worthie & renowned menne, that few of them escaped the Praise of their pens, no, not so much as the painter Apelles, Pigmalion the Carver, nor Arion the the Fidler, but they did eternize by their never dying writings: by reason whereof, English men may be much blamed, eyther of ingratitude or negligence, that have suffred many men to passe unspoken of, in their sweete recording muses, which have as greatly deserved to be inrolled in the Register of Fame, as either the Harper, the Carver, or the Painter. The consideration whereof, moved me the most unsufficient of al others, to take in hand this plesant worke, made too unsavorie through my want of skill: yet I chose rather for to bewray mine own ignorance, then to suffer the well deserving praises of our kind cuntreymen, to lye hidden in the obscure pit of Oblivion. Wherefore if that your Worships shall vouchsafe to shielde under your gentle and curteous protection, this poore Talent of mine being a parcel of my good will, wherein the deeds of your auncient breethren are aymed at; I shall account your favour farre beyond my merit, although the gathering togither of thiese short Remembrances, hath bin unto me no small labour and cost, and by your curteous acceptance, I shall be the more better incouraged to proceede in the Residue of this Historie: the which I humbly Commit to your favourable censures, and wishing unto your all hearts content, and brotherly affection, I humbly rest.

Your Worships in all duty,

Thomas Delony.

To all the good Yeomen of the

GENTLE CRAFT

You that the Gentle Craft professe, list to my words both more and
   lesse;
And I shall tell you many things, of worthy and renownd Kings,
And divers Lords and Knights also, that were Shoomakers long a
   goe;
Some of them in their distresse, delighted in this businesse;
And some, for whom great wait was laid, did save their lives by
   this same Trade:
Other some, in sport and game, delighted much to learne the same.
No other Trade in all this Land, they thought so fit unto their
   hand,
For evermore they stil did find, that shoomakers bore a gallant
   mind.
Men they were of high conceit, the which wrought many a merry
   feat:
Stout of courage were they still, and in their weapons had great
   skill.
Travellers by sea and land, each country guise to understand:
Wrong they wrought not any man, with reason all things did they
   scan,
Good houses kept they evermore, releeving both the sicke and
   poore.
In law no mony would they spend, their quarrels friendly would
   they end.
No malice did they beare to any, but shew'd great favour unto
   many;
Offences soone they would forgive, they would not in contention
   live.
Thus in joy they spent their dayes, with pleasant songs and
   roundelayes,
And God did blesse them with content; sufficient for them He sent:
And never yet did any know, a shoomaker a begging goe:
Kind are they one to another, using each stranger as his brother.
Thus liv'd Shoomakers of old, as ancient Writers have it told:
And thus Shoomakers still would be, so fame from them shall never flee.

To all courteous Readers, health.

How Saint Hugh was son unto the renownd King of Powis, a noble Brittaine borne, who in the prime of his yeares loved the fair Virgin Winifred, who was the only daughter of Donwallo, which was the last King that ever reigned in Tegina, which is now called Flint-shire. But she refusing all offers of love, was only pleased with a religious life. Her father was sent to Rome, and dyed; whose Lady left her life long before. This Virgin therefore, forsook her fathers Princely Palace in Pont Varry, and made her whole abiding in the most sweet pleasant Valley of Sichnaunt, and lived there solitarily, and carelesse of all company or comfort. It chanced that in Summers heat, this fair Virgin being greatly distressed for lack of drink, and not knowing where to get any, there sprung up suddenly a Christall stream of most sweet and pleasant water out of the hard ground, whereof this Virgin did daily drinke: unto the which God himselfe gave so great a vertue, that many people having bene washed therein, were healed of divers and sundry infirmities wherewith they were borne. Moreover, round about this Well, where this Virgin did use to walke, did grow a kind of Mosse, which is of a most swet savour, and the colour thereof is as fresh in Winter as in Summer; so that lying thereon, you would suppose yourselfe to be upon a bed of Down, perfumed with most precious odours. And what of all this; Marry, reade the booke and you shall know; but reade nothing except you reade all. And why so? Because the beginning shews not the middle, nor the middle shews not the latter end.

And so farewell.

The Pleasant History of S. Hugh; and first

Of all, his most constant love to

The fair Virgin Winifred

Conquering and most imperious Love, having seized on the heart of young Sir Hugh, all his wits were set on worke, how for to compasse the love of the fair Virgin Winifred, whose disdain was the chiefe cause of his care, having received many infinite sorrows for her sake: but as a stream of water being stopt, overfloweth the bank, so smothered desire doth burst out into a great flame of fire, which made this male-contented Lover to seeke some means to appease the strife of his contentious thoughts, whereupon he began to encourage himselfe.

Tush Hugh, let not a few froward words of a woman dismay thee; for they love to be intreated, and delight to be wooed, though they would make the world beleeve otherwise: for their denyals proceed more of nicenesse then niggardlinesse, refusing that they would fainest have. What if sometimes Winifred frown on thee? Yet her favours may exceed her frowardnesse. The Sunne is sometimes overcast with clouds so that his brightnessse is not seen. In wars the sorer the fight is, the greater is the glory of the victory; and the harder a woman is to be won, the sweeter is her love when it is obtained: wherefore Ile once again try my fortune, and see what successe my sute shall find.

On this resolution Sir Hugh returned to Winifred, greeting her thus. Now fair Lady, having slept away the remembrance of your sharp answers; I come again in a new conceit, to revive an old sute, and to see if the change of the day will yeeld a change of dolours.

Truly Sir Hugh (quoth shee) if with the change of day you have changed your opinion: your dolour will be driven away well enough: but as touching your suite, it shall be needlesse to repeat it, because I am not going to preferre it.

Stay there (quoth Sir Hugh) I will preferre it, so that you will accept it.

Now (quoth she) I will accept it, if you will preferre it, in sending it back to the place from whence it proceeded, and I would to God I could send you away as soon as your suite.

Why then belike I am not welcome (said Sir Hugh).

Yes (quoth shee) as welcome to me, as a storme to a distressed Mariner: I muse greatly that reason will not rule you, nor words win you from your wilfulnesse: if you were as weary to wooe as I am wearied to heare you, I am perswaded that long since you would have ceased your vaine suite. You think by these perswasions to turn my opinion, but as well you may think that you may quench fire with oyle; therefore I pray you good Sir Hugh, be not so tedious unto me, nor troublesome to your selfe.

Come, come (quoth he) all this will not serve your turn, ponder with thy selfe Winifred that thou art fair. O that thou wert as Favorable; thy beauty hath bound me to be thy servant, and never to cease till I see another obtaine thee, or my selfe be possessed of my hearts content. Thou art a Kings daughter, and I a Princes sonne: staine not the glory of true Nobility with the foule sin of obstinacy but be thou as kind, as thou art courtly, and gentle as thou art noble, and then shall our strife soon end.

Winifred perceiving that the further off she was to grant love, the more eager he was to desire, shifted him off thus: Sir although your overhastinesse drive me into the greater doubtfulnesse, yet let me intreat you, if you love me, to give me but one months respite to consider on this matter; and it may be that upon my better deliberation it shall be pleasing unto you, and nothing at all discontent me.

Fair love (quoth he) far be it from my heart to deny so kind a request; I am content to stay a month from thy sight, were it two or three, upon condition, that thou wouldest then grant me thy good will: three months, although it be very long, yet it will come at last; and I could be content for that time to be dead for thy sake, insomuch that my life might be renewed by thy love.

Nay (quoth Winifred) stay three months, and stay forever; by this a Maid may see how ready men are upon a light occasion to take long daies, whose loves are like a Fernebush, soone set on fire, and soon consumed: and seeing it is so, in faith Sir Hugh, I do mean to try you better before I trust you.

Pardon me fair Winifred (said Sir Hugh) if my tongue do outslip my wit: in truth I speak but to please thee, though to displease my selfe: but I pray thee, let it not be three houres, nor three quarters of an houre, if thou wilt.

Nay, nay (quoth she) your first word shall stand: after three months come to me again, and then you shall know my mind to the full, and so good Sir Hugh be gone: but if I do ever heare from thee, or see thee betwixt this time and the time prefixed, I will for ever hereafter blot thy name out of my booke of Remembrances, and never yeeld the that courtisie which thou at this time so earnestly intreatest for.

Sir Hugh upon these words departed, betwixt hope and dread, much like to a man committing a trespasse, that stayed for the sentence of life or death.

O unhappy man (quoth he) how hath my over slippery tongue lengthened the time of my sorrow? She of her selfe most courteously requested of me but one months stay, and I most willingly and undiscreetly added thereto eight weks more of misery: much like the Hind, that having a knife given him to paire his nailes, did therewith murder himselfe. Now I could wish that the Sun had Eagles wings, swiftly to fly through the faire firmament, and finish six dayes in one dayes time.

With that he began to count the dayes and houres that were in three months, falling (in a manner) to dispaire with himselfe when he found them so many in number: and therewithall melancholily and sadly he went to his Fathers house, where his brother Griffith found by his countenance the perfect map of a pensive lover: wherupon he said unto him.

Why how now brother? Hath Winifreds fair beauty so greatly wounded you, as you cannot speak a merry word to your friends, but sit in a corner, as if you were tonguelesse like a Stork? Tush brother, women are like shadowes, for the more a man follows them the faster they run away: but let a man turn his course, and then they will presently follow him. What man? Pluck up a good heart: for there are more women now, then lived in the time of our old father Adam.

O (said Hugh) were there ten thousand times more then there are now, what were that to me, if Winifred be unkind? Yet is she the oyle that still maintaines the lampe of my light, and without her there is nothing comfortable to my sight.

Then (replied Griffith) you are as much troubled in love, as a Goat in an ague, and as blind as a Flie in October, that will stand still while a man cuts off his head. Come, goe a hunting with me, that will drive away your overfond conceits, and you shall see that these three months will come upon you as a quarter day upon a poore man that hath never a penney ready towards the payment of his rent.

CHAPTER II

How beautifull Winifred being overmuch superstitious, forsook her fathers wealth and lived poorely by a springing Fountain, from whence no man could get her to go; which Spring to this day is called Winifreds Well.

Winifred, who had but of late yeeres, with her own father, received the Christian Faith, became so superstitious, that she thought the wealth of the world for ever would have ben an heavy burthen for her soule, and have drawne her mind from the love of her Maker; wherefore forsaking all manner of earthly pomp, she lived a long time very poorely, hard by the side of a most pleasant springing Well; from which place, neither her friends by intreaty, nor her foes by violence could bring her: which Sir Hugh hearing, he went thither immediately after unto her, which was the time limited by them both, and finding her mind altogether altered, he wondered not a little what she meant. And when he approached near unto the place where she sate, all suted in simple attire, he saluted her with these words.

All health to fair Winifred: I trust (my Dear) that now the Destinies have yeelded a convenient oportunity for me to finish my long begun sute, with the end of my former sorrowes. Long and tedious hath the winter of my woes beene, which with nipping care hath blasted the beauty of my youthfull delight which is like never again to flourish except the bright Sunshine of thy favour do renew the same: therefore (fair Love) remember thy promise made unto me, and put me no more off with unpleasing delayes.

She (which all this while sat solemnly reading in her booke) lent little eare unto his words; which he perceiving, pluckt her by the arme, saying: Wherefore answereth not my fair Love, to her dearest perplexed friend?

What would you have (quoth she?) Can I never be quiet for you? Is there no corner of content in this world to be found?

Yes Winifred (said he) content dwells here, or no where: content me, and I will content thee.

If my content may be thy content, then read this book, and there rests content (said Winifred) and if thou refuse this, then think not to find content on earth.

Sir Hugh replied, What, is this all the reward I shall have for obeying your heart-cutting commandment? Have I thus long hoped, and find no better hap? You wot well that it is now three long months since these eyes took comfort of thy beauty, and since that time that my bleeding heart hath received joy in thy great gentlenesse.

I have forgot you quite (said she); what three months is that you speak of? For my part I assure you, that it is as farre out of my mind, as you are from the mount of Calvary.

Fair Winifred (quoth he) have you forgotten me, and therewithall my love, which was so effectually grounded upon your good liking? You told me that now I should receive an answer to my content.

O Sir (quoth she) you have stayd over-long, and your words are in my hearing, as unprofitable as snow in harvest: my love is fled to heaven, from whence no earthly man can fetch it, and therefore build not in vaine hope, nor do thou deceive thy selfe by following an unprofitable suit: if ever I love earthly man, it shall be thee, insomuch as thou hast deserved an earthly Ladies love; but my love is setled for ever, both in this world and in the world to come: and this I most earnestly intreat thee to take for a finall answer.

With that Sir Hugh turning his head aside, wept most bitterly, and in going away, he glanced his eye still back again after his love, saying to himselfe: O unconstant women, wavering and uncertain, how many sorrows are fond men drawn into by your wily inticements? who are also swallowed up in the gaping gulf of Care, while they listen after the heartliking sound of your inchanting voices. O Winifred, full little did I thinke that so hard a heart could have ben shrouded under so swet and loving a countenance: but, seeing that my good will is thus unkindly requited, I will altogether abhor the sight of women, and I will seek the world throughout, but I will find out some blessed plot, where no kind of such corrupt cattell do breed.

Hereupon all in hot hasty humour he made preparation for to goe beyond the Seas, suiting himselfe after the nature of a melancholy man; and arriving in France, he took his journey towards Paris, which City (at that time) was well replenished with many goodly fair women, as well as Britain, though to his thinking nothing so lovely, but neverthelesse what they wanted in beauty, they had in bravery: which when Sir Hugh saw, he suddenly departed from that place, counting it the most pernicious place in the whole Countrey; and from thence he went into Italy, where he found such stately Dames, and lovely Ladies, whom Nature had adorned with all perfection of outward beauty, whose sight put him again in remembrance of his fair Love which like fresh fuell newly augmented the flame of his burning desire, O (said he) how unhappy am I to be haunted by these heart tormenting fiends, bewtiching the eyes of simple men with Angel-like faces , and, like the enchanting Circes, brining them to a labyrinth of continuall woes.

O Winifred, they peevishness hath bred my dangers, and done thy selfe no good at all. Thou sitest weping by a Cristall streame, where is no need of water, while I wander up and down, seeling to forget thee; thou never remembrest me, having drawn the foutaine of mine eyes dry through thy discourteous disdain. Might I never see any of thy sex, my heart would be more quiet, but every place where I come puts me in mind of thy perfections, and therewithall renews my pain: but I will from hence as soon as possible I can, though not so soon as I would, for feare lest these swet serpents should sting me to death with delight.

Hereupon he passed on so far, that at length he came to a City situated in the Sea, and compassed with the wide Ocean. Here (quoth Sir Hugh) is a fit place for a melancholy men; where it is supposed no women do live, insomuch that their delicate bodies cannot abide the salt savour of the mounting waves: if it be so, there will I make my residence, counting it the most blessed place under heaven. But he was no soonr set on land, but he beheld whole troops of lovely Ladies, passing up and down in most sumptuous attire, framing their gestures answerable unto their beauties and comely personages.

Nay now I see (quoth Sir Hugh) that the whole world is infected with these deceiving Syrens, and therfore in vain it is for me to seek for that I shall never find; and therewithall sought for some house wherein he might hide himselfe from them. But by that time he was set to supper, comes a crue of Courtlike Dames richly attired, and with wanton eyes and pleasant speech they boldly sate down by him; and perceiving him to be a stranger, they were not strange to allure him to their delight: wherefore while he sate at meat, they yeelded him such mirth as their best skill could afford; and stretching their nimble fingers, playing on their swet sounding instruments, they sung this ensuing song, with such cleare and quavering voices, as had ben sufficient to allure chaste hearted Xenocrates unto folly: and still as they did sing, Sir Hugh answered in the last line, insomuch as it seemed to be a dialogue betwen them; and in this manner following, the women began their song.

The Curtizans Song of Venice

Ladies.	*Welcome to Venice, gentle courteous Knight,*
	  Cast off fond Care, and entertain Content:
	If any here be gracious in thy sight,
	  Do but request, and she shall soon content:
	Loves wings are swift, then be not thou so slow.

Hugh.	*Oh that faire Winifred would once say so.*

Ladies.	*Within my lap lay down thy comely head,*
	  And let me stroke those golden lockes of thine:
	Looke on the teares that for thy sake I shed,
	  And be thou Lord of any thing is mine;
	One gentle look upon thy love bestow.

Hugh.	*Oh that fair Winifred would once say so.*

Ladies.	*Embrace with joy thy Lady in thine armes,*
	  And with all pleasures passe to thy delight:
	If thou dost think the light will work our harmes,
	  Come, come to bed, and welcome all the night;
	There shalt thou find, what Lovers ought to know.

Hugh.	*Oh that fair Winifred would once say so.*

Ladies.	*Give me those pearles as pledges of thy love,*
	  And with those pearles the favour of thy heart:
	Do not from me thy sugred breath remove,
	  That double comfort gives to every part.
	Nay stay Sir Knight, from hence thou shalt not go.

Hugh.	*Oh that fair Winifred would once say so.*

When Sir Hugh had heard this song, and there withall noted their wanton gestures, he began to grow suspicious of their proffers, and, thinking in himselfe, that either they sought his destruction, as the Syrens did to Ulysses; or that they intended to make a prey of his purse, as Lais did of her lovers: and therefore supposing some adder to lie lurking under the fair flowers of their proffered pleasures, he determined the next morning after (with all speed) to depart from the City. So when he had with good discretion avoided their company, while he lay tormented with restlesse thoughts on his still tossed bed, began thus to meditate:

Now I well see mine own vanity, that is as ill pleased with womens favour as their frowns; how often have I with heart-sighing sorrow complained of womens unkindnesse, making large invectives against their discourtesies? And yet here where I find women as kind as they are faire, and courteous as they are comely, I runne into a world of doubts, and as suspitious of their fair proffers, as I was earnest to win Winifreds favour: it may be (quoth he) that it is the nature of this gentle soyle to breed as kind creatures, as the Country of Brittaine breeds coy Dames.

Undoubtedly, had my love first taken life in this kind and courteous Climate, she would have bene as kind as they. If I mis-judge not of their gentlenesse, because I have always bene inured to scornfulnesse; methinks they are too fair to be harlots, and too bold to be honest but as they have no cause to hate me that never hurt them, so have they little cause to love me, being a far stranger borne, and to them a man altogether unknown.

But it may be that this time of the yeare is onely unfortunate for lovers; as it is certainly known to all men, that every season of the yeare breeds a sundry commodity, for Roses flourish in June, and Gilly flowers in August, and neither of them both do so in the cold winter. Such as seek for fruit on the saplesse trees in the month of January lose their labours as well as their longing: then why should I covet to gather fruits of love, when I see that love is not yet ripe? Now let me observe the season that yeelds the swetest comfort to love-sicke persons, and so I may reape the joyfull fruits of hearts content: I will therefore return to my former Love, hoping now to find her as friendly, as at my departure she was froward; I will once again intreat her, and speak her exceeding fair; for, with many drops the hardest stone is pierced; so also with many importunate intreaties a flinty heart may be moved to some remorse. I take no pleasure at all in any place, but onely in her presence, with the which she continually graceth a running streame; far be it from her mind to kisse her own shadow in the Chrystall spring, and to be in love with her own similitude; for so she might be spoiled as Narcissus was: for it is commonly seene, that sudden danger follows fond opinions.

So with this and the like thoughts he drove out the night, till the Suns bright eye began to peep at his chamber window; at what time dressing himselfe he went to the water side, where he found a ship ready to transport rich merchandise into the Westerne Ilands, in the which Sir Hugh became a passenger. But when they were put off to sea, there arose so sudden a storme, and of so long continuance, that no man looked for life, but expected every moment present death; so that the Mariners quite forsooke the tackle, and the

Master the helme, committing themselves to God, and their ship to the mercy of the swelling seas, by whose furious waves they were sometime tossed up towards heaven, and anon thrown down to the deep of hell. In which extremity Sir Hugh made this lamentation:

O unhappy man, how eagerly doth mischance pursue me at my hele; for betwixt my Love on the land, and danger of life on the sea, it hath made me the wretchedst man breathing on earth.

Here we may see that miseries have power over men, and not men over miseries. Now must I die far from my friends, and be drenched in the deepe, where my bodie must feed the fishes that swim in the rich bottom of the sea. Therefore fair Winifred, the chiefe ground of my griefes, here will I sacrifice my last teares unto thee, and poure forth my complaints.

Oh how happy should I count my selfe, if those fishes which shall live on my bodies food, might be meate for my Love! It grieveth me much to think that my poore bleeding heart, wherein thy picture is engraven, should be rent in pieces in such greedie sort; but thrice accursed be that fish, that first seteth his nimble teeth thereon, except he swimme therewith unto my Love, and so deliver it as a present taken from me.

Had my troubled stars allotted me to leave my life in the pleasant valley of Sichnant, then no doubt but my Love with her fair hands would have closed up my dying eyes, and perhaps would have rung a peale of sorrowfull sighs for my sake.

By this time was the weather-beaten Bark driven upon the shore of Sicilie, where the men had safety of their lives, although with losse of their ship and spoile of their goods: but they had no soonr shaken off their dropping wet garments on the shore, but that they were assaulted by a sort of monstrous men that had but one eye apiece, and that placed in the midst of their foreheads, with whom the tempest-beaten Souldiers had a fierce fight, in which many of them were slain, and divers of them fled away to save themselues; so that in the end Sir Hugh was left alone to Fortune in a double fray: and having at last quite overcome all his adversaries, he went his way, and so passing up the country in dark night, in the end he lost his way, and was so far entered into a great dark wildernesse, that he could not devise with himselfe which way he should take to get out, where he was so cruelly affrighted with the dreadfull cry of fierce Lyons, Beares, and wilde Bulls, and many thousand more of other dangerous and cruell ravenous beasts, which with greedy mouths ranged all about for their prey, in which distresse, Sir Hugh got him up to the top of a tree, and being there, brake out into this passion:

O Lord (quoth he) hast Thou preserved me from the great perill and danger of the Sea, and delivered me out of the cruell hands of monstrous men, and now suffer me to be devoured of wilde beasts? Alas, that my foule sins should bring so many sundry sorrows on my head.

But for all this may I thank unkind Winifred, whose disdain hath wrought my destruction. Woe worth the time that ever my eyes beheld her bewitching beauty. But hereby we may see that the path is smooth that leadeth to danger. But why blame I the blamelesse Lady? Alas, full little did she know of my desperate courses in travell. But such is the fury that hants frantick Lovers, that never feare danger untill it fall and light upon their own heads.

But by that time that the day began to appeare, he perceived an huge Elephant with stiffe joynts stalking towards him, and presently after came a fiery tongued Dragon, which suddenly assaulted the peacefull Elephant, in whose subtle encounter the wrathfull Dragon with his long wrinkling taile did so shackle the hinder feet of the Elephant together, that like a prisoner fast fettered in irons, he could not stir a foot for his life; at what time the furious Dragon never left till he had thrust his slender head into the Elephants long hooked nose, out of which he never once drew it, untill by sucking the Elephants blood, he had made him so feeble and weake, that he could stand no longer upon his feet; at which time the fainting Elephant with a grievous cry, fell down dead upon the Dragon: so with the fall of his weighty body, burst the Dragon in pieces, and so killed him; whereby their bloods being mingled together, it stained all the ground where they both lay, changing the green grasse into a rich scarlet colour.

This strange fight betwixt these two beasts, caused good Sir Hugh to judge that nature had planted betwixt them a deadly hatred, the fire whereof could not be quenched, but by the shedding of both their hearts blood. Now when Sir Hugh saw that grim Death had ended their quarrell, and perceiving no danger neare, he came down from the tree, and sought to find out some inhabited town, but being intangled in the woods, like the Centaure in his Labyrinth, he could by no means get out, but wandered in unknown passages, leading him to many perils.

At last another Elephant met him, who according to his kind nature never left him till he had conducted him out of all danger, and brought him out of the Wildernesse into the way again; whereby Sir Hugh at the length came in sight of a Port-town,where in foure dayes after he imbarked himselfe in a ship bound for Britaine, and at last obtained the sight of his native Country where he arrived in safetie, though in very poore sort, coming on shoare at a place called Harwich, where for want of money he greatly lamented, and made much moane. But meeting with a merry Journey-man Shoomaker dwelling in that town, and after some conference had together, they both agreed to travell in the Country, where we will leave them, and speak of Winifred, and of her great troubles and calamities.

CHAPTER III

How fair Winifred was imprisoned, and condemned to die for her Religion: and how Sir Hugh became a Shoomaker, and afterward came to suffer death with his Love: showing also how the Shoomakers tools came to be called Saint Hughs bones, and the trade of Shoomaking, The Gentle Craft.

Anon after that the Doctrine of Christ was made known in Brittaine, and that the worship of heathen Idols was forbidden, yet many troubles did the Christians endure by the outragious bloodthirstinesse of divers wolvish tyrants, that by the way of invasion set footing in this Land, as it fell out in the dayes of Dioclesian, that with bloudy minds persecuted such as would not yeeld to the Pagan law: amongst which the Virgin Winifred was one, who for that she continued constant in faith, was long imprisoned.

During which time Sir Hugh wrought in a shoomakers shop, having learned that trade through the courteous directions of a kind Journey-man, where he remained the space of one whole yeere; in which time he had gotten himselfe good apparell, and everything comely and decent. Notwithstanding though he were now contented to forget his birth, yet could he not forget the beautie of his Love, who although she had utterly forsaken him, yet could he not alter his affection from her, because indeed affections alter not like a palefaced coward. The wildest Bull (quoth he) is tamed being tied to a Fig-tree; and the coyest Dame (in time) may yeeld like the stone Carchædonis, which sparkles like fire, and yet melts at the touch of soft wax. Though Roses have prickles, yet they are gathered; and though women seem froward, yet will they shew themselves kind and friendly. Neither is there any wax so hard, but by often tempering, is made apt to receive an impression: Admit she hath heretofore been cruell, yet now may she be courteous. A true hearted Lover forgets all trespasses: and a smile cureth the wounding of a frown. Thus after the manner of fond Lovers he flattered him selfe in his own folly, and in the praise of his fair Lady, he sung this pleasant Ditty here following.

> *The pride of Brittain is my hearts delight,*
> *My Lady lives, my true love to requite:*
> *And in her life I live, that else were dead,*
> *Like withered Leaves in time of Winter shead.*

> *She is the joy and comfort of my mind,*
> *She is the Sun that clearest sight doth blind;*
> *The fairst flower that in the world doth grow,*

Whose whitenesse doth surpasse the driven snow.
Her gentle words more swet then honey are,
  Her eyes for clearenesse dims the brightest star:
O were her heart so kind as she is faire,
  No Lady might with my true love compare.

A thousand griefs for her I have sustained,
  While her proud thoughts my humble sute disdained:
And though she would my heart with torments kill,
  Yet would I honour, serve, and love her still.

Blest be the place where she doth like to live:
  Blest be the light that doth her comfort give:
And blessed be all creatures farre and neer,
  That yeeld relief unto my Lady dear.

Never may sorrow enter where she is,
  Never may she contented comfort misse:
Never may she my proffered love forsake,
  But my good will in thankfull sort to take.

Thus feeding his fancy with the swet remembrance of her Beauty, being never satisfied with thinking and speaking in her praise, at length he resolved himselfe to go into Flint-shire, where he might sollicite his suit anew again: but coming neere to the place of her residence; and hearing report of her troubles, he so highly commended her faith and constancy, that at length he was clapt up in prison by her, and in the end he was condemned to receive equall torment, for a triall of his own truth.

But during the time that they lay both in prison, the Journeymen Shoomakers never left him, but yeelded him great reliefe continually, so that he wanted nothing that was necessary for him; in requital of which kindnesse he called them Gentlemen of the Gentle Craft and a few dayes before his death, he made this Song in their due commendations.

Of Craft and Crafts-men more and lesse,
  The Gentle Craft I must commend:
Whose deeds declare their faithfulnesse,
  And hearty love unto their freind:
The Gentle Craft in midst of strife,
  Yeelds comfort to a carefull life.

A Prince by Birth I am indeed,
            The which for Love forsooke this Land:
And when I was in extreme need,
            I tooke the Gentle Craft in hand,
And by the Gentle Craft alone,
            Long time I liv'd, being still unknown,

Spending my dayes in swet content,
            With many a pleasant sugred Song:
Sitting in pleasures complement,
            Whilst we recorded Lovers wrong:
And while the Gentle Craft we us'd,
            True Love by us was not abus'd.

Our shooes we sowed with merry notes,
            And by our mirth expell'd all mone:
Like Nightingales, from whose swet throats,
            Most pleasant tunes are nightly blown;
The Gentle Craft is fittest then,
            For poore, distressed Gentlemen:

Their minds do mount in courtesie,
            And they disdain a niggards feast:
Their bodies are for Chivalry,
            All cowardnesse they do detest.
For Sword and Shield, for Bow and Shaft,
            No man can stain the Gentle Craft.

Yea sundry Princes sore distrest,
            Shall seek for succour by this Trade:
Whereby their greifes shall be redrest,
            Of foes they shall not be afraid.
And many men of fame likewise,
            Shall from the Gentle Craft arise.

If we want money over night,
            Ere next day noone, God will it send,
Thus may we keepe our selves upright,
            And be no churle unto our friend:
Thus do we live where pleasure springs,
            In our conceit like petty Kings.

Our hearts with care we may not kill,
Mans life surpasseth worldly wealth,
Content surpasseth riches still,
And fie on knaves that live by stealth:
This Trade therefore both great and small,
The Gentle Craft shall ever call.

When the Journey-men Shoomakers had heard this Song, and the fair title that Sir Hugh had given their Trade, they engraved the same so deeply in their minds, that to this day it could never be razed out: like a remembrance in a Marble stone which continueth time out of mind.

But not long after came that dolefull day, wherein these two Lovers must lose their lives, who like two meeke Lambs were led to the slaughter: the bloody performance thereof was to be done hard by that fair Fountain, where the Love-despising Lady made her most abode: and because she was a Kings daughter, the bloody Tyrant gave her the priviledge to chuse her own death: to the which she passed with as good a countenance, as if she had ben a fair young Bride prepared for marriage.

(viz.) When they were come to the place of execution, and mounted upon the Scaffold, they seemed for beauty like two bright Stars, Castor and Pollux; there they embraced each other with such chaste desires, as all those that beheld them, admired to see how stedfast and firme both these Lovers were, ready in hearts and minds to heaven itselfe.

At what time the Lady turned her selfe to Sir Hugh, and spake to this effect: Now do I find thee a perfect Lover indeed, that having setled thy affection above the Skies, art ready to yeeld thy life for thy Love, who in requitall thereof, will give the life for ever.

The Love of earthly creatures is mixed with many miseries, and interlaced with sundrie sorrows: and here grief shall abate the pleasures of Love, but be well assured that joy shall follow the same.

Thou didst wooe me for love, and now have I won thee to love: where setling both our selves upon God His love, we will love one another; and in token of that heavenly love, receive of me I pray thee a chaste and loving kisse from my dying lips.

Fair Winifred (quoth he) it is true indeed; I never loved truly, untill thou taughtest me to love, for then my love was full of discontent, but now altogether pleasing, and more sweet is the thought thereof then any tongue can expresse. The thing that I ever before called Love, was but a shadow of love, a sweetnesse tempered with gall, a dying life, and a living death, where the heart was continually tossed upon the seas of tempestuous sorrows, and wherein the mind had no calme quietnesse: and therefore blessed be the time that I ever learned this love.

With that he was interrupted by the Tyrant, who said, You are not come hither to talk but to dye; and I have sworn you both shall die at this instant.

Thou Tyrant (sad Sir Hugh) the very like sentence is pronounced against thy selfe; for Nature hath deemed that thou shalt die likewise, and albeit the execution thereof be something deferred, yet at length it will come, and that shortly, for never did Tyrant carry grey haires to the grave.

The young Lady desired first to die, saying to Sir Hugh, Come dear friend and learne magnanimity of a Maide: now shalt thou see a silly woman scorn death at his teeth, and make as small account of his cruelty, as the Tyrant doth of our lives, and there withall stript up her silken sleeves, and committed her Alabaster armes into the Executioners foule hands, having made choice to die in bleeding: at what time being pricked in every vain, the scarlet blood sprung out in plentifull sort, much like a precious fountain lately filled with Claret Wine.

And while she thus bled, she said: Here do I sacrifice my blood to him that bought mee, who by his blood washt away all my sinnes, O my sweet Saviour, thus were thy sides pierced for my transgressions, and in this sort sprung thy precious blood from thee, and all for the love thou bearest unto mankind: I feele my heart to faint, but my soule receiveth strength, I come swet Christ, I come. And therewithall her body fainting, and the blood failing, like a Conduit suddenly drawn drie, the young Princesse fell down dead, at what time a pale colour over-spread her fair face, in such comely sort, as if a heape of Roses had been shadowed with a sheet of pure Lawn.

But it is to be remembred, that all the while the young Princesse bled, her blood was received into certain basons, which being in that sort saved together, the Tyrant caused it to be tempered with poyson, and prepared it to be the last drink that Sir Hugh should have, saying; That by her love whom he so dearely loved, he should receive his death. And thereupon incontinently, without any further delaying of time, he caused a cup of that most deadly poysoned blood to be delivered into his hands, who with a lovely and cherfull countenance received the same, and then uttered his mind in this manner.

O thou cruell tyrant (quoth he) what a poore spite is this to inflict upon a dying man, that is as carelesse how he dies, as when he dies? Easie it is for the to glut me with blood, although with blood thou art not satisfied. Swet blood (quoth he) precious and pure, how fair a colour dost thou cast before mine eyes? Sweet I say wast thou, before such time as this ill-savouring poyson did infect thee: and yet as thou art, I nothing despise the. O my dear Winifred, full little did I think, that ever I should come to drinke of thy heart blood.

My greedy eye that glutton-like did feed upon thy beauty, and yet like the Sea was never satisfied, is now with thy gore blood fully gorged. Now may I quench my thirsty desire with love, that like hot, burning coals set my heart in such an extreme heat, that it could not be quenched before this time; for if fair

Winifred could spare any love from heaven, assuredly she left it in her blood; her sweet, heart blood I mean, that nourished her chast life: see, here is a caudle to cool my vain affections. Far be it that any true Lover should ever taste the like.

But this punishment have the just heavens poured upon me, for the preferring the love of an earthly creature, before the love of an heavenly Creator; Pardon, O Lord, the foule sinnes of superstitious Lovers, that while they make Idols of their Ladies, they forget the honour of thy Divine Majesty. Yet doth it do my heart much good to think that I must bury swet Winifreds blood in my body, whose love was lodged long ago in my heart: and therewithall, drinking the first draught, he said, O Lord, me seemeth this potion hath a comfortable taste, far doth it surpasse that Nectar wherewith the gods were nourished.

Well (said the Tyrant) seeing it pleaseth thee so well, thou shalt have more, and therewith another cup of the same blood was given him to drink.

Yes come (quoth he) my thirst is not quenched; for the first draught gave me but a taste of sweetnesse, and like a longing woman, I desire the rest; and with that he drank the second draught. The third being delivered him, he took the cup into his hand, and looking about, he said: Lo here, I drinke to all the kind Yeomen of the Gentle Craft, the dearest draught of drinke that ever man tasted of.

I drink to you all (quoth he) but I cannot spare you one drop to pledge me. Had I any good thing to give, you should soon receive it: but my life the tyrant doth take, and my flesh is bequeathed to the fowls, so that nothing is left but onely my bones to pleasure you withall; and those, if they will do you any good, take them: and so I humbly take my leave, bidding you all farewell.

There with the last draught he finished his life, whose dead carkasse after hanged up where the fowls devoured his flesh, and the young Princesse was contemptuously buried by the Well where she had so long lived. Then had he the title of Saint Hugh given him, and she of Saint Winifred, by which termes they are both so called to this day.

CHAPTER IV

How the Shoomakers stole away Saint Hughes bones, and made them working tools thereof, and the vertue that they found in the same: whereby it came, that when any man saw a Shoomaker travelling with a pack at his back, they would presently say: There goes Saint Hughes bones.

Upon a time it chanced, that a company of Journey-men Shoomakers passed along by the place where Saint Hughes dead body was hanging, and finding the flesh pickt cleane off from the bones, they entred thus into communication among themselves.

Never was Saint Hugh so bare (quoth one) to carry never a whit of skin upon his bones; nor thou never so bare (said another) to beare never a penny in thy purse. But now seeing you talk of Saint Hugh, it brings me in remembrance of the Legacy that he gave us at his death.

What was that said the rest?

Marry (quoth he) I will tell you. When the gentle Prince saw that the cruelty of the time would not suffer him to be liberall to his friends, but that his life was taken away by one, and his flesh given to others, he most kindly bequeathed his bones unto us.

Tush (quoth another) that was but to shew his mind towards the Shoomakers, because he had of them received so many favours: for alas, what can the dead mans bones pleasure the living?

No (quoth another) I can tell you there may be as great vertue

found in his bones, as the braines of a Weasill, or the tongue of a Frog.

Much like (answered the rest) but I pray thee shew us what vertue is in those things you speak of.

(Quoth he) I will tell you. The braines of a Weasill hath this power, experientia docet, that if the powder thereof be mingled with the Runnet, wherewith women make their Chese, no mouse dares ever touch it: In like manner, the tongue of a water-frog hath such great force in it, that if it be laid upon the breast of any one sleeping, it will cause them tell whatsoever you shall demand; for by that means Dick Piper knew he was a Cuckold. Again, I know that those that are travellers are not ignorant, that whosoever puts but six leaves of Mugwort in his shooes, shall nere be weary, though he travell thirtie or fortie miles on foot in a forenoon.

That indeed may be true, (quoth one) for by the very same hearb my last Dame kept her Ale from sowring: and it is said, that where houseleek is planted, the place shall never be hurt with thunder. Pimpernell is good against Witchcraft; and because my sister Ioane carrieth alwayes some about her, Mother Bumby could not abide her: Therefore what vertue a dead mans bones may have, we know not till we have tryed it.

Why then (said the third man) let us soon at night steal Saint Hughes bones away, and albeit the Tyrant will be displeased, yet it is no theft, for you say they were given us, and therefore we may the bolder take them, and because we will turn them to profit, and avoyd suspition, we will make divers of our Tools with them, and then if any vertue do follow them, the better we shall find it.

To this motion every one gave his consent, so that the same night Saint Hughes bones were taken down, and the same being brought before a sort of shoomakers, there they gave their opinion; That it was necessary to fulfill the will of the dead, and to take those bones in as good a part, as if they were worth ten thousand pounds; whereupon one steps out, and thus did say:

> *My friends, I pray you list to me,*
> *And mark what S. Hughes bones shall be.*
>
> *First a Drawer and a Dresser,*
> *two wedges, a more and a lesser:*
> *A pretty block three inches high,*
> *in fashion squared like a die,*
> *Which shall be called by proper name,*
> *a Hel-block, the very same.*
> *A Hand-leather and a Thumb-leather likewise,*
> *to pull out shoo-threed we must devise;*
> *The Needle and the thimble,*
>   *shall not be left alone,*
> *The Pincers and the pricking Aule,*
>   *and the rubbing stone.*
> *The aule steele and tackes,*
>   *the Sow-hairs beside,*
> *The Stirrop holding fast,*
>   *while we sowe the cow-hide,*
> *The whetstone, the stopping-stick,*
>   *and the paring knife:*
> *All this doth belong*
>   *to a Journeymarn's life,*
> *Our Apron is the shrine*
>   *to wrap these bones in:*
> *Thus shrowded we Saint Hugh*
>   *in gentle Lambs skin.*

Now all you good Yeomen of the Gentle Craft, tell me now (quoth he) how like you this?

As well (replyed they) as Saint George doth of his horse, for as long as we can see him fight with the Dragon, we will never part from this Posie.

And it shall be concluded that what Iourney-man soever he be hereafter, that cannot handle the Sword and Buckler, his Long Sword, or a Quarter staffe, sound the Trumpet, or play upon the Flute and beare his part in a three mans Song: and readily reckon up his Toole in Rime; except he have born Colours in the field, being a Lieutenant, a Sergeant or Corporall, shall forfeit and pay a pottle of wine, or be counted for a colt: to which they answered all viva voce Content, content, and then after many merry Songs, they departed.

And never after did they travell without these tools on their backs: which ever since were called Saint Hughes bones.

CHAPTER V

How Crispianus and his brother Crispine, the two sons of the King of Logria, through the cruelty of the Tyrant Maximinus, were fain in disguised manner to seek for their lives safety, and how they were entertained by a Shoomaker in Feversham.

When the Roman Maximinus sought in cruell sort, to bereave this Land of all her noble youth or youth of noble blood, The vertuous Queene of Logria (which now is called Kent) dwelling in the city Durovernum, alias Canterbury, or the Court of Kentishmen, having at that time two young Sons, sought all the means she could possible to keep them out of the Tyrants claws; and in this manner she spake unto them.

My dear and beloved sons, the joy and comfort of my age, you see the danger of these times and the stormes of a Tyrants raigne, who having now gathered together the most part of the young Nobilite, to make them slaves in a forraign Land, that are free born in their own Countery, seeketh for you also, thereby to make a cleare riddance of all our borne Princes, to the end he might plant strangers in their stead. Therefore (my sweet sons) take the counsell of your mother, and seek in time to prevent ensuing danger, which will come upon us suddenly as a storme at sea, and as cruelly as a Tyger in the wildernesse: therefore suiting your selves in honest habits, seek some poore service to shield you from mischance, seeing necessity hath priviledged those places from Tyranny. And so (my sons) the gracious Heavens may one day raise you to deserved dignitie and honour.

The young Lads seeing their mother so earnest to have them gone, fulfilled her commandment, and casting off their attire, put homelie garments on, and with many bitter tears, took leave of the Queen their mother, desiring her before they went, to bestow her blessing upon them.

O my sons (quoth she) stand you now upon your ceremonies? Had I leasure to give you one kisse, it were something; the Lord blesse you, get you gone, away, away, make hast I say, let not swift time overslip you, for the Tyrant is hard by: with that she pushed them out of a backe doore, and then set her selfe down to weep.

The two young Princes, which like pretty lambes went straying they knew not whither, at length, by good fortune, came to Feversham, where before the dayes peep, they heard certaine Shoomakers singing, being as pleasant as their notes, as they sate at their businesse, and this was their Song:

Would God that it were holiday,
*   hey dery down down dery:*
That with my Love I might goe play,
*   with woe my heart is weary:*
My whole delight is in her sight,
*   would God I had her company,*
*   her company,*
Hey dery down, down adown.

My Love is fine, my Love is fair,
*   hey dery down, down dery:*
No Maid with her may well compare,
*   in Kent or Canterbury;*
From me my love shall never move,
*   would God I had her company,*
*   her company,*
Hey dery down, down adown.

To see her laugh, to see her smile,
*   hey dery down, down dery:*
Doth all my sorrows clean beguile,
*   and make my heart full merry;*
No griefe can grow where she doth goe,
*   would God I had her company, &c.*
Hey dery down, down adown.

When I do meet her on the green,
*   hey dery down, down dery:*
Methinks she lookes like beauties Queene,
*   which makes my heart full merry*
Then I her greet with kisses sweet,
*   would God I had her company, &c.*
Hey dery down, down adown.

My love comes not of churlish kind,
*   hey dery down, down dery;*
But bears a gentle courteous Mind,
*   which makes my heart full merry,*
She is not coy, she is my joy,
*   would God I had her company, &c.*
Hey dery down, down adown.

> *Till Sunday come, farewell my dear,*
> > *hey dery down, down dery.*
> *When we do meet we'll have good chear,*
> > *and then we will be merry:*
> *If thou love me, I will love the,*
> > *and still delight thy company, &c.*
> *Hey dery down, down adown.*

The young Princes perceiving such mirth to remain in so homely a cottage, judged by their pleasant notes, that their hearts were not cloyed with over many cares, and therefore wished it might be their good hap to be harboured in a place of such great content.

But standing a long time in doubt what to do, like two distressed strangers, combating twixt hope and feare; at length taking courage, Crispianus knocked at the doore. What knave knocks there (quoth the journeyman) and by and by, down he takes his quarter staffe and opens the doore, being as ready to strike as speak, saying: What lacke you? To whom Crispianus made this answer:

Good Sir, pardon our boldnesse, and measure not our truth by our rudenesse; we are two poore boyes that want service, stript from our friends by the fury of these warres, and therefore are we enforced succourlesse to crave service in any place.

What, have you no friends or acquaintance in these parts to go to (said the shoomaker) by whose means you might get preferment?

Alas Sir (said Crispianus) necessitie is despised of every one, and misery is toden down of many; but seldome or never relieved: yet, notwithstanding, if our hope did not yeeld us some comfort of good hap, we should grow desperate through distresse.

That were great pitie (said the Shoomaker) be content, for as our Dame often tells our Master, A patient man is better than a strong man. Stay a while and I will call our Dame to the doore, and then you shall heare what she will say.

With that he went in, and forth came his Dame, who beholding the said youths, said: Now alas, poore boyes, how comes it to passe that you are out of service? What, would you be Shoomakers, and learn the Gentle Craft?

Yes forsooth (said they) with all our hearts.

Now by my troth (quoth she) you do look with honest true faces. I will intreat my husband for you, for we would gladly have good boyes; and if you will be just and true, and serve God, no doubt you may do well enough: Come in my lads, come in.

Crispianus and his brother, with great reverence, gave her thanks; and by that time they had stayed a little while, down came the good man, and his wife hard at his heels, saying: see husband, these be the youths I told you of, no doubt but (in time) they will be good men.

Her husband looking wishtlie upon them, and conceiving a good opinion of their favors, at length agreed that they should dwell with him, so that they would be bound for seven years. The youths being contented, the bargain was soon ended, and so set to their business; wherat they were no soonr setled, but that great search was made for them in all places; and albeit the Officers came to the house where they dwelt, by the reason of their disguise they knew them not: having also taken upon them borrowed names of Crispianus and Crispine.

Within a few days after, the Queene their mother was by the tyrant taken; and for that she would not confesse where her sons were: she was laid prisoner in Rochester Castle: whereunto she went with as cherfull a countenance, as Cateratus did, when he was led captive to Rome: and coming by the place where her sonnes sat at work, with a quick eye she had soon spyed them and looke how a dying coal revives in the wind, even so at this sight she became suddenly red: but making signes that they should hold their tongues, she was led along: whom seven yeers after her sons did never see. But as men stand amazed at the sight of Apparitions in the ayre, as ignorant what successe shall follow, even so were these two Princes agast to see their own mother thus led away, not knowing what danger would ensue thereof.

Notwithstanding, they thought good to keep their service as their lives surest refuge: at what time they both bent their whole minds to please their Master and Dame, refusing nothing that was put to them to do, were it to wash dishes, scoure kettles, or any other thing, whereby they thought their Dames favour might be gotten, which made her the readier to give them a good report to their Master, and to do them many other services, which otherwise they should have missed; following therein the admonition of an old Journey-man, who would alwayes say to the Apprentices:

> *Howsoever things do frame,*
> *Please well thy Master, But chiefly thy Dame.*

Now by that time, these two young Princes had truely served their Master the space of foure or fiue yeers, he was grown something wealthy, and they very cunning in the trade; whereby the house had the name to breed the best workmen in the Countrey: which report in the end prefer'd their Master to be the Emperours Shoomaker: and by this means, his servants went to Maximinus Court every day: but Crispianus and Crispine fearing they should have bene known, kept themselves from thence as much as they could. Notwithstanding, at the last perswading themselues, that Time had worne them out of knowledge, they were willing in the end to go thither, as well to hear tidings of the Queen their Mother as also for to seek their own preferment.

CHAPTER VI

How the Emperours fair daughter Ursula, fell in love with young Crispine coming with shooes to the Court; and how in the end they were secretly married by a blind Frier.

Now among all the Shoomakers men that came to the Court with shooes, young Crispine was had in greatest regard with the fair Princesse, whose mother being lately dead, she was the only joy of her father, who always sought means to match her with some worthy Romane, whose renown might ring throughout the whole world.

But fair Ursula, whose bright eyes had entangled her heart with desire of the Shoomakers favour, despised all proffers of love, in regard of him. And yet notwithstanding she would oft check her own opinion, in placing her love upon a person of such low degree, thus reasoning with her selfe.

Most aptly is the god of Love by cunning Painters drawn blind, that so equally shoots forth his fiery shafts: for had he eyes to see, it were impossible to deal in such sort, as in matching fair Venus with foule Vulcan, yoking the Emperiall hearts of Kings to the love of beggars, as he did by Cofetua, and as now in my selfe I find how mad a thing it would seem to the eyes of the world, that an Emperors daughter should delight in the favour of a simple Shoomaker.

O Ursula take heed what thou dost, stain not thy royalty with such indignity. O that Crispines birth were agreeable to his person! for in mine eye, there is no Prince in the world comparable to him: if then while he is clothed in these rags of servitude, he appear so excellent, what would he be, were he in Princely attire! O Crispine, either thou are not as thou seemest, or else Nature, in disgrace of Kings, hath made the a Shoomaker.

In these humours would the Princesse often be, especially at Crispines approach, or at his departure; For, as soon as ever he came within her sight with shooes, a sudden blush like unto a flame of lightning would strike in her face, and at his departure an earthly pale colour, like to the beams of the bright Sunne obscured by cole-blacke clouds. But after many weary conflicts with Fancy, she fully resolved, at his next coming, to enter in communication with him, but imagining his stay from Court over long, on the sudden she sent presently for him, finding great fault in the last shooes he brought her. At which time Crispine most humbly on his knee gently craved pardon for all such faults as she then found, promising amendment in the next shooes she should have.

Nay (quoth she) Ile shew thee, they are too low something in the instep; also the hel is bad, and besides that, they are too strait in the toes.

You shall have a pair made (said he) shall fit you better, for none shall set a stitch in them but mine own selfe.

Do, said the Princesse, but let me have them so soon as thou canst; and therewith Crispine departed.

The Princesse then all solitary, got her selfe into her chamber, entred there into consideration, and found within her selfe great trouble and sorrow, while her tongue, the hearts advocate, was not suffered to speak. At last she heard Crispines voice, enquiring of the Ladies in the great Chamber for the Princesse, who answered, That having taken little rest the night before, she was now laid down to sleep, and therefore they willed him to come again some other time.

Asleep, replied the Princesse! I am not asleepe, bid him stay: what hasty huswife was that which sent him hence? Call him again quickly I would advise you.

And therewithall changing melancholly into mirth, she arose up from out of her bed, and as a bright starre shooting in the Element, she swiftly got her forth to meet the shoomaker, whose fair sight was to her as great a comfort as Sunshine is before a showre of raine.

How now (quoth she) hast thou brought me a pair of shooes?

I have, gracious Madam (quoth he).

Then (quoth the Princesse) come thy selfe and draw them on: therewith she sitting down, lifted up her well proportioned legge upon his gentle knee. Where, by that time her shooes were drawn on, she had prepared a good reward for her shoomaker, and giving him a handfull of gold, she said: Thou hast so well pleased me in making of these shooes, that I cannot but reward thee in some good sort, therefore shoomaker, take this, and from henceforth let no man make my shooes but thy selfe. But tell me Crispine, art thou not in love, that thou dost smug up thy selfe so finely, thou wast not wont to go so neatly: I pray thee tell me what pretty wench is it that is mistresse of thy heart?

Truely, fair Madam (quoth he) If I should not love, I might be counted barbarous, for by natures course there is a mutuall love in all things: the Dove and the Peacock love intirely, so doth the Turtle and the Popinjay; the like affection the fish Musculus beareth unto the huge Whale, insomuch that he leadeth him from all danger of stony rocks, and as among birds and fishes, so amongst plants and trees the like concord is to be found, for if the male of palme trees be planted from the female, neither of both prosper: and being set one neer another, they do flourish accordingly, imbracing with joy the branches one of another. And for mine own part, I am in love too; for first of all, I love my Maker, and next, my good Master and Dame. But as concerning the love of pretty wenches, verily Madam, I am cleare: and the rather do I abstain from fixing my fancy on women, seeing many sorrowes do follow the married sort, that for a dramme of delight have a pound of pain.

That is (answered the Princesse) where Contention setteth the house on fire, but where true love remaines, there is no discontent: and what can a man more desire for this worlds comfort, but a vertuous wife, which is reported to be a treasure inestimable. Therefore Crispine, say thy minde, if I prefer thee to a wife, every way deserving thy love, wouldst thou take it well?

Truly Madame (said Crispine) if I should not accept of your good will, I should shew my selfe more unmannerly then well nurtured: but seeing it pleaseth you to grace me with your Princely countenance, and to give me libertie to speak my mind, this is my opinion: If I were worthy to choose a wife, then would I have one fair, rich, and wise; first, to delight mine eye; secondly, to supply my want; and thirdly, to govern my house.

Then (said the Princesse) her beauty I will refer unto the judgement of thine own eyes, and her wisedome unto the triall of Time; but as concerning her portion, I dare make some report, because it well deserveth to be praised: For at her marriage thou shalt have a bagge full of rare vertues with her.

Truly Madam (quoth Crispine) such coynes go not currant among Tannars; and I know, if I should go therewith to the Market, it will buy me no soale-leather. Notwithstanding, when I do see her, I will tell you more of my mind.

The Princesse taking him aside, privately walking with him in a fair Gallerie, said; in looking upon me, thou mayest judge of her, for she is as like me as may be.

When Crispine heard her say so, he right prudently answered: I had rather Madam she were your own selfe, then like your selfe: and although my words savour of presumption, yet with your favour I dare boldly pronounce it, that I hold my selfe worthy of a Queen, if I could get her good will. And were it not danger to match with your Excellency, if so it should please you it should not dislike me.

Then said the Princesse; Now shoomaker I see thou hast some courage in thee: and doubt thou not, that if I were of that mind, but I would be as ready to guide thee from the dangerous rocks of my fathers wrath, as the fish called Musculus is for the Whale: But, couldst thou not be contented to die for a Ladies love?

No Madam (quoth he) if I could keep her love, and live.

Then live faire friend (answered she) enjoy my love, for I will die rather then live without thee.

Crispine hearing this, was stricken into an extasie of joy, in such sort, as he wist not whether he were asleep, or dreamed: But by that time he had summoned his wits together, with the plighting of his faith, he opened his estate and high birth unto her, shewing all the extremities that he and his brother had ben put unto since the death of their royall Father, and of the imprisonment of the Queen their Mother.

The which when fair Ursula with great wonder heard, giving him an earnest of her love, with a sweet kisse; she said; My deare Love, and most gentle Prince, ever did I think, that more then a common man was shrowded in these poore habiliments, which made me the bolder to impart my mind unto thee, and now dread no more my Fathers wrath, for the fire thereof was long agoe quenched.

No, no, (quoth Crispine) an Eagles thirst is never expelled, but by blood. And albeit your father have now (perhaps) qualified the heat of his fury by the length of time, yet if he should understand of this my love to thee, it would cause him to rake out of the ashes, hot burning coals of displeasure again: and then might my life pay a deare price for thy love. Therefore (my deare Ursula) I desire thee, even by the power of that love thou bearest to me, to keepe secret what I have shewed thee, nothing doubting but that in time, I may find release of these miseries; in the mean space we will be secretly married, by which holy knot, we may as well in body, as in heart, be unseparately tied together.

To this Ursula consented most gladly, and thereupon told him that she would meet him in her fathers Park, at any houre he would appoint, which she might do the more easily, in respect she had a key to one of the garden doores, which gave present passage into the Park. The day and houre being concluded upon, they parted for this time, both of them indued with such content, as in all their lives they never found the like.

And at this time there was in Canterbury a blind Frier that in many yeers had never seen the Sun; to this man did Crispine go, thinking him the fittest Chaplain to chop up such a marriage, who meeting with him at Christ-church one evening after the Antheme, broke with him after this manner.

God speed good father: there is a certain friend of mine that would be secretly married in the morning betimes; for which purpose he thinks you the fittest man to perform it in all the Cloister: and therefore, if you will be diligent to do it, and secret to conceale it, you shall have foure angels for your pains.

The Frier being fired with the desire of his gold, rubbing his elbow and scratching his crown, swore by the blessed Book that hung by his knee, that he would be both willing and constant to keep it in secret. Tush young man, you may trust me, I have done many of these feats in my dayes; I know that youth are youth, but they would not have all the world wonder at their doings: and where shall it be, said the Frier?

(Quoth Crispine) at Saint Gregories Chappell, and because you shall not make your boy acquainted therewith, I my selfe will call you in the morning. Good father be not forgetfull to observe the time, at two of the clock is the houre, and therefore look you be ready when I shall call you.

I warrant you (replied the Frier:) and because I will not oversleep my selfe, I will for this night lie in my clothes, so that as soon as ever you call, I will straight be ready.

Then father I will trust you (quoth Crispine) and so departed.

When he came to his Masters, he made not many words, but so soon as he had supt on Sunday at night, he went to his chamber, and laid him down upon his bed, making no creature in the house privy to his intent, not his own brother, his minde still running on his faire Mistresse, and the happie houre that will tie them both in one: never was there hunger-starved man that did long more for the sweet approch of wholesome food, than did Crispin for two a clock. And so soon as the silent night had drawn all things to rest, Crispine got him up, and to Canterbury goes he, to meet his Rose-cheked Lady in her Fathers Park, who also took hold of Times forlock, and like clear Cynthia shaped her course to seek out Sol in the Meridian. But so soon as her searching eye had spied him, she commended his vigilancie, saying: He well observed his houre.

O my deere (quoth he) rich preys do make true men theves: but finding thee here so happily, I will fetch the Frier straight.

He had no soonr called at the Friers doore, but he presently heard him; and groaping the way down, he opened the doore, and along they went together. But the Frier, finding his journey longer then he expected, said; That either Saint Gregories Chappell was removed, or else he was not so good a footman as he was wont to be.

That is likely enough (said Crispine:) for how much the older you are since you went this way last, so much the weaker you are to travell. But be you content, now we are at the last come to the place, and therefore good Frier, make what speed you may.

I warrant you (quoth he) and therewithall he puts his Spectacles on his nose.

The fair Princesse perceiving that, laughed heartily, saying, Little need hath a blind man of a paire of Spectacles.

True Mistress (said he) as little need hath an old man of a young wife; but you may see what use is: Though I be blind and can see never a letter, yet I cannot say Masse without my Booke and my Spectacles; And then he proceeded to solemnize their marriage, which being finished, the Frier had his gold, and home he was led.

In the mean time the Princesse stayed still in the Park for her Bridegroom; where when he came, on a bank of sweet primroses, he pluckt the rose of amorous delight: and after, the Princesse came to her Fathers Palace, and Crispine to his Masters shop.

CHAPTER VII

How Crispianus was prest to the warres, and how he fought with Iphicratis the renowned Generall of the Persians, who made warre upon the Frenchmen: shewing also the occasion that a Shoomakers sonne is said to be a Prince born.

In the mean time that Crispine was secretly busied about his marriage, his brother Crispianus the same night, with many other, was prest to wars into the Countrey of Gaul, now called France, which made his Master and Dame full of woe, who had committed to his government the whole rule of the house. And when Crispine came home, they told him what chance had hapned, and demanded where he had been. They said, they were glad he had so well escaped.

Crispine excusing himselfe so well as he could, said he was sorrie for his brothers sudden departure: notwithstanding, the joy of his late mariage mitigated much of his sorrow; to whom in his brothers absence, his Master gave the oversight of his houshold, which place he guided with such discretion, as thereby he got both the good will of his Master, and the love of the houshould. And as he sate one day at his worke, he sung this song in commendation of marriage: himselfe sung the Ditty, and his fellowes bore the burthen.

> *Among the joyes on earth, though little joy there be,*
> *hey down down adown, fine is the silken twist,*
> *Among the married sort most comfort I do see:*
> *hey down down adown, beleeve it they that list.*
> *He that is a married man, hath beauty to embrace,*
> *hey down down adown, and therefore mickle woe:*
> *He liveth in delight, and is in happie case,*
> *hey down down adown, in faith we think not so.*
> *His wife doth dresse his meate, with everything most meet,*
> *hey down down adown, fair women love good chear:*
> *And when he comes to bed, she gives him kisses sweet,*
> *hey down down adown, for thanks he payes full deare.*

A hundred honey sweets, he hath when that is done,
     hey down down adown, the truth is seldome known:
He hath in a little time a daughter or a son,
     hey down down adown, God grant they be his own.
A wife is evermore, both faithfull true and just,
     hey down down adown, 'tis more then you do know:
Her husband may be sure, in her to put his trust,
     hey down down adown, most are deceived so.
While he doth ride abroad, she looks unto his house,
     hey down down a down, the finest cloth is torn:
And when he comes, she gives him brawn and sowse,
     hey down down adown, and oftentimes the horn.

How now, what is that you say? (quoth Crispine).

Nothing (quoth they) but only beare the burden of your Song. And surely we think it great pity that you are not married, seeing you can sing so well in the praise of marriage.

Truly (quoth he) were it not for that holy Institution, what would the world be but a brood of haplesse bastards, like to the cursed seed of Cain, men fit for all manner of villany, and such as would leave behind them a race of runnagates, persons that would live as badly as they were lewdly begotten.

The rest of the Journey-men hearing him enter into such a deep discourse of the matter, began thereof to demand many questions: but seeing it appertaines not to our matter, weele leave them to their disputation: and in the mean space I will shew you something of Crispianus, who is now in France, with many other Noble Britains, whom Maximinus sent thither to aide the Gauls against the mightie force of Iphicratis the Persian Generall, who had at this time invaded their Countrey with a great power.

The day of battel being appointed, the Armies met in the field, at what time both the Generals like two Lyons filled with wrath in their proud march viewed one another, breathing forth on both sides words of disdain, and thus the Generall of the Gauls began:

Thou insulting Commander of the Easterne troups, how durst thou set thy ambitious foot within our territories? Cannot the confines of Persia content thee, nor those conquered Kingdomes already in they hand, but that with unsatiable desire thou must come to usurp our right? Know thou, that the undaunted Gauls do scorn thee: for albeit that Alexander-like, thou seekst to subdue the whole world, flattering thy selfe in thy fortunes, yet never think that the son of a shoomaker shall bend our neck to a servile yoke. Therefore in our just right we are come to give thee hire for thy pride, and by the force of our swords to beat down the Scepter of thy proud thoughts.

The renowned Iphicratis upon these words made this replie: Now may I report, that the Gauls can do something, finding them such good scolds: But know this that I come not to raile, but to revenge these contemptuous speeches, and with the points of sturdie

Launces to thrust them down your throats again. Indeed, my fathers trade is a reproach unto me, but thou art a reproach to thy father: but thou shalt understand that a Shoemakers son is a Prince born, his fortune made him so, and thou shalt finde no lesse.

And hereupon the trumpets sounding to a charge, and the drums striking a alarum, there followed a sore and cruell fight: wherein Crispianus like a second Hector laid about him, hewing down his foes on every side. Whose valiancy and Princely courage was noted of all the Gauls.

And this fierce fight ended with the nights approach, each Army tooke their rest. At what time the Noble Generall of the Gauls sent for Crispianus, and receiving him with sundry kind imbracements into his Tent, he demanded of what birth he was.

To whom Crispianus shaped this answer: Most worthy Generall, my birth is not mean, and my secrets lesse, but by trade I am a Shoomaker in England.

A Shoomaker! (said the Generall). If such fame waite upon shoomakers, and such magnanimity follow them, well were it for us, if all the people in the Kingdome were Shoomakers. And as great thanks I am to give Maximinus for sending me such a Souldier, as he may be proud to have such a subject: and now right sorrie am I, that ever I reproached famous Iphicratis, with his Fathers trade, seeing I find it true that Magnanimity and Knightly Prowesse, is not alwayes tied within the compasse of Noble blood. And for my own part, I will so honourably requite thy deservings, that thou shalt blesse the time thou ever camest into these wars.

The next morning the Generals joyned battell again, resolving in this fight either by death or victory, to make an end of these troubles, where the souldiers on each side strove for the golden wreath of renown. The two Generals meeting in the battell, fought most couragiously together; in which bloody conflect the Prince of the Gaules was thrice by Iphicratis unhorsed, and as many times of Crispianus mounted again: but in the end the great Commander of the Easterne Army, so mightily prevail'd, that he had seized on the person of the French Prince, and was carrying him captive to his Colours.

But so highly was Crispianus favoured of Fortune, that he and his followers met him in the pride of his conquest: who then all besmeared in the Persian blood, set upon Iphicratis, and so manly behaved himselfe, that he recovered the Prince again, and in despight of the Persians, brought him to his Royall Tent: in which encounter the Noble Iphicratis was sore wounded, by reason whereof the Souldiers had rest for three or foure dayes: in which space Iphicratis sent to the Prince of Gauls, to know what kin he was, that in such valiant sort rescued him out of his hands; saying; that if he would serve him, he would make him ruler over a mighty Kingdome.

The French Prince sent him word, that it was a right hardy Brittaine, which had performed that honourable service; but no Knight, though well deserving greater dignity, but a Shoomaker in England and thus (quoth he) a Shoomakers son was by a Shoomaker foiled.

When Iphicratis understood this, he sent word again to the Gauls that for the favour of that worthy man, he would not only cease the wars, but forever after be a friend to the Gauls: which joyfull message when the French King understood, most willingly he imbraced the unlooked for tydings of happie peace: and thereupon made Crispianus a knight.

After the which there was a great feast ordained, whereunto the renowned Iphicratis was invited, and the two generals, with Crispianus, friendly met together. Thus the sowre war was ended with sweet feasting: and Iphicratis soon after departed out of the Country with his Army, and never after annoyed them.

Then the french King, writing his Letter of thanks unto the Emperour Maximinus, did therein certifie him of the Princely acts of Crispianus, whereby he was brought into the emperours favour; and with these letters Crispianus returned into England.

CHAPTER VIII

How the Lady Ursula finding her selfe to be with child, made her great moan unto her husband Crispine, and how he provided for her a secret place, where she was delivered.

In the mean space the Lady Ursula finding her selfe to be with child, and her unknown husband coming one day with Shooes unto her, she made her moan unto him, saying: O Crispine how shall we do? The time of my sorrow and shame draweth on; I feel that living in my womb, which, I fear, will bring death upon us all.

Why my dear Lady (answered he) art thou with child? Keep thy chamber close, and wittily excuse thy grief, untill I have found means to procure our safety.

But dost thou mean faithfully (said she) wilt thou not deceive me, and for fear of my fathers wrath fly the country?: if thou shouldest do so, then were I the wretchedst Lady alive. Forsake me not sweet Crispine, whatsoever thou doest, but take me with thee wheresoever thou goest: it is not my fathers frowns that I regard, so I may have thy favour, what do I care for a Princely Pallace: an homely Cottage shall content me in thy company. O my Love, I will rather learne to spin hemp for thy shoo-threed, than live without thee in the greatest pleasure.

I will not leave thee my deare Love (quoth he) by that faith I vow, which I plighted to thee at our blessed marriage; and therefore be contented, and it shall not be long before I do return.

Leaving thus his sad Lady he came home, and secretly broke the matter unto his Dame, desiring her counsell in this his extremity.

What, how now (quoth she) hast thou got a Maid with child? Ah thou whorson villaine, thou hast undone thy selfe, how wilt thou do now? Thou hast made a faire hand; here is now sixteen pence a week beside sope and candles, beds, shirts, biggins, wastcoats, headbands, swadlebands, crosse-cloths, bibs, tailclouts, mantles, hose, shooes, coats, petticoats, cradle and crickets, and beside that a standing-stole, and a posnet to make the child pap; all this is come upon thee, besides the charges of all her lying in. Oh Crispine, Crispine, I am heartily sorry for thee.

But in good faith, if I knew the quean that hath brought thee to this folly, I would have her by the face I swear to you: for though I speak it before thee (Crispine) thou art a proper fellow, and thou mightest have done full well if thou hadst had grace. God hath done his part on thee: and with that she began with kindnesse to weep. Whereupon her husband coming in, asked what she ailed:

O man (said she) Crispine!

Why, why, what of Crispine? Tell me. Why speakst thou not?

We shall lose a good servant, so we shall.

What servant shall we lose foolish woman? (quoth he). Tell me quickly.

O husband! By Cock and Pie, I swear, Ile have her by the nose.

Who wilt thou have by the nose? What the Devill, art thou mad, that thou wilt not answer me?

Crispine, who at his Masters coming in shunned the roome, lending an ear unto these words, went unto his Master, and said unto him, Sir, these foure yeeres have I served you, and the fifth draweth neer unto an end; as I have found you a good Master to me, so I trust you have had no great cause to complain of me, though (through ignorance) I have sometimes made offence: and knowing at this instant, no man so neer a friend unto me as your selfe, I have thought good to impart my secret counsell to you: something I did presume upon my Dames favour: which made me open that unto her, which now I wish I had not discovered. Notwithstanding, resting more upon your discretion then her secrecie, I would desire your counsell in a matter that concerns me very neer.

Verily (said his Master) if it be a thing wherein I may do thee good, thou shalt find that I will not fall from thee in thy sorrows, and therefore be not abashed to declare thy mind: for I swear, if I may procure the right, thou shalt put up no wrong.

Why then sir, thus it is (quoth he) my will running before my wit, I have gotten a Maiden with childe, and I wot not in this case what to do, that I might preserve the Maid from shame, and my selfe from discredit: beside, I doubt if it be known, it will cost me my life: therefore in such case good Master be secret.

Tush man feare not (quoth he) it is a matter of nothing: but I pray thee, now tell me, what a wanton Wagtaile is it that thou hast clapt thus under the apron?

O Master (quoth he) the Kings faire daughter Ursula is my Love, and she it is that lives in care for my sake.

Passion of my heart thou whorson Knave (quoth his Master) thou art a dead man. I marvell how the devill thou camest to be so bold with her. Surely thou hast drawn on her shooes on Sunday, I may say, thou hast left so good a token behind: but in truth my boy I commend thee, that thou wouldest shoot at the fairest.

Yea sir (quoth Crispine) and I have hit the mark I trow, and do verily beleeve, that none will shoot so neere again.

Nay sweare not (said his Master) many may aim at faire marks, and more then one man hits them now and then: but what wouldest thou have me to do in this case?

My good Master (quoth Crispine) the troth is, she is my wife; and the very same night my brother was prest to the warres, I was married to her: and if you could tell me how she might be delivered of her burden without any suspition, I should not only remain beholding to you while I lived, but would also gratifie your kindnesse in such sort as should content you.

His Dame all this while listned to their talk, and when she understood he spake of the Kings daughter, and that he had married her, she said: Now Gods blessing on thy heart Crispine, that thou art so carefull for thy wife, but it maketh me wonder she would marrie a Shoomaker, and a poore fellow too.

Master and Dame (quoth Crispine) seeing I have begun, Ile shew you a further matter, as strange as the other. The necessity of these times makes many Noble personages to mask in simple habite, as Jupiter did in a shepherds weed, and the truth is, that Lady Ursula is not ignorant, that by matching with me she hath wedded a Prince, and you may say that these five yeeres two Princes have served you obediently, under the simple borrowed names of Crispine and Crispianus. Our Royall Father was slaine by the Emperour Maximinus, and the Queen our Mother lies yet imprisoned, and your poore house, and these leather garments, have been our life of defence against the blood-thirsty tyrant.

Now you see, that though there were hate towards us in the Father, yet there is love yeelded us by the Daughter. This must be kept for a certaine time from the knowledge of him, lest our lives pay a deare ransome for our loves.

Well Crispine (quoth his Dame) be of good cheare, for I have a device in my head, how to get thy Love out of her Fathers Pallace, that she may be brought to bed in mine own house, without either hurt to thee, or dishonour to her, if thou wilt do as I wish thee. When you do perceive that she grows neere unto the time of her travell, I would wish you to worke such means, as to set some tree on fire late in the night, that standeth somewhat neere one of the Beacons upon the Sea coast, whereby it will follow, that such watchmen as watch at our Beacons, supposing the Beacons at the Sea coast to be of fire, will set theirs on fire also. Then will there be a great hurly burly, with the preparation of men at Armes on all sides, to withstand a supposed foe, that which they shall never find: then (as you know) Maximinus with his houshold will be in most fear, because he is most hated, so that whilest he is abroad, the rest of his houshold will every one of them seek for their safegard, amongst the which, let faire Ursula be one, who by that means singling her selfe alone, may take up my house, and here she may closely be kept till she be delivered, taking upon her the name and habite of a simple woman.

But the troth of this matter (quoth Crispine) I doubt it will soon be perceived and found out, then how shall Lady Ursula do, for she will straight be missed.

Tush thats no matter (quoth his Dame) and missed let her be, untill such time as she is in better case to go abroad again, for in such a tumult as then will be, they will suppose many things, that one mischance or other is befallen her: or if she be in health, that she hath wandred into the woods, or some other uncouth place; where she might best provide for safety: and when she comes home again, I warrant the Crispine she will be welcome.

Then said his Master, I like my wives device well; and therefore by my consent put it in practice.

Whereunto Crispine consented, and so making the Lady privie to the purpose, at length it was put in execution, at what time there was crying out on all sides, Arme, Arme, Arme: our enemies are coming upon us.

Where? (quoth they).

At Rutupium said one.

At Aruvagus Castle said another.

(Quoth the third) it is at Doris.

I tell you (quoth the fourth) it is at Duur.

And all this is but Dover (said the fifth man) and at Dover it is undoubtedly, therefore, hast, hast, and away; for never was there more neede: so that Maximinus was almost at his wits end, as one not knowing which way to turn, the cries of the people came so thicke, one after another. The waiting gentlewomen left their Princesse and sought their owne safetie. Thus while some were busie in carying out the Kings treasure; others hiding the plate, and others the goods, Ursula had an easie passage into the Shoomakers house.

The young Prince Crispine was gone with the rest of the town towards Dover, where when they came, there was nothin to do; which when Maximinus saw, he was not a little glad the wars were so soon ended: But when he came to the Court and missed his daughter, there was posting up and down in every place to seek her but all in vain, for no man could meet with her, for which he made a great lamentation, making a Proclamation throughout the whole Country, that whosoever could bring her to him, he should not onely have a Princely reward, but also, if he were a man of Noble blood, he should be honoured with the marriage of his fair daughter. This was good news to Crispine, who was not to learn to make profit thereof.

But by that time his Lady was light, Crispianus his eldest arrived into England with great honour, as before you have heard. And before he went to the Court, he thought it good to visit his old Master, who came also in good time to the christening of his brothers child, which when he with wonder beheld, noting what a strange accident there was, that Maximinus daughter should be his brother's wife. But after that he had in Princely manner saluted the new delivered Lady, talking the infant in his arms, he kissed it, saying: Now I will say and swear (said he) that a Shoomakers Son is a Prince born, joyning in the opinion of Iphycratis, and henceforth Shoomakers shall never let their terme die.

Then turning to his Master and Dame (he said) how much dear Master and Dame, are we bound to your favours, that have maintained our honours with our happiness; for by that means, I hope we shall make a joyfull conclusion of our sorrowfull beginnning, and will so work that the Emperour shall confirm what is alreadie begun; I mean, the honour due to these Princely Lovers, and, together with our happy fortunes, procure our mothers liberty.

Hereupon within a short time after, he made preparation to the court, he attired himselfe in Princely manner, and with a most knightly grace he delivered to Maximinus, the King of Gaul's letter, where he certified the Emperor of the honourable deeds performed by Crispianus, whereupon he received him to great favour, and said unto him, Right renowned Knight, for that great honour thou hast done me in France, I will honour thee with anything which thou shalt command that standeth with the Majesty and credit of an Emperor to give.

Then I beseech your Highnesse (quoth he) to grant me the life, and liberty of my dear Mother, that late Queen of Logria.

Art thou her son? (said Maximinus). Although thy father was my foe, yet I must needs say, he was a most couragious and warlike Prince: thy suit is granted. And once I had a daughter worthy of thy love, but unconstant Fortune hath bereft mee of that blisse; but had it pleased the faire Heavens to have left her me till this day, I would have made the more honourable by her match: But seeing that my wishing doth nothing profit thee, take hence the richest jewell I have, and be thou next my selfe in authority: with that he took from his owne necke a Coller of most precious Diamonds, and gave it to Crispianus, saying, be thou as fortunate as Policrates.

CHAPTER IX

How fair Ursula came before her father with Crispine her husband, who was joyfully received by him, and in the end had his good will to confirme the mariage betwixt them, whereupon there was great joy on both sides. And the Shoomakers in honour of this happy day, made a joyfull Song.

Within a certaine space after, word was brought to the Emperor, that his daughter was with a Shoomaker, come to the Court; whereat Maximinus was stricken into a sudden joy, saying: An Honourable Shoomaker may he be that hath brought my fair daughter again. Welcome my sweet Ursula, and in good time welcome to thy father, and welcome also is this happy young man, that hath so fortunately brought thee; and turning to Crispianus he said: Noble sir Knight, take here my daughter to wife.

Not so dear Father (quoth she) this man hath best deserved my love, that hath preserved my life, and his wife will I be.

Why Ursula (said her Father) wilt thou darken the sun-shine of my joy, with the clouds of foule obstinacy, and yoke thy selfe so unequally? This man is a Prince.

And this mans son is another (quoth she.)

That is strange (said the Emperour) can that child be a Prince, whose father is but a Shoomaker?

Then answered Ursula, My Royall Father, a Shoomakers son is a Prince born.

Most gracious Lord (quoth Crispianus) the very like sentence did I hear the renowned Iphicrates pronounce to the King of Gauls, when he upbraided him with his birth: with that Crispines Dame presented the child to the Emperour; and faire Ursula was very diligent to uncover the childs face, and held it to her Father.

Why daughter (quoth he) art thou not ashamed to honour a base borne brat so much? Hence with the Elfe, and therewithall pusht it from him: whereat his daughters teares trickled down her cheeks, and so kissing the child, gave it again to the woman.

What (said Maximinus) dost thou love the child so well, that thou must kisse it, and weep for it?

I have cause deare Father (quoth she) for that this childs mother lay in my mothers belly.

At these words the Emperor suspected something, and demanded of Crispine of what parentage he was. And then knowing that he was Crispianus brother, all the controversie was ended, and their secret mariage confirmed openly, with great joy and triumph: at which time the Shoomakers in the same town made Holiday: to whom Crispine and Crispianus sent most Princely gifts for to maintain their merriment. And ever afterward, upon that day at night, the Shoomakers make great cheare and feasting, in remembrance of these two Princely brethren: and because it might not be forgotten, they caused their names to be placed in the Kalender for a yeerly remembrance, which you shall find in the moneth of October, about three dayes before the Feast of Simon and Jude.

The Shoomakers Song on Crispianus night.

Two Princely brethren once there were,
*   right Sonnes unto a King;*
Whose father tyrant Maximus
*   to cruell death did bring:*
Crispianus one was call'd,
*   the eldest of the two;*
Crispine was the others name,
*   which well had learn'd to wooe.*
These brethren then were after fain,
*   from fathers house to flie:*
Because their foes, to spoil their lives
*   in privy wait did lie,*
Into a kind shoomakers house,
*   they suddenly stept in;*
And there to learn the Gentle Craft,
*   did presently begin.*
And five yeers space they lived so,
*   with great content of mind;*
So that the Tyrant could not tell,
*   whereas he shoud them find:*
Though every day to Court they came,
*   with shooes for Ladies feet;*
They were not known by their attire,
*   they us'd themselves so meet.*

At length unto the furious wars
        was Crispianus prest:
Whereas his knightly prowesse then
        he tried above the rest.
But Crispine found them better sport –
        would I had Crispine been:
The Kings fair daughter Lov'd him well,
        as it was after seen.
The length of this fair Ladies foot,
        so well did Crispine know,
That none but he could please her mind,
        the certain truth is so.
Came he by night, or else by day,
        he was most welcome still;
With kisses sweet she did him pay,
        and thanks for his good will.
So oft these lovers twain did meet,
        by day and eke by night:
That at the last the Lady said,
        she should be shamed quite:
What was the matter, tell me true,
        that so her sorrow bred?
Her Shoomaker most daintily
        had got her Maidenhead.
But he at length so wisely wrought,
        as doth the Story tell:
Her fathers right good will he got,
        and every thing was well.
And Crispianus came again
        from warres victoriously:
Then Shoomakers made Holiday,
        and therefore so will I.
And now for Crispianus sake,
        this wine I drinke to the,
And he that doth this marke mistake,
        and will not now pledge me:
He is not Crispianus friend;
        nor worthy well I wot,
To have a Lady to his Love,
        as Crispine he hath got.

CHAPTER X

How Sir Simon Eyer being at first a Shoomaker, became in the end Mayor of London, through the counsell of his wife: and how he broke his fast every day on a Table that he said he would not sell for a thousand pounds: and how he builded Leadon Hall.

Our English Chronicles do make mention, that sometime there was in the honourable City of London a worthy Mayor known by the name of Sir Simon Eyer, whose fame liveth in the mouths of many men to this day, who albeit he descended of mean parentage; yet by Gods blessing, in the end he came to be a most worthy man in the Commonwealth.

This man being brought young out of the North Countrey, was bound prentice to a shoomaker, bearing then the name of the Gentle Craft (as still it doth.) His Master being a man of reasonable wealth, set many journey-men and prentices to work, who followed their businesse with great delight, which quite excludeth all wearinesse, for when servants do sit at their work like Dromedaries, then their minds are never lightly upon their businesse: for it is an old proverb.

> *They prove servants kind and good,*
> *That sing at their businesse like birds in the wood.*

Such fellows had this young Lad, who was not behind with many Northern Jigs, to answer their Sothern Songs. This youth being the youngest prentice in the house, as occasion served, was often sent to the Conduit for water, where in short time he fell acquainted with many other prentices comming thither for the same intent.

Now their custome was so, that every Sunday morning divers of these prentices did use to go to a place neer the Conduit, to break their fast with pudding pies, and often they would take Simon along with them: but upon a time it so fell out, that when he should draw money to pay the shot with the rest, that he had none, whereupon he merrily said unto them: My faithfull friends, and Conduit companions, treasurers of the water-tankard, and main pillers of the pudding house, I may now compare my purse to a barren Doe, that yields the Keeper no more good then her empty carkasse: or to a bad nut, which being opened hath, never a kernell: therefore, if it will please you to pardon me at this time, and excuse me for my part of the shot, I do here vow unto you, that if ever I come to be Lord Mayor of this City, I will give a breakfast unto all the prentices in London.

We will take your word (quoth they) and so they departed.

It came to passe, that Simon having at length worn out his yeers of Apprentiship, that he fell in love with a maiden that was a neer neighbour unto him, unto whom at length he was married, and got him a shop, and laboured hard daily, and his young wife was never idle, but straight when she had nothing to do, she sat in the shop and spun: and having lived thus alone a yeer or thereabout, and having gathered something together, at length he got him some prentices, and a Journey-man or two, and he could not make his ware so fast as he could have sold it, so that he stood in great need of a Journey-man or two more.

At the last, one of his servants spying one go along the street with a fardell at his back, called to his Master, saying, Sir, yonder goes Saint Hughes bones, twenty pounds to a penney.

Run presently (quoth he) and bring him hither.

The boy running forth called to the man, saying; Good fellow come hither, here is one would speak with you.

The fellow being a Frenchman, that had not long been in England, turning about, said: Hea? What you sea? Will you speak wed me, Hea? What you have? Tell a me, what you have, Hea? And with that coming to the stall, the good man askt him if he lackt work. We par ma foy (quoth the Frenchman).

Hereupon Simon took him in, and to worke he went merrily, where he behaved himselfe so well, that his Master made good account of him, thinking he had been a Bachelor; but in the end it was found otherwise.

This man was the first that wrought upon the low cut shoo with the square toe, and the latchet overthwart the instep, before which time in England they did weare a high shooe that reached above the ankles, right after the manner of our husbandmens shooes at this day, save onely that it was made very sharp at the toe turning up like the tail of an Island dog: or as you see a cock carry his hinder feathers.

Now it is to be remembred, that while John Denevale dwelt with Simon Eyer, it chanced that a Ship of the Ile of Candy was driven upon our Coast, laden with all kind of Lawns and Cambricks, and other linnen cloth: which commodities at that time were in London very scant, and exceeding dear: and by reason of a great leak the ship had got at Sea, being unable to sail any further, he would make what profit he could of his goods here.

And being come to London, it was John Denevales chance to meet him in the streets, to whom the Merchant (in the Greek tongue) demanded where he might have lodging, for he was one that had never been in England before; and being unacquainted, wist not whither to go: but while he spake Greek, John Denevale answered him still in French, which tongue the Merchant understood well: and therefore being glad that he had met with one that could talk to him, he declared unto him what tempests he had indured at Sea, and also how his ship lay upon the Coast with such commodities as he would sell.

Truly sir, quoth John, I am my selfe but a stranger in this Country, and utterly unacquainted with Merchants, but I dwell with one in the City that is a very honest man, and it may be that he can help you to some that will deale with you for it, and if you think it good, I will move him in it, and in the mean space, Ile bring you where you may have very good lodging, and tomorrow morning I will come to you again.

Sir (said the Merchant) if you please to do me that favour, Ile not only be thankfull unto you for the same, but also in most honest sort will content you for your pains: and with that they departed.

Now so soon as John the Frenchman came home, he moved that matter unto his Master, desiring him that he would do what he could for the Merchant. When his Master had heard each circumstance, noting therewith the want of such commodities in the Land, cast in his mind as he stood cutting up his worke, what were best to be done in this case, saying to his man John, I will think upon it betwixt this and the morning, and then I will tell the my mind: and therewithall casting downe his cutting Knife, he went out of his shop into his Chamber, and therein walking up and down alone very sadly ruminating hereon: he was so far in his muse, that his wife sending for him to supper two or three times, he nothing regarded the maids call, hammering still this matter in his head.

At last his wife came to him saying, Husband, what mean you that you do not come in to supper? Why speak you not man? Hear you, good husband, come away, your meat will be cold: but for all her words, he stayed walking up and down still like a man that had sent his wits a woll-gathering, which his wife seeing, pulled him by the sleeve, saying: Why husband in the name of God, why come you not? Will you not come to supper to night? I called you a good while ago.

Body of me, wife (said he) I promise thee I did not hear thee.

No, faith, it seemeth so (quoth she) I marvell whereupon your mind runneth.

Beleeve me wife (quoth he) I was studying how to make my selfe Lord Mayor and thee a Lady.

Now God help you (quoth she) I pray God make us able to pay every man his own, that we live out of debt and danger, and drive the Woolf from the doore, and I desire no more.

But wife (said he) I pray thee now tell me, Doest thou not think that thou couldest make shift to bear the name of a Lady, if it should be put upon thee?

In truth husband (quoth she) Ile not dissemble with you, if your wealth were able to beare it, my mind would beare it well enough.

Well wife (replied he) I tell thee now in sadnesse, that, if I had money, there is a commodity now to be bought, the gains whereof would be able to make me a gentleman forever.

Alas husband, that dignitie your trade allows you already, being a squire of the Gentle Craft, then, how can you be lesse than a gentleman, seeing your sonne is a Prince borne?

Tush wife (quoth he) those titles do onely rest in name, but not in nature: but of that sort had I rather be, whose lands are answerable to their vertues, and whose rents can maintain the greatnesse of their minde.

Then sweet husband, tell me (said his wife) tell me, what commodity is that which you might get so much by? I am sure your selfe hath some money, and it shall go very hard but Ile procure friends to borrow one forty shillings, and beside that, rather then you shall lose so good a bargain, I have a couple of crowns that saw no Sun since we were first married, and them also shall you have.

Alas wife (said Simon) all this comes not neere that matter: I confesse it would do some good in buying a few backs of leather, but in this thing it is nothing: for this is Merchandise that is precious at this time and rare to be had, and I heare whosoever that will have it, must lay down 3,000 pounds ready money. Yea wife, and yet thereby he might get three and three thousand pounds profit.

His wife hearing him say so, was inflamed with desire thereof, as women are (for the most part) very covetous: that matter running still in her mind, she could scant finde in her heart to spare him time to go to supper, for very eagernesse to animate him on, to take that bargain upon him. Wherefore, so soon as they had supt, and given God thanks, she called her husband, saying: I pray you come hither, I would speake a word with you: That man is not alwayes to be blamed that sometimes takes counsell of his wife: though womens wits are not able to comprehend the greatest things, yet in doubtfull matters they often help on a sudden.

Well wife, what mean you by this? (said her husband).

In truth (quoth she) I would have you plucke up a mans heart, and speedily chop up a bargain for these goods you speak of.

Who I? (quoth he). Which way should I do it, that am not able for three thousand pounds, to lay down three thousand pence?

Tush man (quoth she) what of that? Every man that beholds a man in the face, knows not what he hath in his purse; and whatsoever he be that owes the goods, he will no doubt, be content to stay a month for his money, or three weekes at the least: and I promise you, to pay a thousand pounds a week, is a pretty round payment, and I may say to you, not much to be misliked of.

Now husband, I would have you in the morning goe with John the Frenchman to the Grecian Merchant, and with good discretion drive a sound bargain with him, for the whole fraught of the ship, and thereupon give him halfe a dozen Angels in earnest, and eight and twenty dayes after the delivery of the goods, condition to deliver him the rest of his money.

But woman (quoth he) dost thou imagine that he would take my word for so weighty a masse of money, and to deliver his goods upon no better security?

Good Lord (quoth she) have you no wit in such a case to make shift? Ile tell you what you shall do: Be not known that you bargain for your owne selfe, but tell him that you do it in the behalf of one of the chief Aldermen in the City; but beware in any case, that you leave with him your own name in writing, he being a Grecian cannot read English: and you have no need at all to shew John the Frenchman, or if thou shouldst, it were no great matter, for you can tell well enough that he can neither write nor read.

I perceive Wife (quoth he) thou wouldst fain be a Lady, and worthy thou art to be one, that dost thus imploy thy wits to bring thy husbands profit: but tell me, if he should be desirous to see the Alderman to confer with him, how shall we do then?

Jesus have mercy upon us (quoth she) you say women are fooles, but me seemeth men have need to be taught sometimes. Before you come away in the morning, let John the Frenchman tell him, that the Alderman himselfe shall come to his lodging in the afternoon; and receiving a note of all the goods that be in the ship, he shall deliver unto him a bill of his hand for the payment of his money, according to that time. Now sweetheart (quoth she) this Alderman shall be thine own selfe, and Ile go borrow for the all things that are necessary against that time.

Tush (quoth her husband) canst thou imagine that he, seeing me in the morning, will not know me again in the afternoon?

O husband (quoth she) he will not know thee, I warrant thee: for in the morning thou shalt go to him in thy doublet of sheepskins, with a smuched face, and thy apron before thee, thy thumb-leather and hand-leather buckled close to thy wrist, with a foule band about thy neck, and a greasie cap on thy head.

Why woman (quoth he) to go in this sort will be a discredit to me, and make the Merchant doubtfull of my dealing: for men of simple attire are (God wot) slenderly esteemed.

Hold your peace good husband (quoth she) it shall not be so with you, for John the Frenchman shall give such good report to the Merchant for your honest dealing (as I praise God he can do no lesse) that the Grecian will rather conceive the better of you, than otherwise: judging you a prudent discreet man, that will not make a shew of that you are not, but go in your attire agreeable to your trade. And because none of our folks shall be privy to our intent, tomorrow weel dine at my cousin John Barbers, in Saint Clements Lane, which is not far from the George in Lumbard Street, where the Merchants strangers lie. Now Ile be sure that all things shall be ready at my cousin Johns, that you shall put on in the afternoon. And there he shall first of all with his scissers snap off all the superfluous hairs, and fashion thy bushy beard after the Aldermans grave cut: then shall he wash thee with a sweet Camphire Ball, and besprinkle thine head and face with the purest Rose-water; then shalt thou scoure thy pitchy fingers in a bason of hot water, with an ordinary washing Ball: and all this being done, strip thee from these common weeds, and Ile put thee on a very fair doublet of tawny sattin, over which thou shalt have a Cassock of branched damask, furred round about the skirts with the finest foynes, thy breeches of black Velvet, and shooes and stockings fit for such array: a band about thy neck, as white as the driven snow, and for thy wrists a pretty pair of cuffs, and on thy head a cap of the finest black: then shalt thou put on a fair gown, welted round with velvet, and overthwart the back thwart it shall be with rich foyne, with a paire of sweet gloves on thy hands, and on thy forefinger a great seale-ring of gold.

Thou being thus attired, Ile intreat my cousin John Barber, because he is a very hansome young man, neat and fine in his apparell (as indeed all Barbers are) that he would take the pains to wait upon you unto the Merchants, as if he were your man, which he will do at the first word. And when you come there, tis not for you to use many words, because one of you cannot understand the other, so that it will be sufficient with outward curtesie, one to greet another; and he to deliver unto you his notes, and you to give to him your bill, and so come home.

It doth my heart good, to see how trimly this apparell doth become you, in good faith husband, me seems in my mind, I see you in it already, and how like an Alderman you will looke, when you are in this costly array. At your return from the Merchant, you shall put off all these clothes at my cousins again, and come home as you did go forth. Then tell John the Frenchman, that the Alderman was with the Merchant this afternoon, you may send him to him in the morning, and bid him to command that his Ship may be brought down the River: while she is coming about, you may give notice to the Linnen Drapers, of the Commodities you have coming.

Enough Wife (quoth he) thou hast said enough, and by the grace of God, Ile follow thy counsell, and I doubt not but to have good fortune.

CHAPTER XI

How Simon Eyer was sent for to my Lord Mayors to supper, and shewing the great entertainment that he and his wife had there.

Anon after, supper time drew neer, she making her selfe ready in the best manner she could devise, passed along with her husband unto my Lord

Mayors house: and being entred into the great Hall, one of the Officers there certified to my Lord Mayor, that the great rich Shoomaker and his wife were already come. Whereupon the Lord Mayor in courteous manner came into the Hall to Simon, saying: You are most heartily welcome good Master Eyer, and so is your gentle bedfellow. Then came forth my Lady Mayoresse and saluted them both in like manner, saying: Welcome good Master Eyer and Mistresse Eyer both, and taking her by the hand, set her downe among the Gentlewomen there present.

Sir (quoth the Lord Mayor) I understand you are a Shoomaker, and that it is you that hath bought up all the goods of the great Argozy.

I am indeed my Lord of the Gentle Craft, quoth he, and I praise God, all the goods of that great Argozy are my own, when my debts are paid.

God give you much joy of them, said the Lord Mayor, and I trust you and I shall deale for some part thereof.

So the meat being then ready to be brought in, the guests were placed each one according to his calling. My Lord Mayor holding Simon by the hand, and the Ladie Mayoresse holding his wife, they would needs have them sit neer to themselves, which they then with blushing chekes refusing, my Lord said thus unto them, holding his cap in his hand:

Master Eyer and Mistresse Eyer, let me intreat you not to be troublesome, for I tell you it shall be thus: and as for these Gentlemen here present, they are all of mine old acquaintance, and many times wee have been together, therefore I dare be the bolder with them: and albeit you are our neighbours also, yet I promise you, you are strangers to my Table, and to strangers common courtesie doth teach us to shew the greatest favour, and therefore let me rule you in mine house, and you shall rule me in yours.

When Simon found there was no remedy, they sat them downe, but the poore woman was so abashed, that she did eate but little meat at the Table, bearing herselfe at the table with a comely and modest countenance: but what she wanted in outward feeding, her heart yeelded to with inward delight and content.

Now so it was, many men that knew not Simon, and seeing him in so simple attire sit next my Lord, whisperingly asked one another what he was. And it was enough for Simons wife with her eyes and eares, to see and hearken after every thing that was said or done.

A grave wealthy Citizen sitting at the table, spake to Sirnon and said, Sir in good will I drink to your good health, but I beseech you pardon me, for I know not how to call your name.

With that my Lord Mayor answered him, saying: his name is Master Eyer, and this is the Gentleman that bought all the goods that came in the black Swan of Candy, and before God, though he sit here in simple sort, for his wealth, I do verily beleeve he is more sufficient to bear this place then my selfe. This was a man that was never thought upon, living obscure amongst us, of none account in the eyes of the world, carrying the countenance but of a Shoomaker, and none of the best sort neither, and is able to deal for a bargain of fie thousand pounds at a clap.

We do want many such Shoomakers (said the Citizen), and so with other discourse drove out supper.

At what time rising from the Table, Simon and his wife receiving sundry salutations of my lord Mayor and his Lady, and of all the rest of the worshipfull guests, departed home to their own house: at what time his wife made such a recitall of the matters; how bravely they were entertained, what great chear was there, also what a great company of Gentlemen and Gentlewomen were there, and how often they drank to her husband and to her, with divers other cricumstances, that I beleeve, if the night had bene six months long, as it is under the North pole, they would have found talke enough till morning.

Of a truth (quoth she) although I sate close by my Ladies side, I could eat nothing for very joy, to heare and see that we were so much made of. And never give me credit husband, if I did not heare the Officers whisper as they stood behind me, and all demanded one of another, what you were, and what I was: O (quoth one) do you see this man? Mark him well, and marke his wife well, that simple woman that sits next my Ladie: what are they? What are they? (quoth another). Marry this is the rich Shoomaker that bought all the goods in the great Argozy: I tell you there was never such a Shoomaker seen in London since the City was builded. Now by my faith (quoth the third) I have heard much of him today among the Merchants in the street, going betweene the two Chains: Credit me husband, of mine honesty this was their communication. Nay, and do you not remember when the rich citizen drank to you (which craved pardon, because he knew not your name) what my Lord Mayor said? Sir (quoth he) his name is Master Eyer, did you marke that? And presently thereupon he added these words: This is the Gentleman that bought, and so forth. The Gentleman understood you, did you heare him speake that word?

In troth wife (quoth he) my Lord uttered many good words of me, I thank his honour, but I heard not that.

No (quoth she) I heard it well enough: for by and by he proceeded further, saying: I suppose, though he sit here in simple sort, he is more sufficient to beare this charge then my selfe. Yea (thought I) he may thanke his wife for that, if it come so to passe.

Nay, said Simon, I thank God for it.

Yea, and next him, you may thanke m(quoth she). And it did her so much good to talk of it, that I suppose, if she had lived to this day, she should yet be prating thereof, and if sleep did not drive her from it.

And now seeing that Simon the Shoomaker is become a Merchant, we will temper our tongues to give him that title, which his customers were wont to do, and from henceforth call him Master Eyer, who, while he had his affairs in hand, committed the government of his shop to John the Frenchman, leaving him to be a guide to his other servants, by means of which favour, John thought himself at that time to be a man of no small reputation.

CHAPTER XII

How John the Frenchman fell in love with one of his Masters Maids: and how he was crossed through the craft of Haunce the Duchman.

At the same time there was dwelling in the house, a jolly lusty wench, whose name was Florence, whom John the Frenchman loved dearly well, and for her onely sake he brought many a good bottle of wine into the house, and therwithall, so soon as their Master and Mistresse were gone to bed, they would oftentimes make merry amongst themselves; which Haunce, a Journey-man in the same house perceiving, sought to crosse them as much as in him lay, thereby to bring his own purpose the better to passe, which was to joyn the Maidens favour to his owne affection.

And because the Frenchman had greatest gains under his master, and being thereof no niggard when he had got it, the maids did much delight in him, and little esteemed the Duchman, though his good will were as great towards her as the other: for they could not be in any corner of the house together, nor could they meet in any place abroad, but the Duchman would still watch them.

Upon a time, Florence being at Market, her Love John went forth of the shop to meet her, and Haunce stayed not long behind, who at length espied them, and heard his fellow John questioning with her in this sort.

What Florence, what you have in your basket? Hea, let mee see what you buy.

Marrie John (quoth she) I have bought Beefe and Mutton, and other things. Come, come, must you peep into my basket (quoth she) away, for shame away.

Be Got Florence, me will see a little: ha, ha! Florence, you buy the pudding, hea? You love de puddings? Florence hea?

Yea sir (quoth she) what if I do love puddings? What care you?

Of my tra, Florence, if I be your husband me will give you pudden, shall warren.

My husband? (quoth she). In faith Sir, no, I mean not to marrie a Frenchman.

What Florence, de Frenchman be de good man: but Florence, me will give you a pinte of wine by my treat.

O, I cannot stay now, I thank you, John.

What (quoth he) Florence, no stay with your friend? I shall make you stay a little time.

And so with that, taking her by the hand, into the Tavern they do, and Haunce the Duchman following them, and sate close in the next roome, and by that means he heard all that they said, and that they appointed the next Sunday to go to Islington together, and there to be merry: and so, the maid hasting away, they departed.

Well (quoth Haunce secretly to himselfe) it shall go hard by but Ile disappoint you.

Sunday in the afternoon being come, John the Frenchman, according to his appointment, went before to Islington, leaving Florence to come after, with another Maid which dwelt in the same house, whilest he prepared good chear for their coming: and the more to make her merrie, he hired a noise of musitians to attend their pleasure.

And as it after happended, his fellow Haunce prevented this sport, who watching in the fields for Florence, at length he spied her coming: to whom he said, Well met fair Florence, your friend John hath changed his mind, for whereas he appointed you to meet him at Islington, you shall lose your labour so to do, for he is not there.

No? How so? (said Florence).

The reason is this (said Haunce) so farre as I can understand by him, he thinks you are verie fickle and inconstant, and because it was his chance this morning, to see you speak to a young man that passed by, he saith verrily, that you are a marvellous great dissembler: and in this humour he is gone I know not whither.

And this is even so? (said Florence). Ile tell thee what Haunce, because he hath made the privie to his mind, I will shew thee somewhat of mine. Doth he suspect me because I did but speake to one? Nay, if he be so jealous now, what will he be hereafter? And, therefore insomuch that it is so, let him go to the Devill, he shall very well find, that I will set as light be him, as he doth by me. Did the knave get leave of my Mistris for me to come abroad this day, and doth he now serve me thus? Well, this shall teach me wit, in faith, and so she turns back again.

Nay (quoth Haunce) seeing you are now abroad, let me intreat you to go to Hogsdon, and I will bestow a messe of cream upon you.

In the end she was won, and as they walked together, Haunce spake thus unto her: I know not what cause John the Frenchman hath given you, to bear him so good will, as I perceive you do, but in my mind, he is a far unmeet match for you. And thus much I know, he is of a very mistrustfull nature, a wavering mind, and deceitfull heart, he did professe great good will to you in outward shew, but I have heard him speak most shamefully of you behind your back, making his vaunts, that he had you at a beck of his finger, and how that for a pint of Wine be could cause you to follow him up and down over all the Citie, Florence, I am a fool to tell you thus much, it may be you will scarce beleeve it, and, for my part, I will not urge you thereunto: but in troth, look what I tell you, it is for good will, because I have been sorrie to see you abused.

I thank you good Haunce (quoth she) I may beleeve it well enough: but from henceforth I know what I have to do: I confesse indeed, that I have drunk with him abroad, but it was at his own earnest intreaty, neither could I ever be quiet for the knave, he doth so follow me up and down in every place; but, seeing, I know his dissimulation to be such, if I do not requite him in his kind, trust me no more: and now I am heartily sorrie that I was so foolish as to follow him this day at his appointmnet: but seeing he hath served me thus, he shall not know of my coming out of doors, and therefore good Haunce, do not tell him that you met me this day in the fields.

Nay in faith, Florence (quoth he) I will not onely be secret to thee, but will also from henceforth acquaint thee with all my proceedings.

And having eaten their creame, Haunce brought her some part of the way homeward: and taking his leave of her, he went back to see if he could meet with John the Frenchman, who having stayed at Islington for Florence until almost night, and she not coming, he and the Musicians together were faine to eat up the meat, without more company, which caused John the Frenchman to swear like a Turk.

And as he was coming homeward over the fields chaffing and fretting to himselfe, who should he meet withall but Haunce the Duchman: who said to him: what John, who thought to meet you here?

Here thou seest I am now (said John): but when came you from home?

Marry but even now (quoth Haunce).

And who is at home? (said John).

The other answered, there was no body but their mistresse, and the maid Florence, with the rest of the household.

Is Florence at home? (said John). The Devill take her for me, she hath maid a right fool of me indeed.

How so? (quoth Haunce). Then the other in a great chafe, said: Be Got shall be revenged, Florence mock an me too mush, too mush she make me beleeve she love me, and me tink so too, and, be Got, she made me a Jack Fool.

When Haunce heard him say so, he said: Alas good John, she love thee? If you think so, you are greatly deceived: for she is the scoffingest quean in London: And I have heard her behind your back, to mock and flout you, saying: Doth shitten John think that I will marry him? In faith Sir no.

When the Frenchamn heard this, he stampt like a mad-man, and bit his thumb, saying: Mordue me shall be revenged, be Got: shitten John? Call a shitten John, hea? A de put in corryon, a meshant, shitten John, no better name but shitten John?

It is as I tell you (quoth Haunce): and moreover, she said she scorned to come after you to Islington, saying, she would see you hanged first.

Well be no matter; she no love me, me no love she, but me shall go home, me shall, and beat as a stockfish.

Na, do not so (said Haunce) but let her alone: for it is no credit for you to beat a woman: and besides that, if you should, our Master would turn you out of doores; therefore be quiet a while, and be secret in that I have told you, then shall you see how she useth you.

In this humour they departed: at what time, John, full of melancholy, stood frowning by the fire side: and as the Maid went up and down the house about her businesse, he cast looks on her, as fierce as a Panther; but she, by reason of the Duchman's tale to her, shews her selfe as scornfull as he was currish, and not once cast her eye towards him, and thus they drove out the time of a senight or a fortnight.

CHAPTER XIII

How Master Eyr was called upon to be Sheriffe of London, and how he held his place with worship.

In this space Master Eyer following his businesse, had sold so much of his Merchantize as paid the Grecian his whole money: and yet had resting to himselfe three times as much as he had sold, whereof he trusted some to one Alderman, and some to another, and a great deal amongst substantiall Merchants; and for some had much ready money, which he imployed in divers merchantizes: and became Adventuruer at Sea, having (by Gods blessing) many a prosperous voyage, whereby his riches dailie increased.

It chanced upon a time, that being in his study, casting up his accounts, he found himselfe to be clearly worth twelve or thirteen thousand pounds, which he finding to be so, he called his wife to him and said:

The last day I did cast up my accounts, and I finde that Almighty God of his goodnesse hath lent me thirteen thousand pounds to maintain us in our old age, for which his gracious goodnesse towards us, let us with our whole hearts give his glorious Majesty eternall praise, and therewithall pray unto him, that we may so dispose thereof, as maybe to his honour, and the comfort of his poore members on earth, and above our neighbours may not be puffed up with pride, that, while we think on our wealth, we forget God that sent it to us, for it hath been an old saying of a wise man, that abundance groweth from riches, and disdain out of abundance: of which God give us grace to take heed, and grant us a contented mind.

So soon as he had spoken this, they heard one knocking hastily at doore: whereupon he sent Florence to see who it was, the Maiden coming again, told her Master it was one of my Lord Mayors Officers that would speake with him. The Officer being permitted to come in, after due reverence, he said: Sir, it hath pleased my Lord Mayor, with the worshipfull Aldermen his brethren, with the counsell of the whole Communaltie of the honourable City, to chuse your worship Sheriffe of London this day, and have sent me to desire you to come and certifie your mind therein, whether you be contented to hold the place or no.

Master Eyer hearing this, answered he would come to his Honor and to their Worships incontinent, and resolve them what he was minded to do; and so the Officer departed.

His wife, which all this while listned unto their talke, hearing how the case stood, with a joyfull countenance meeting her husband, taking him about the neck with a loving kisse, said, Master Sheriffe, God give the joy of thy name and place!

O wife (quoth he) my person is farre unworthy of that place, and the name far exceedes my degree.

What, content your selfe, good husband (quoth she) and disable not your selfe in such sort, but be thankfull unto God for that you have, and do not spurn at such promotion as God sendeth unto you; the Lord be praised for it, you have enough to discharge the place whereto you are called with credit: and wherefore sendeth God goods but therewithall to do him and your Countrey service?

Woman (quoth he) it is an old Proverb: Soft fire makes sweet mault: for such as take things in hand rashly, repent as suddenly: to be Sheriffe of London it is no little cost. Consider first (quoth he) what house I ought to have, and what costly ornaments belong thereto, as hanging of Tapistry, cloth of Arras, and other such like, what store of Plate and Goblets of Gold, what costly attire, and what a chargeable train, and that which is most of all, how greatly I shall stand charged beside to our Soveraigne Lord the King, for the answering of such prisoners as shall be committed to my custody, with an hundred matters of such importance, which are to such an Office belonging.

Good Lord Husband (quoth she) what neede all these repetitions? You need not tell me it is a matter of great charge: notwithstanding I verily think many heretofore have with great credit discharged the place, whose wealth hath not in any sort been answerable to your riches, and whose wits have been as mean as your own: truly Sir, shall I be plain? I know not anything that is to be spoken of, that you want to performe it, but only your good will: and to lack good will to do your King and Countrey good were a signe of an unworthy subject, which I hope you will never be.

Well wife (said her husband) thou dost hold mee here with prittle prattle, while the time passeth on, tis high time I were gone to Guild Hall, I doubt I shall appear too unmannerly, in causing my Lord Mayor and the rest to stay my leisure.

And he having made himselfe ready, meet to go before such an Assembly as he went unto, he went out of doores, at what time his wife called after him, saying: and holding up her finger. Husband, remember, you know what I have said: take heed you dissemble not with God and the world, look to it husband.

Go to, goe to, get you in (quoth he) about your businesse, and so away he went.

So soon as he was gone out of sight, his wife sent one of her men after him to Guild Hall to hearken and hear, whether her husband held his place or no; and if he do, bring me word with all possible speed.

I will Mistresse (quoth her man).

Now when Master Eyer came to Guild Hall, the Lord Mayor and his brethren bade him heartily welcome, saying: Sir, the communaltie of the City having a good opinion of you, have chosen you for one of our Sheriffes for this yeer, not doubting but to find you a fit man for the place.

My good Lord, (quoth he) I humbly thank the City for their courtesie and kindnesse, and I would to God my wealth were answerable to my good will, and my ability were able to bear it. But I finde my selfe insufficient; I most humbly desire a yeers respite more, and pardon for this present.

At these words, a grave Commoner of the City standing up, with due reverence spake thus unto the Mayor: My good Lord, this is but a slender excuse for Master Eyer to make: for I have often heard him say, and so have divers others also, that he hath a Table in his house, whereon he breakes his fast every day, that he will not give for a thousand pounds: wherefore (under your Lordships correction) in my simple judgement, I think he that is able to spare a thousand pounds in such a dead commoditie, is very sufficient to be Sheriff of London.

See you now (quoth my Lord) I muse Master Eyer, that you will have so lame an excuse before us, as to take exceptions at your own wealth, which is apparently proved sufficient; you must know Master Eyer, that the Commons of London have searching eyes, and seldome are they deceived in their opinion, and therefore looke what is done, you must stand to it.

I beseech you my Lord (quoth Master Eyer) give mee leave to speake one word. Let it be granted, that I will not give my Table whereon I breake my fast for a thousand pounds, that is no consequence to prove it is worth so much; my fancy to the thing is all: for doubtlesse no man here would give me a thousand shillings for it when they see it.

All is one for that (quoth my Lord Mayor) yet dare I give you as much wine as you will spend this yeer in your Shrivaltie to let me have it.

My good Lord (quoth he) on that condition I will hold my place, and rest no longer troublesome to this company.

You must hold (said my Lord) without any condition or exceptions at all in this matter: and so they ended.

The Assembly being then broken up, the voice went, Master Eyer is Sheriffe, Master Eyer is Sheriffe. Whereupon the fellow that Mistresse Eyer sent to observe how things framed, ran home in all hast, and with leaping and rejoycing said: Mistresse, God give you joy, for you are now a Gentlewoman.

What, quoth she, tell me sir sawce, is thy Master Sheriffe, or no? And doth he hold his place?

Yes Mistris, he holds it now as fast as the stirrop doth the shooe while we sow it.

Why then (quoth she) I have my hearts desire, and that I so long looked for, and so away she went.

Within a while after came her husband, and with him one of the Aldermen, and a couple of wealthy Commoners, one of them was he that gave such great commendations of his Table, and comming to his doore, he said, You are welcome home good Master Sheriffe.

Nay, I pray you come in and drink with me before you go. Then said he, Wife, bring me forth the pasty of Venison, and set me here my little Table, that these Gentlemen may eat a bit with me before they go.

His wife which had beene oft used to this terme, excused the matter, saying; The little Table! Good Lord husband, I do wonder what you will do with the little Table now, knowing that it is used already? I pray you good Husband, content your selfe, and sit at this great Table this once. Then she whispered him in the eare, saying; What man, shall we shame our selves?

What shame? (quoth he) tell not me of shame, but do thou as thou art bidden, for we are but three or foure of us, then what should we do troubling the great Table?

Truly (answered she) the little Table is not ready: now good Husband, let us alone.

Trust me, we are troublesome guests (said the Alderman) but yet we would fain see your little Table, because it is said to be of such prize.

Yea, and it is my mind you shall (quoth Master Eyer): therefore he called his wife again, saying: good Wife, dispatch and prepare the little Table: for these Gentlemen would faine have a view of it.

Whereupon his wife seeing him so earnest, according to her wonted manner, came in; and setting her selfe down on a low stoole, laid a fair Napkin over her knees, and set the Platter with the pasty of Venison thereupon, and presently a cheare was brought for Master Alderman, and a couple of stools for the two Commoners: which they beholding, with a sudden and hearty laughter, said; Why Master Sheriffe, is this the table you held so deare?

Yes truly (quoth he).

Now verily (quoth they) you herein have utterly deceived our expectation.

Even so did you mine (quoth he) in making me Sheriffe: but you are all right heartily welcome, and I will tell you true, had I not thought wondrous well of you, you had not seene my Table now. And I think, did my Lord Mayor see it as you do, he would repent his bargain so hastily made. Notwithstanding I account of my Table never the worse.

Nor have you any cause (quoth they) and so after much pleasant talk, they departed, spreading the fame of Master Sheriffes little table ouer the whole City.

But you must now imagine, that a thousand cares combred the Sheriffe, in providing all things necessary for his Office: at what time he put off his Shoomakers shop to one of his men, and set up at the same time the signe of the Black Swan swimming upon the Sea, in remembrance of that ship, that first did bring him his wealth: and before that time the sign of the Black Swanne was never seen nor known in any place in or about the Citie of London.

CHAPTER XIV

How Haunce having circumvented John the Frenchmans Love was by him and others finely deceived at the Garden.

Now at that time John the Frenchman, and fair Florence were both at variance, as you heard before, by the Duchmans dealing, by which subtilty he sought means to win favour for himselfe, which John the Frenchman perceived, and therefore went about not onely to prevent him, but to take revenge on him for his deceitfulnesse. And meeting Florence as she went to the Garden for flowers, he began to talk thus unto her. What, Florence, you goe to the Garden?

And how then (quoth she) what have you to say to that?

Me sea nothing, but you be discontent; you no speake a me, you no look a me; nor you no drink with me, nor noting, ah Florence, how chance dat?

Go get the hence, prating fool (quoth she) I drinke with thee? Thou shalt be pie-peckt first.

Pie peck? What be pie-peckt a hea? Be Got, Florence, you make me a Jacke-nape, you mock a me, and call me shitten Jan, and you be so proud, because Haunce love you, dat shall be marvell: but and if you call mee shitten John any more, par ma foy, shall not put up, shall not take at your hands.

Who told you, that I called you shitten John (quoth Florence) I never called you so.

No Florence! You no call a me shitten John? A so meshant villain pulard Haunce tell a me so.

I never said so (quoth Florence). But Haunce told me that you made your boast that I was at a beck of your finger; and that you could make me follow you up and down the whole City for a pinte of Wine; no, I would you should well understand, I will not follow a better man then you.

Of my fet Florence, me never say so.

No? Yes (quoth she) but you did, I can tell you by a good token, for that very time that I should have met you at Islington, you said it, and made me a fool to come over the fields to you, and when all came to all, you sent Haunce to tell me you were gone there hence long agone.

Ah cet tokin, Haunce (quoth John) be des ten bon, tis true, for me tarry dere more den one, two, tree hour, and had provide shopon, de rabit, de creame, de pudding pie, and twenty ding more.

Well, howsoever it was, I am sure I was made an asse betwixt you, and for that cause I will beware how I shew kindnesse again to any: therefore, John I pray you be gone, and seek some other company, for you shall not go with me.

No? (said John). Well den, adieu, Florence, and so they departed.

Now it is to be understood, that Haunce had promised Florence to meet her in the Garden, and to bring with him a bottle of wine, and there in the presence of a maid or two more, to make themselves sure together: and she, for that purpose, had carried with her a good corner of a venison pasty. But there was an English Iourney-man in the house called Nicholas that understood thereof, who, meeting with John the Frenchman, he made him privie thereunto, saying; Trust me John, if thou wilt be ruled by me, we will not onely disappoint this match, but also with their good chear make ourselves merry. John, who was glad and readie to do the Duchman any injurie, consented to follow Nicolas his counsell in any thing.

Then (quoth Nicholas) it shall be thus: I will go to the Garden, and stay for Haunce his comming with the Wine, and in the mean space do thou hide thy selfe under one of the hedges of the Garden on the other side, and with thee take a couple of pots, and let the one be empty, and the other filled with water, and when Haunce is come into the Garden with his bottle of wine (now he will not let me see it by his good will) notwithstanding Ile observe well where he doth set it down, and then will I finde the meanes, while they are busie in toying and talking, to convey the bottle of wine through the hedge to thee, and likewise the venison: then emptying the bottle, thou shalt fill it with water, and thrusting it through the hedge again, it shall be set where first it was found, which being done, thou shalt hastily rap at the Garden doore, at what time they shall be told that it is my Master or Mistresse, which they hearing, will be in such a maze, that on a sudden they will not know which way to turn themselves, especially for the conveying away of Haunce: Now when you have knockt twice or thrice, and that you heare no body come to the doore, get you away, and stay for mee at the Rose in Barking, and there we will drink up their wine, eat up the venison: and this being done, weele laugh them to scorne.

Truly Nicholas (quoth John the Frenchman) this will be brave, and thereupon they prepared themselves to do the feat. Nicholas therefore got him into the Garden, and by and by after comes Haunce with the bottle of Wine, who knocking at the garden doore, was straight let in: but seeing Nicholas there, he secretly set his bottle in a corner: but Nick, who had as searching eyes as Argos in his businesse, quickly did as before he had determined, and instead of wine set the bottle downe again, where he first found it, full of water.

Then comes John, and lustily knocks at the doore.

There is our Master and Mistresse (quoth Nicholas).

Alas (quoth Florence) what shall we do for Haunce? Then rapt he at the doore again. Alas (quoth she) get you over the hedge.

Shall I open the doore? (quoth Nick). O no, said Florence, not yet good Nick.

With that he knockt more hastily. Anon, anon (quoth she). Hence Haunce: Go to the doore Nick.

Who is there? (quoth he). And with that opening the doore found just no body. Truly Florence (said he) they are gone whosoever they were. God be with you, I can stay no longer.

When he was departed, the Maids wished that Haunce had been there again. Alas, poore fellow (quoth they) is he gone, and he left his bottle behind him?

Marry I am glad that it is no worse (quoth Florence): And now, that the wine is here, we will drink it for his sake, and I have here a morsell of Venison, that will give it a good relish: and therewithall looking for it, she found the cloak, but the meat gone. Now a vengeance on it (quoth she) one skurvy Cur or other hath got into the garden, and tooke away the meat!

O God, what ill luck is that (quoth the maid): a murren on that Curre that got it: but seeing it is gone, farewell it.

Well (said Florence) here is the wine yet, I know it is excellent good: for he told me he would bring a bottle of the best Renish wine that in London could be bought: and I am certain he is as good as his word. But beleeve me Joane, he is as kind hearted, and as loving a fellow as ever professed love to any: I assure you, that here is a cup of Wine that the King might drink thereof: but how shall us do for a glasse?

Weele drink it out of the bottle (said Joane).

Not so (quoth Florence) I do love to see what I drink, and therefore Ile borrow a glasse at the next house.

And while she goes for a glasse (said Joane to her selfe) Ile have a taste of it before she returns again: and then setting her hand unto the bottle and the bottle to her mouth she drank a good draught, and finding it to be something thin in the going down, she said to Besse that sat by: Credit me now, but for the name of Wine, I have drunk as good water.

It is Renish wine (quoth Besse) and that is never strong.

At which words Florence entred with a glas: and powring it out into the glasse, she extolled the colour, saying, see what a brave colour it hath, it is as clear, I do assure you, as rock water: and therewithall drinking it off, she said, it drinks very dead: Of a troth (quoth she) this is but bad Wine, it is even as dead as a doore naile: and so filling the glasse again, she gave it unto Besse.

She tasting thereof, said: Passion of me, this is plain water.

Water (said Joane). It is water? Let me taste of it once again: by my Maiden-head, it is water indeed (quoth she).

Water (said Florence) you have played the drabs in drinking out the Wine, and filling the bottle again with water.

Of my faith (quoth Joane) you say not true in saying so: I would you did understand, we played not the drabs in any such sort, but Haunce rather played the knave that brought us water instead of Wine.

Nay (quoth Florence) I dare swear for him that he would not serve you so, for all the wealth my Master is worth. And I am perswaded it was no body but your selves that did it: but in faith you might have dealt so with another, and not with me.

Nay then (quoth they) you needed not to serve us so, to cause us to drink water instead of Wine: and we would you should think, although you be Master Sheriffes Maid, we love our mouths as well as you do yours for your life, and it was but an homely recompence for our good will, I tell you true; neither do we care how little we come to be thus deluded.

Go to, go to (said Florence) you are like to Penelopes puppy, that doth both bite and whine, I know you well enough.

Know us? (quoth Joane). What do you know by us? We defie you for anything you can say by us. Know us? Nay, it were well if thou didst know thy selfe, and hearest thou? Though thou hast thy companions to meet the at thy pleasure, and we have not: no, know us? We are known to be as honest as thou art, or else we should be sorry: and so she departed in a chafe.

Now John the Frenchman and Nicholas having eaten the venison, and drunk up the wine, came back again time enough to hear all this strife, whereat they greatly rejoyced. But so soon as Florence did meet with Haunce again, she kept no small stir for mocking her with a bottle of water: about the which they fell at variance, in such sort that they were not friends for a long time after.

But during the time that Haunce was out of favour, Nicholas sought the Maids friendship by all the means he might, but in vain was his pains spent therein: for, although Florence (outwardly) seemed much displeased, yet Haunce had her heart still, and in processe of time obtained great favour: the matter was grown so foreward, that the performance of their mariage was forthwith appointed, which they intended should be celebrated at the Abbey of Grace on Tower Hill. Notwithstanding, this matter was not kept so close, but that their secret dealings were known; and Nicholas purposing to deceive the Duchman, made John the Flenchman privy thereunto, saying; John, it is so, that this night at midnight Masse, Florence and Haunce do intend secretly to be married, and they have appointed the Frier to do it so soon as the Tapers are all put out, because they will not be seen of any: Therefore John, if now you will be my friend, I do not doubt but to marry her my selfe, and so to give the Duchman the slampam, and bore him through the nose with a cushin.

Ha (quoth John) be Got me shall do as you sea, and therefore Nicholas tell a mee what you do.

Mary John (quoth he) you know the Duchman loveth to drink well, and by that he loveth, weele cause him to lose his Love, for we will get him out to the Taverne, and there cause him to be disguised, that he shall neither be able to stand nor go; and while he lies parbreaking his mind, Ile go and marriy the Maid.

The Frenchman hearing this, scratcht his head, and rubbing his elbow, said, Ma foy, Nicholas, dis be de fine trick: how shall wee get him forth a doores?

Excellent well (quoth Nicholas) for there is a new Iourney-man come to Town with Sir Hughes bones at his back, and you know, that we being of the Gentle Craft, must go give him his welcome, and I will tell Haunce thereof, who being now very jocund, by reason that his mariage is so neer, will not deny to come, I know. Therefore you and the stranger Journey-man shall go before to the Taverne, and then I will go fetch him.

A beene, content, content (said John).

And so to the Taverne he hasted with the strange man. Anon comes Nicholas and Haunce, and with them two or three Journey-men more, and all to the new Journey-man: sitting down, they get Haunce in the midst, called for wine lustily, and such varieties, as the Duchman was soon set packing; for every one sought to overcharge him; and being himselfe of a good kind to take his liquor, spared not to pledge every man. At what time in the midst of his cups, being well whitled, his tongue ran at random (as wine is the bewrayer of secrets) so it proved by him, for there he opened to his companions all his whole mind, saying, My hearts, for all I sit here, I must be a married man ere morning.

God give you joy (quoth they).

But who shall you marry (said Nick). Florence?

Yea Florence (said the Duchman) that is the Lasse that I do love, and all the world cannot deceive me of her now, I am the man that must have her Maidenhead, and this night we must be married at the Abbey of Grace; and if you be good fellows, go with me to Church; will you go with me?

Will we go with thee? (said John Frenchman) that we will.

O John (said Haunce) I have wiped your nose, and Nicks too, you must weare the willow Garland.

Well, what remedy (quoth they) it is the better for you.

But in faith Haunce, seeing it is so (quoth Nick) weele have one pottle of wine more, that we may drinke to the health of our lo fair Bryde.

Ile pledge her if it be a gallon (quoth Haunce).

Be my fet and trot (said John) weele have a gallon. Hea Drawer, where be you? I pray you bring me a gallon of de best Claret, and a gallon of de best Sack, shall make merry i'fet: What Florence be merrie and I no know?

But by the time this Wine was drunk, Haunce was laid up for walking any more that night. When Nick perceived that, he stole suddenly out of the Tavern, and went to meet Florence at the appointed place: but John quickly missing him, knew straight whereabout he went, got him presently to the Constable of the Posterne Gate, and told him, that Nick had laid a man for dead in Tower street, and that he was gone to save himselfe under the priviledge of the Abbey of Grace, but (quoth he) if you will go along, I shall bring him out with fair words unto you, and then I desire you to clap him up to answer this matter in the morning.

But where dwell you? (said the Constable).

I do dwell with Master Alderman Eyer (quoth John) and there you shall have me at all times.

The Constable did as John bade him, and committed Nicholas to prison. In the mean space, Florence, and an old woman of Tower street, said that they did go to a womans labour, and by that means they passed along by the Watch, and to the Abbey of Grace they came. They had not long been there, but that John Frenchman meeting them, sayd; Florence, well met, here is a fit place to finish that I have long looked for.

John (quoth she) thou art like an evill spirit that must be conjured out before a body shall get any quietnesse, urge not me upon any such matters for you be not the man I looke for, and therefore, as taking little pleasure in your presence, as of your proffers, I would be very glad to see your back.

What (said John) have you no compassion upon a poore man? You be hard-hearted indeed.

But as he was uttering these speeches, it was his wives chance to hear his tongue, being newly come from the Barge at Billinsgate, and at that time going toward Saint Katerines to see if she could meet with some of her Countrry folks that could tell her any tydings of her husband; but as I said, hearing his tongue, and knowing him by his speech, she said: What, John Denevale? May husband John Denevale? What make you wed pretty wence hea?

At which words John was stricken into such a dump, that he wist not what to say: notwithstanding, hearing Florence to ask if she was his wife, he answered and said, Yea.

O thou dissembling fellow (quoth she) is it even so? Didst thou say thou wast a Batcheller, seeking to marry me, and hast a wife alive? Now fie on the: O good Lord, how was I blest to escape him: nay, now I see that Haunce may have a wife in Flaunders too, although he be here: and therefore, by the grace of God, I will not marry a stranger.

O (quoth John) I thought my wife had been dead, but seeing she is alive, I will not lose her for twenty thousand crowns.

So Florence departed and left John with his wife.

Now, Haunce never waking untill it was the next day at noon; when he saw he had overslept himself, being very sorry, he went home, not knowing how to excuse his folly to Florence; whom she utterly forsook, as well in regard of his drunkennesse, as for that being a stranger, he might, like John the Frenchman, have another wife living. But Nicholas (that all this while lay in prison) being brought before the Alderman Eyer, rehearsed the truth, and, craving pardon for his offence, was without more ado delivered. And Florence being called before him, he made up the match between her and his man Nicholas, marrying them out of his house with credit, giving them a good stock to begin the world withall: also for John Frenchman he did very much, and shewd himselfe a good Master to his man Haunce, and to all the rest of the servants.

CHAPTER XV

How Master Alderman Eyer was chosen Lord Mayor of London, and how he feasted all the Prentices on Shrove Tuesday.

Within a few yeers after, Alderman Eyer, being chosen Lord Mayor of London, changing his copy, he became one of the Worshipfull Company of Drapers, and for this yeer he kept a most bountifull house. At this time it came into his mind what a promise once he made to the Prentices, being at breakfast with them at their going to the Conduit, speaking to his Lady in this wise: Good Lord (quoth he) what a chance have we had within these thirty yeares? And how greatly hath the Lord blessed us since that? Blessed be his Name for it.

I do remember, when I was a young prentice, what a match I made upon a Shrove Tuesday morning, being at the Conduit, among other of my Companions; trust me wife (quoth he) tis worth the hearing. And Ile tell the how it fell out.

After we had filled our Tankards with water, there was some would needs have me set down my Tankard, and go with them to breakfast (as many times before I had done) to which I consented: and it was a breakefast of Pudding-pies. I shall never forget it. But to make short, when the shot came to be paid, each one drew out his money, but I had not one penny in my purse, and credit I had none in the place; which when I beheld, being abashed, I said; Well my Masters, do you give me my breakfast this time; and in requitall thereof, if ever I be Mayor of London, Ile bestow a breakfast on all the Prentices of the City: these were the words, little thinking (God wot) that ever it would come to passe: but such was the great goodnesse of our God, who setteth up the humble, and pulleth down the proud, to bring whom he pleaseth to the seat of Honour. For as the scripture witnesseth, Promotion cometh neither from the East, nor from the West, but from him that is the giver of all good things, the mighty Lord of heaven and earth. Wherefore wife seeing God hath bestowed that upon me that I never looked for; it is reason that I should perform my promise: and being able now, Ile pay that which then I was not able to do: for I would not have men say that I am like the Ebon tree, that neither beares leaves nor fruit. Wherefore wife, seeing that Shrove Tuesday is so neer at hand, I will upon that day performe my promise; which upon that day I made.

Truly, my Lord (quoth she) I shall be right willing thereunto.

Then answered my Lord, as thou dost love me let them want neither Pudding-Pies nor Pancakes, and look what other good chear is to be had, Ile referre all to your discretion.

Hereupon great provision was made for the prentices breakfast: and Shrove Tuesday being come, the Lord Mayor sent word to the Aldermen, that in their severall Wards they should signifie his minde to the Citizens, to crave their favours, that their Prentices might come to his house to breakfast; and that for his sake they might play all the day after. Whereupon it was ordered, that at the ringing of a Bell in every Parish, the Prentices should leave work, and shut in their shops for that day, which being ever since yearly observed, it is called the Pancake Bell.

The prentices being all assembled my Lord Mayors house was not able to hold them, they were such a multitude; so that besides the great Hall, all the Gardens were set with Tables, and in the backside Tables were set, and every other spare place was also furnished: so that at length, the Prentices were all placed; and while meat was bringing in, to delight their eares, as well as to feede their bodies, and to drown the noise of their pratlings, Drums and Trumpets were pleasantly sounded: that being ended, the Waits of the City, with divers other sorts of Musick played also to beguile the time, and to put off all discontent.

After the first service, were all the Tables plentifully furnished with Pudding-pies and Pancakes, in very plentifull manner, and the rest that remained was given to the poore. Wine and Ale in very great measure they had given; insomuch, that they had no lack, nor excesse to cause them to be disordered. And in the midst of this their merriment, my Lord Mayor in his Scarlet gown, and his Lady in like manner went in amongst them, bidding them all most heartily welcome, saying unto them, that his promise so long ago made, he hath at length performed. At what time they (in token of thankfulnesse) flung up their Caps, giving a great shout, and incontinently they all quietly departed.

Then after this, Sir Simon Eyer built Leaden-Hall, appointing that in the midst thereof, there should be a Market kept every Monday for Leather, where the Shoomakers of London, for their more ease, might buy of the Tanners, without seeking any further. And in the end, this worthy man ended his life in London with great Honour.

A new love Sonnet

Maide

All hayle sweet youth, fair Venis graft,
*   Cheife Master of the Gentle Craft,*
How comely seemes thou in my sight,
*   Like Phebus in the heavens bright*
That never was in cupids pound,
*   Or from his shaft received a wound;*
For by thy mirth it doth appeare
*   Thy minde is free from griefe and care.*

Shoomaker

Faire Maid, you speak no more but truth,
        For why the freedome of my youth,
I value at too high a rate,
        To linke myselfe with any mate;
There is no comfort on the earth,
        Compared to a freeborne mirth,
When fairest beauties me orethwart,
        I look the better to my heart.

When beauteous Nymphs do me surprise,
        I shut the Casements of mine eyes,
For he is a fond and foolish Elfe,
        That loves a maid losing himselfe,
To fall in love is such a thing,
        From whence sometimes doth mischief spring,
I wish well unto women-kind,
        But for to wed I have no minde.

Maide

What if your Casements chance to ope,
        And give affection so much scope,
As to encounter with a Dame,
        Why then methinks it were no shame,
For you to love and not to speake,
        And by degrees the Ice to breake:
But if you speak and so obtaine,
        Then have you found your hearte againe.

It were a shame for Maids to woe,
        But men may speak and so may you,
If that occasion offerd be,
        God Cupids blind and cannot see,
But shoots at randome here and there,
        O therefore Edmond, have a care,
At unawares you may be hit,
        No pollicy can hinder it.

But O unhappy women kinde,
        That toxicated are in mine,

And know not how to vent the same,
> *Without the losse of our good name,*
They count us bold if now and than,
> *We do not look upon a man,*
And look we may, but dare not speak,
> *Much lesse our mindes unto them break.*

Shoomaker

Would I were worthy for to know
> *The cause of this your griefe and wo,*
For why, your words and looks declare,
> *Your minde is overcharg'd with care,*
If that your heart be fled away,
> *And it be taken for a Stray,*
The man that hath it Ile perswade
> *To take some pity on a Maid.*

This young man struck this faire maid mute,
> *She wanted one to pleade her Sute,*
Faine would she speak, but was afraid,
> *This is the case of many a Maid,*
He was the man whom she loved best,
> *Her heart did lodge within his breat,*
Although to him it was unknown
> *Untill at last he lost his owne.*

Cupid the god of love came downe,
> *And on this man young Man cast a frowne,*
He bent his bowe and sent a dart,
> *That struck the young man to the heart,*
And, cause the Maid should win the prize,
> *He opened the Shoomakers eyes,*
So when her beauty he beheld,
> *He gladly yeelded up the field.*

With folded Armes along he walkt,
> *And thus unto himselfe he talkt,*
O what are we that vainly trust
> *In our weak strengths that are but dust;*
I durst have sworne no living wight

Could move me from my sweet delight,
    But now I see and feele the smart,
        Mine eyes too soon deceive my heart.

He that before was grown so stout,
        And strong enough to keep love out,
Is vanquisht now and made to yeeld,
        And did both win and lose the field:
He conquered her to him unknown,
        She conquerd him, and made him her own:
Thus maids with men are dallying still,
        Till they have brought them to their will.

Alas (quoth he) how am I crost,
        Beholding her, my self Ive lost;
Now beauty is become a snare,
        The which hath brought me to dispaire;
If she no other man had lovd,
        I might have hoped she might be movd;
But she another doth affect,
        And I must dye without respect.

She noting of his passion then,
        As Maids will do that love young Men;
And finding the occasion fit,
        Mark here a wily wenches wit;
Delayes prove dangerous she knew,
        And many Maids have found it true:
Thus in her selfe resovd to speak,
        She unto him her mind did break.

(Quoth she) young man, it is your lot,
        The god of love hath laid a plot,
The net was spread, the bird is caught,
        And I have found the thing I sought:
Though Men are strong and women weak,
        Stout hearts will yeeld before theyl break;
And Women sometimes win the field
        When men are willing for to yeeld.

With that the Nimphs and Rurall Swaines,
        Come straightway tripping ore the plaines.

The Satyres made them Pipes of Reeds,
  And brought in Musik more than needs;
The syrens sung such somgs of mirth,
  That brought King Oberon from the earth;
The Fairies with their Fairy king,
  Did dance about them in a ring.

 Chorus.

All health and happinesse betide,
  The Shoomaker and his sweet bride,
Lo thus we sing and thus we dance,
  Till we have brought love in a trance,
Thus pleasures sweet this couple grace,
  Both linckt together in sweet imbrace,
The neighbouring hils and dailes resound,
  With Eccho of our pleasant sound.

Whilst thus they sung their Roundalayes,
  God Cupid crownd their heads with bayes,
The bride lookt like the Queen of May,
  The shookmake led her away,
Where now they live in quiet peace,
  And love doth more and more increase,
Thus love you see, can finde a way,
  To make both Men and Maids obey.

 How a Shoomakers widdow fell in love with her man.

These three years John I have been deep in love,
  And nere till now had time my mind to move.
Speak, Canst thou love me though I am thy Dame?
  I would not have the daunted, Fie, for shame.
Old proverb, spare to speak and spare to speed,
  Thou wantst a wife and I a husband need.

 His Answer

Mistris I am in love as well, tis true,
  But to speak truth, in truth I love not you,
I have a Maid in Chase, as sweet a Lasse,

In my conceit I think, as ever was:
Pray then, forbeare, it never shall be said
    I took a widdow and forsook a Maid.

Reader observe whats written by the Poet,
    Women and maids love men, but few will shew it.

FINIS

The Gentile Craft

The Second Part

Being a most merrie and pleasant Historie, not altogether unprofitable nor anyway hurtfull: verie fit to passe away the tediousnesse of the long winter evenings.

By T.D.

Newly corrected and augmented

Haud curo invidam

London

Printed by Elizabeth Purslow, dwelling neere

Christ Church, 1639

To the Master and Wardens of the

Worshipfull company of the Cordwaynors

In London, all continuance of health and per-

fect brotherley affection.

Once more hath good will emboldened me, to present unto your Worships, my worthles labour, to manifest the good affection I beare to this fraternity: and finding, you lent a gentle looke on the first part of this History, I have beene the more bolde to proffer you the second: for having bound my selfe by promise to performe it: and you perhaps clayming promise as a debt, expecting payment, I bent my study to keepe touch: whereupon I tender this small trifle unto you, onely craving at your worships hands, a good opinion of my poore endevours. And albeit this pamphlet doth not minister matter worthy your grave view: yet in regard of the subject, I trust you will deigne to esteeme it, sith so well as I could, though not so well as I would, I have sought herein to procure your delight: and although you finde not all the men spoken of, which is promised in the first part, yet thinke it no faintnes in me, but fault of good instruction: and againe, for as much as these men here mentioned were all of this Citie (whose story grew longer then I supposed) and the other of the country: I thought good so to breake off, and to defer their story to another time, when I may more perfectly speake thereof. In the meane space I commend your Worships to the protection of the most highest.

Your Worships in all he may.
T.D.

To the Courteous Readers

Health.

Gentle Reader, you that vouchsafe to cast curteous lookes into this rude Pamphlet: expect not herein to find any matter of light value, curiously pen'd with pickt words, or choise phrases but a quaint and plaine discourse, best fitting matters of merriment, seeing wee have herein no cause to talke of Courtiers or Scholers. Notwithstanding, if you find your selfe over charged with melancholy, you may perhaps have here a fit medicine to purge that humour, by conferring in this place with Doctor Burket: or if you meet with round Robin, he may chance ryme it away. I tell you among Shoomakers is some solace, as you shall see by Tom Drums entertainment, and other mad merry prankes playd by the Greene-King of S. Martins. If that will not suffice, you may in meeting with Anthony now now, have such a fit of mirth, with his firking Fiddle, that it shall be a great cause to expell choler. And so I leave you to your owne liking, whether you will enter to see this sport or no: stand backe, I pray, roome for a Gentleman, for you cannot come in under a groat.

CHAPTER I

Containing the History of Richard Casteler: and the first of his love.

The lovely Maidens of the Citty of Westminster, noting what a good husband Richard Casteler was and seeing how diligently hee followed his businesse, judged in the end he would prove a rich man: for which cause many bore unto him very good affection, and few there was that wished not themselves to be his wife: insomuch that he having the custome of all the pretty Wenches in the Citty, by that meanes knew the length of every Maidens foot so well, that he above all other best pleased them. On the Sundayes when he came into the Church, the Maides eyes were so firmely fixed on him, that hee could neither looke forward, backeward, nor on any side, but that he should be sure to have a winke of one, a smile of another, the third would give a nod: and to be briefe, they would all cast on him such gracious lookes, that it was easie to guesse by their outward countenance, their inward good will.

And when in his Holy-dayes attire he past along the streets, the Maidens (after their businesse was done) standing at their Masters doores and spying him, would say thus one to another: Now verily, there goes a proper civill young man, wise and thrifty: yea such a one as in time will prove wondrous wealthy, and without all doubt, will come to great credit and preferment.

These and the like words would they use of him continually, whereby he had among them such a generall good opinion, that as he stood a dayes at his cutting boord, he should be sure to have twenty cursies made him in an houre, by Maidens that past up and downe: some would bestow on him dainty sweet nosegayes, of the fairest flowers they could find, and other some would bring him handkerchers of Cambrick, and divers such like favours, well bewraying their friendship towards him.

But among many that secretly affected him, I will onely tell of twaine, because above all the rest, their merriments doe onely remaine in memorie, the one of them was called Margaret, of the spread-Eagle, but more commonly knowne by the name of long Meg of Westminster: The other was a proper neat wench named Gillian of the George, both of them as wily as they were witty, who among all the Maides in Westminster were reputed to be the best servants; having therefore good wages, they maintained themselues gallantly, and therwithall so honestly, that no man could quip them with bad living, though afterward it fell out otherwise, as in this historie you shall heare.

Margaret was a maiden borne in Lancashire, in height and proportion of body, passing the ordinary stature of women, but there- withall very comely, and of amiable countenance, her strength was agreeable to her stature and her courage as great as them both: she was of a quicke capacitie, and pleasant disposition, of a liberall heart, and such a one as would be sodainely angry, and soone pleased, being readier to revenge her wrongs by weapons, then by words: and therein did shee differ from the nature of other women, because shee could not abide much brabling: and so heedfull was shee of her behaviour in her yonger yeeres, that her good properties far exceeding her portion, she was wooed by divers, but would be won by none, for the man whom shee most loved, least thought upon her. And albeit shee manifested her good will by divers meanes, yet did Richard little regard it, having his mind nothing bent unto marriage, by meanes whereof Margaret grew into such sad conceits as changed her chery cheekes into a greene wan countenance: in-somuch that every one wondred to see her pensivenes.

At last it chanced that Margaret having occasion to go into London, it was her good fortune to meet with Gillian of the George, whom her mistres had sent thither to buy Comfets, and Carawayes, with divers other sweet meates, for that they had a banket bespoken by divers gallant Courtiers, which that night appointed to come thither: but so soone as Margaret spied her, she smiled, saying: Gillian now in good sadnes, wel met, (if thou beest met a maid.)

And ill met (quoth she) not meeting so good a maid as my selfe.

Tush (said Margaret) it is good for us to thinke well of our selves, for there is enough that think ill of us.

Mary I defie them (quoth Gillian) that thinks ill of me, and Irespect as little their speech, as they do my profit. For a woman with a good life, feares no man with an evill tung.

If you bee so hot (quoth Margaret) where the wind blows so cold, what will you be by that time supper is ready, where the fire will be as fierce as your choller is great? And mistake mee not good Gillian, though I said men think ill of us, I meane not thereby that any goe about to blemish our good names, but I suppose they thinke not so wel of us as they might do that doe not love us so well as to marry us.

Nay (said Gillian) if that be all, I am at a good point for though my maiden-head be some what burdensom to beare, yet I had rather keepe it, then bestow it on a bad husband: but though I say it, though I be but a poore wench, I have choise of husbands enough, and such as I am assured in my conscience, would both love me well, and keepe me gallantly.

Wherefore then doe you not marry? (quoth Margaret). In my opinion it is the most pleasingst life that may be, when a woman shall have her husband come home and speake in this sort unto her. How now Wife? How dost thou my sweet-heart? What wilt thou have? Or what dost thou lacke? And therewithall kindly embracing her, gives her a gentle kisse, saying: speake my prettie mouse, wilt thou have a cup of Claret-wine, White-wine, or Sacke to supper? And then perhaps he carves unto her the leg of a Capon, or the wing of a Chicken, and if there be one bit better then other, shee hath the choise of it: And if she chance to long for any thing by and by it is sent for with all possible speed, and nothing is thought too deare to doe her good. At last having well refresht themselves, she sets her silver whistle to her mouth, and calles her maid to cleare the boord: then going to the fire, he sets her on his knee, and wantonly stroking her cheeke, amourously hee chockes her under the chin, fetching many stealing toutches at her rubie lips, and so soone as he heares the Bell ring eight a clocke, he calles her to goe to bed with him. O how sweet doe these words sound in a womans eares? But when they are once close betweene a paire of sheetes, O Gillian then, then.

Why what of that? (quoth she).

Nay nothing (saith Margaret) but they sleep soundly all night.

Truly (quoth Gillian) there be many wives, but few that meete with such kind husbands: but seeing you aske me why I marry not, in troth Meg I would tell thee, if I had time to stay: but I feare I have stood too long pratling here already, and therefore farewell good Meg, when I see the againe, thou shalt know more of my mind.

Nay Gillian heare you (quoth she) go but a little way with me, and I will goe home with you as straight as a line, for I have nothing to buy but a score of Quinces, and couple of Pomegranets, and that shall be done in a trice.

Gillian was contented for her good companies sake to stay a while, and as soone as Margaret had made her market, they settled themselves to goe homeward, where by the way Gillian entred into this communication.

You did even now demand a question of me, and very desirous you were to know why I did not marry when I was so well offered: Trust me Margaret, I take you to be my friend, which makes me the more willing to unfold my fancy, being as well perswaded of your secresie as I am of your amity, and there-upon I am the more willing to make you copartner of my counsailes. Fire in straw will not be hidden, and the flames of affection wil burst forth at length, though it be long kept under. And truth it is that I have forsaken good matches, for I might have had Master Cornelius of the Guard if I would, who as you know is wealthy, and therwithall of very good conversation, yet there was one thing made me refuse his kind offer.

What was that (quoth Margaret) I pray the tell?

(Quoth she) he loved not me so well but I loved another tenne times better, and therefore it is not good for handes to joyne, where hearts agree not. No Meg, no, there is a youth in our street that nearer touches my heart and better pleases my mind, notwithstanding he shall go namelesse, for it is an old proverb, two may keep counsell if one be away.

Nay then (quoth Meg) if you dare not trust me tell no further, notwithstanding, I have had credit in as great matters as yours, for many a man hath put his life in my hands, and found no hurt thereby, and as many women have committed their secrets to me, as men have ventured their bodies with me.

Go to Margaret, you are disposed to jest (said Gillian) but sweare by thy Maidenhead that thou wilt never bewray my liking, nor prevent me in my love, and I will shew thee all.

Nay fie, do not so (quoth Margaret) shew not all for shame, least more see it then my selfe, for so may they blush at thy boldnes, and nothing commend thy modesty: but it is happy that I have a maidenhead left to sweare by: else I perceive I should know nothing of thee.

No trust me (quoth Gillian) for such a one as cannot keepe her Maidenhead, wil never keep a secret, and that made Katherine of the Crane to be such a blab: but now Meg I will proceed to the matter. What doe you thinke by Richard of the Rose, the wakeful cock of Westminster?

Oh he (quoth Meg) is that the man? There is no reason I should thinke amisse of him that every man commends: neverthelesse, he is no body in respect of riches, being but a yong housekeeper of one yeares standing, a man (God wot) unacquainted with the worlds guise, and to speake truth, nothing comparable to Master Cornelius.

I will tell thee what (quoth Gillian) that man which needeth neither to flatter with his friends, nor borrow of his neighbours hath riches sufficient: and hee is most poore that hath least wit, by which arguments I am able to proove, that the Cock is as wealthy as he is wary, for he will sure be beholding to no body, or to as few as he may, and it is al wayes to be noted that men of such mindes doe never prove beggers.

Margaret hearing Gillian so stoutly to take Richards part, perceived by her vehement speeches the great affection she bore to him, and finding that she was sick of her owne disease, Margaret sought means to remove the cause of her griefe, and thereby thrust her selfe into the greater sorrow: And the policy she used most herein, was to speak altogether in Richards dispraise, seeking thereby to dislodge her love, and the more firmely to plant her owne, whereupon she uttered her mind in this sort.

Well Gillian, seeing you beare so good an opinion of Richard of the Rose, I would not for a bushel of Angels seek to disswade you: but because you request my opinion how I like the man, in troth I will tell thee my mind without fraud or flattery: I confesse that Richard is a gentle young man, curteous and kind, diligent about his businesse, and wary in his dealings, which argues good husbandry. Notwithstanding, I like not these over covetous fellowes, of such greedy mindes, such penny fathers and pinchfistes, that will not part from the paring of their nailes, nor the dropping of their nose, if they thought it would yeeld them but the fourth part of a farthing. Tell me I pray the what joy should a woman have with such a churle, that would grudge at every halfe-penny that is laid out, that in a whole yeare would not leave a farthing worth of mustard unwritten in his booke: And such a one I feare will this Cocke prove, for me thinkes hee lookes with a hungry nose, and, howsoever you think of him, I know not, but I verily feare though hee be a Cocke by name, hee will never prove a Cock of the game. Againe he is but a dwarfe in respect of a man, a shrimpe, a Wren, a hop of my thumbe, such a one as a body might hide in a wrinkle of their buttocks.

Well Meg (quoth shee) you are priviledged to speake your pleasure, but should another thus mistearme him, I would teare her face: I tell the true I had rather have a winner then a waster, a sparer, then a prodigall spender: for when a man in his youth, hath gotten something with paine, he may the better spend it in his age with pleasure, and farre better it is hee should be thought covetous, then carelesse; his stature and proportion of body pleases me well enough, for it is no matter how great hee is, but how good hee is.

But Margaret seeing our talk hath indured so long, that it hath brought us both home, let us at our parting be mindfull of our promises, to keepe secret whatsoever hath been said, for little knowes the young man the depth of my mind, and therefore would I keepe it close, till I saw some signe of good will proceeding from him, for it becommeth not maidens to be woers, though willingly they could wish to wed where they best fancie, and so farewell sweet Margaret.

Adue gentle Gillian (quoth Margaret) until our next meeting, when I hope I shall further understand of your proceedings in your love.

When Meg had thus understood her mind, and saw how the matter went, she sought all meanes possible to prevent her, as hereafter shall be shewen.

CHAPTER II

How Margaret requested Richard to the eating of a Posset at night: And how her Masters buttocks was scalded therewith.

It chanced that against Whitsontide, Margaret stood in need of a new paire of Shooes: Therefore in a morning betimes she came to Richard of the Rose to bespeake them aforehand, and the more to declare her kindnes, and to win his good will, she carried with her a bottle of excellent good Muskadine, which one of the Yeomen of the Kings wine seller had bestowed upon her: and to make it relish the better, she carried with her a dainty peece of powdred beefe, and the tender carkasse of a cold Capon, and thus plesantly began to greet him.

All health to the kind cocke of Westminster, that with the Larke greetes the Sun rising with a cheerefull note, and mounts above many to the love of pretty lasses. Tell me (quoth she) thou bonny Lad, wilt thou take the length of my foote, and make me a good payre of shooes against Sunday?

That I will Margaret (quoth he), therefore let me see thy foote.

There is both my foote and leg (said Meg), I am not ashamed to shew either of them, for I am not legged like a Crane, nor footed like a Flie, and therewith lift up her cloathes to the knee, whereat Richard smiling said, a little higher Meg and shew all.

Whereupon she sodainly replied in this sort: soft, Richard not so, for I will tell the one thing.

Every Carter may reach to the garter,
A Shoomaker he may reach to the knee,
But he that creepes higher shall aske leave of me.

Good reason (quoth Richard) leave is light, which being obtained a man may be bold without offence, but this onely is my griefe, I have never a Last in my shop long enough for thy foot.

Then I would they were all fired (quoth Meg). He that will be counted a good workman must have tooles to fit all persons, and I muse that you which strive to be counted excellent, will want necessaries: Fie Richard fie, thou shouldest never be unprovided especially for women.

Well Meg (quoth he) be contented, consider you are a woman of no ordinary making, but as in height thou ouerlookest all, so in the length of thy foot thou surpassest all: therefore I must have a paire of Lasts made for the nonce, and that shall be done out of hand.

I tell thee Dicke (quoth shee) as high as I am, I am not so high as Paules nor is my foot so long as Graves-end Barge.

Notwithstanding (quoth Richard) a paire of Lasts to fit thy foot will cost as much as a hundred of fagots which will not be bought under ten groats.

If they cost a crown (quoth Meg) let me have them; what man, rather then I will goe without shooes I will beare the charge thereof my selfe and in token that I mean troth, take there the money, thou shalt find me no Crinkler, but one that will reward cunning to the uttermost: I love not to pinch for a penny, or stand upon tearmes for two pence, if I find my shooes good I will not shrinke for a shilling.

In troth (quoth Richard) franke customers are worthy of good ware, and therefore Meg doubt not, for thou shalt have as good a shoe as ever was drawne upon womans foote.

God a mercy for that, sweet Dicke (quoth she) and seeing thou saist so, I will bestow this bottle of wine on thee to breakfast, beside that, I have brought here a modicome that will prove as good a shooing-horne to drawe downe a cup of Muskadine as may be: and therewithall she pluckt out her powdred beefe and her colde Capon.

Richard seeing this, with thankes to Margaret for her meat, reacht out a couple of joyne stooles, and after that they had laid a cloth thereon, they downe did sit, at which time many merry speeches did passe betweene them. And at that very time there was in the same shoppe, amongst a great many other men a pleasant jorney man called round Robin, being a wel trust fellow short and thicke, yet very active and pleasantly conceited: for singing hee was held in high reputation among all the Shoomakers in Westminster, and he would scant speake any thing but in rime. This jolly companion seeing them bent so well to their breakfast, and nothing at all to respect him, in the place where he sate cast out these merry speeches unto them.

> *Much good doe it you masters, and well may you fare,*
> *Beshroe both your hearts and if you do spare:*
> *The wine should be nought as I judge by the smell,*
> *And by the colour too I know it full well.*

Nay faith (quoth Meg) that's but a jest,

> *Ile sweare* (quoth Robin) *tis none of the best.*

Tast it (quoth Meg) then tell me thy mind:

> *Yea marry* (quoth Robin) *now you are kind.*

With that Margaret filling a cup brim full, gave it into his hand saying: Now tast it Robin and take there the cup.

> *Nay hang me* (quoth Robin) *if I drinke it not up.*

By my Maiden-head (quoth Margaret) I see that thou art a good fellow: and to have the drinke it up, is the thing that I crave.

> *Then sweare* (quoth Robin) *by the thing you have,*
> *For this to sweare I dare be bold:*
> *You were a maid at three yeares old.*
> *From three to foure, five, sixe, and seaven,*
> *But when you grew to be eleven,*
> *Then you began to breed desire;*
> *By twelve your fancy was on fire:*

At thirteene yeares desire grew quicke,
And then your maiden-head fell sicke:
But when you came unto fourteene,
All secret kisses was not seene:
By that time fifteene yeares was past,
I guesse your maiden-head was lost.
And I pray God forgive me this,
If thinking so I thinke amisse.

Now by my honesty (quoth Meg) you doe me mighty wrong to thinke so ill of me: for though indeed I confesse, I cannot excuse myselfe, for women are not Angels, though they have Angels faces: for to speake the truth might I have had my owne hearts desire when time was, I would rather have chosen to lye with a man then a maid, but such merry motions were out of my mind many a deere day agoe, and now vow that a maiden I will die.

By this wine (quoth Robin) *I dare sweare you lye,*
For were I as my master by this good light,
You would leese your maiden-head ere twelve a clock anight.
With high derry derry,
If it be not gone already.

Nay (quoth Margaret) your Master scornes me, he keeps all his gownes for Gillian of the George: a pretty wench I confesse, having a proper body but a bad leg, she hath a very good countenance but an ill coulour, and you talk of desire, but her desire I doubt will bring her the greene sicknesse, if your master like a good Phisition give her not a medicine against that malady.

Why Margaret (quoth Richard) hath she told you so much of her mind, that you know her griefe so well?

It may be she hath (quoth Margaret) but whether she did or no, it is sufficient that I know so much: But I thinke (quoth Margaret)
you are not so besotted to make any account of a Tallow cake.

No, faith (quoth Robin) *a nut-browne girle,*
Is in mine eye a Diamond and a Pearle:
And she that hath her cheekes cherry red,
Is ever best welcome to a young mans bed.

Certainly (quoth Richard) which is the best or worst I know not yet, nor doe I meane hastily to prove; and as for Gillian of the George, as she hath no reason to hate me, so she hath no cause to love me: but if she doe, it is more favour then I did ever merit at her hand, and surely were it but in regard of her good will, I am not to scorne her nor for her favour to feed her with floutes, but for her good thoughts of me to think well of her, though not so well as to make her my wife.

Well said Master (quoth Robin).

> *In this sort grind you still,*
> *So shall we have mo sackes to mill.*

Trust me (quoth Margaret) I speake not this so much to disgrace Gillian, as for the regard I have to your credit: but to make an end of Gillian and this jest altogether, let me entreat you soone at night to come to our house; and thinke this, though your cheere chance to be small, your welcome shall be great. I know that this Summer (and especially against these holy-daies) you will worke till ten, and I promise you by eleven I will have as good a posset for you, as ever you did taste on in your life. My master is an old man, and he commonly goes to bed at nine, and as for my mistris, I know where she will be safe till midnight masse be ended, so that for an houre we may be as merry as pope John: what say you Richard (quoth she), will you come?

In troth Margaret (quoth he) I heartily thank you for your good will, I would willingly come but I love not to be from home so late.

> *I thinke so* (quoth Robin) *least you should misse Kate,*
> *But take my counsell, when you are with Meg:*
> *Suppose you have got fine Kate by the leg.*

Robin (said he) thou art so full of thy rime, that often thou art without reason; thou seest that Margaret hath been at cost with us to day, and it is more then good manners to charge her further, before we have made amends for this: and beside that, late walking in the evening brings young men into much suspition.

Tush (quoth Margaret) once and use it not, is not such a matter: therefore sweet Richard you shall come, and you shall not say me nay, therefore I charge you on paine of displeasure not to faile, and forget not to bring round Robin with you, and so farewell.

> *No, faith* (quoth Robin) *it shall not need,*
> *I am bidden already and so God speed.*

Who bad thee? (quoth Margaret).

What are thy wits so unsteady?
You did bid me (quoth Robin) *have you forgot already?*

Why then I pray thee good Robin (said Meg) do not forget in any case,
and put thy Master in mind thereof if he should chance to change his opinion,
or overslip the time through greedines of work, for, ifaith Robin if thou bring
him along with thee, I will thinke the better of thee while I live.

Why then (quoth he).

And as I am no knight,
We will come to eate the posset soone at night.

Now Margaret was no sooner gone, and Richard at his cutting boord, and
Robin set on his stoole, but in comes Gillian of the George, bringing in her
aporne the corner of a Venison Pastie, and a good deale of a Lambe pye, who
with a smyling countenance entring the shop, bidding Richard good morrow,
askt if he had broke his fast?

Yes verily (quoth Richard) I thank long Meg, we have beene at it this
morning, and had you come a little sooner you had found her heere, for she
went away but even now, and I verily thinke she is scant at home yet.

Tis a lusty wench (quoth Robin) *gentle and kind,*
And in truth she beares a most bountifull mind.

Gillian hearing Robin to enter into Megs commendations, began to grow
jealous of the matter: out upon her foule stammell (quoth she) he that takes
her to his wife shall be sure of flesh enough, let him get bread where he
can: tis such a bold betrice, she will acquaint her selfe with every bodie.
Notwithstanding this I will tell you, Richard, the lesse she comes in your
company, the more it will be for your credit. And howsoever she deserves it,
God knowes, I cannot accuse her, but I promise you she hath but a hard report
among many. But letting her rest as she is, see here what I have brought you,
and with that she gave him the Venison and the rest, and drawing her purse,
she would needs send for a quart of wine. Richard sought to perswade her to
the contrary, but she would not be intreated; what man, quoth she, I am able
to give you a quart of wine.

That's spoke like an Angell (quoth Robin).

And this I doe thinke,
If you be able to give it, we be able to drinke.

Hereupon the wine was fetcht, and so they sate them downe to their meate, at what time they fed not so heartily on the Venison pasty, but Gillians eye fed as greedily on Richards favour: and as soone as the wine was come, she pluckt out of her pocket a good peece of sugar, and filling a glasse of wine tempered wel therwith, she drank to him saying: here Richard to all that love you and me, but especially to him whom I love best.

Let it come (quoth Richard) I will pledge him, whosoever it be.

> *So will I* (quoth Robin) *without any faile,*
> *Were it the best Hipocras, I would turn it ouer my naile.*

Then Gillian looking round about spoke to this effect: verily Richard, here is a pretty house, and every thing hansome by Saint Anne, I see nothing wanting but a good wife to keep all things in his due kind.

Whereunto Robin made this answer.

> *Now speake thy conscience, and tell me good Gill,*
> *Wouldst not thou be that good wife, with a good will?*

Who I? Alas (quoth she) your Master scornes me, he looks for a golden girle, or a girle with gold, that might bring him the red ruddocks chinking in a bag, and yet possible he were better to have one with lesse money, and more huswifery: for my owne part I thanke God, and in a good time may I speake it, I would not come to learne of never a woman in Westminster, how to deale in such affaires.

I thinke no lesse (quoth Richard) and therefore I pray God send you a good husband, and one well deserving so good a wife.

With that Gillian fetcht a great sigh, saying; Amen I pray God, for it is a sinful thing to leade a sinfull life, except:

Nay, say your mind, speake your mind (quoth Richard).

Why (quoth she) it is written, that we shall give an account for every idle word, and that ill thoughts are as bad as wanton deeds:

It is true (quoth Richard).

Then God helpe us all (quoth Gillian) but if I were married, I should remove a great many of them.

Why then marry me (quoth Robin) and thereby prevent the perill of bad thoughts.

Harke in thy eare Robin (quoth she) I would thy Master would say as much and then he should soone know my mind.

Ha, ha (quoth Robin*) ifaith, you drab,*
And would you have him to stampe the crab?

Why what is the matter? (quoth Richard).

Nay nothing (quoth Gillian) but that I was bold to jest with your man, and I hope you will not be offended if he and I talke a word or two.

There is no reason I should (quoth Richard) and therefore conferre at your pleasure, and the whilest I will be busie with the Lambe pye.

Then Gillian rounding Robin in the eare, spoke in this sort unto him. I perceive you can spie day at a little hole: you may see Robin, love is like an unruly streame that will over-flow the banks if the course be once stopt, as by my speeches no doubt you have noted: neverthelesse how forcible soever fancy is, it is thought small modesty in a maiden to lay open her heart in those cases, but I am of opinion that affection growing as strong in a woman as a man, they ought to have equall priviledge, as well as men to speake their minds. Robin, I take the to be an honest fellow, and it is the part of a man in cases of honest love to assist poore maidens: counsell, the key of certainty, which makes me to require both thy counsaile and help. In truth Robin to be plaine, I love thy Master with all my heart: and if thou wouldst be so much my friend to break the matter unto him and therewithall to procure his good liking to me, I would bestow on thee as good a sute of apparell as ever thou wast master of in thy life.

Whereunto Robin answered, saying,

Heers my hand Gillian, at thy request
Ile make a vow Ile doe my best,
But for my apparell grant me this,
In earnest first to give me a kisse.

There it is (quoth Gillian) and I doe protest, that upon that blessed day, when he gives his happy consent to be my husband, at the delivery of thy apparell I will make that one kisse twenty, and hereupon shaking hands, they came to the table and set them downe againe.

Richard marking all, said nothing, but at her approach to the boord tooke the glasse and drunk to her, giving her thankes for her cost and kindnes: she gladly accepting the same, bending her body instead of cursie, tooke it at his hands, and with a winke drunk unto Robin, and so taking her leave of them both as light as a Doe she ran speedily home.

So soone as she was gone, Robin told his Master it was the pleasantest life in the world to live a Batcheler, during which time he could neither want good cheere nor good company.

I mary (quoth Richard) but what I get one way I spend another way, while I passe the time in trifling about nothing: you see (quoth he) here is a forenoone spent to no purpose, and all by the means of a couple of giglets, that have greater desire to be playing with a man, then to be mindfull to follow their busines: but if I live I will sodainly avoid both their delights and their loves. I tell thee Robin, I account their favours full of frawd, and their inticements daungerous, and therefore a man must not be won with faire words as a fish with a baite.

Well Master (quoth Robin) all is one to me, whether you love them or loath, but yet soone at night let not the posset be forgot.

Beleeve me (quoth Richard) if I rest in the mind I am in now, I meane not to be there at all.

O then you will loose her love (quoth Robin) for ever and ever Amen.

That (said his Master) is the onely thing that I request, for the love of a shroe is like the shadow of a cloude that consumeth as soone as it is seene, and such love had I rather loose then find.

> *But yet* (quoth Robin) *this once follow my mind.*
> *Though by her love you set but light,*
> *Let us eate the posset soone at night:*
> *And afterward I will so deale,*
> *If you will not my trickes reveale:*
> *That they shall trouble you no more,*
> *Though by your love they set great store:*
> *For one another they shall beguile,*
> *Yet thinke themselves well pleas'd the while.*

Verily (quoth his Master) if thou wilt doe so, I wil be Megs guest for this once, and happy shall I thinke my self to be so well rid of them.

Hereupon being resolved, they plyde their worke hard till the evening, and when the Sunne was crept under the earth, and the Stars up in the skies, Richard having his shop window shut in, and his doores made fast, he with his man Robin tooke their direct way to the spread Eagle, where they no sooner knockt at the doore, but Margaret came downe and let them in, with such a cheerefull countenance, as gave perfect testimony of their welcome.

Now Richard (quoth she) I will witnesse you are a man of your word, and a man that hath a respect of his promise: I pray you hartily come neere, for to have you come in my office, is my desire.

But tell us first (quoth Robin) *was your office never a fire?*

Yfaith no (quoth she) you see the kitchin is large and the chimney wide.

But how many rookes (quoth Robin) *hath the goodnes of your kitchin tride?*

I know not (said Meg) how many or how few:

Trust me (quoth Robin) *I thinke even so.*

Goe to (quoth Meg) I smell out your knavery, and guesse at your meaning, but taking it to be spoken more for mirth, then for malice, I let them passe. Then taking Richard by the hand, she bad him sit downe, saying, good Richard think yourselfe welcome, for in troth I have never a friend in the world that can be better welcome.

I thank you good Margaret (said he).

I thank her still (quoth Robin) *with thanks of every degree,*
For you that have all the welcome, shall give all thanks for mee.

Why Robin (quoth Meg) be not offended for thou art welcome to me.

Ifaith (quoth he) *you bid me welcome when you have nothing else to do.*

Herewithall Margaret very neatly laying the cloth, with all things necessary, set a dainty minst pie on the boord, piping hote, with a great deale of other good cheere, and having sent another maid of the house for a pottle of wine, they fell to their meat merrily, whereof when they had eaten and drunk, Margaret stepping from the boord went to reach the posset, but while she had it in her hands she sodainly heard one comming down the stairs.

Gods precious (quoth she) my Master comes, what shift shall we make to hide the posset, if he chance to see it, we shall have more anger then ten possets are worth. With that she quickly whipt into the yard and set the posset downe upon the seat in the privy-house, thinking it there safest out of sight, for her Master being an old crabbed fellow, would often steale downe to see what his maids were a doing, but God wot that was not the cause, for the old man being raised by the loosenes of his body, came hastily downe to pay tribute to Ajax, where when he was come, he clapt his buttocks into the posset, wherewith being grievously scalded, he cried out saying, alacke, alacke, help maids, help, or I am spoild for ever; for some spirit or divell in the foule bottome of the privie hath throwne up boyling leade upon my buttocks. And in this case like one dauncing the trench more he stampt up and downe the yard, holding his hips in his hands.

Meg that better knew what the matter was then her master, ran into the house of office with a spit in her hand, as if she had beene purposed to broch the divell, and there casting the well spiced posset into the midst of the puddle, taking the bason away, said, how now Master, what is the matter, who hath hurt you, or are you not hurt at all?

Hurt (quoth her master) I tell thee Meg, never was man thus hurt, and yet I am ashamed to shew my hurt.

Bring me a Candle (quoth Meg) I tell you, Master, it is better all should be shewen, then all should be spoyled: and there with casting by his shirt, spied both his great cheekes full of small blisters, whereupon she was faine with all possible speed to make him a medicine with sallet oyle and houseleeks, to asswage the fury of an unseene fire. And by meanes of this unhappy chance, Richard with his man was faine secretly to slip away, and to goe home without tasting the posset at all: which was to Robin no small griefe, and yet they could both of them scant stand for laughing, to thinke how oddly this jeast fell out.

> *I am* (quoth Robin) *forty yeares old and more,*
> *Yet did I never know posset, so tasted before:*
> *I thinke his eyes in his Elbowes he had,*
> *To thrust his arse in the posset, or else he was mad.*

His master answering said, beleeue me Robin, I never knew the like in my life, but by the grace of God I will never goe there no more to eate a posset: and so going to bed they slept away sorrow till morning.

At what time Margaret coming thither told them she was very sorie they were so suddenly broke from their banket; but Yfaith, Richard (quoth she) another time shall make amends for all.

CHAPTER III.

How the Cocke of Westminster was married to a Dutch maiden, for which cause Long Meg, and Gillian of the George wore willow Garlands.

Richard Casteler living a long time a Batchelor in Westminster, after many good proffers made unto him, refusing all, hee at last linked his love to a young Dutch maiden dwelling in London, who besides that, was of proper personage, and comely countenance, and could doe divers pretty feates to get her owne living. To this pretty soule went Richard secretly a wooing, who for halfe a yeare set as light by him, as hee did by the Maidens of Westminster. And the more hee was denyed, the more desirous hee was to seeke her good will, much like to an unruly patient, that most longes after the meate hee is most forbidden: and such is the fury of fond Lovers, to esteeme them most precious, that are to them most pernitious: he scornfully shunnes such as gently seekes him, and wooes her earnestly that shakes him off frowardly: but while he was thus busied to make himselfe blessed by matching with a Mayden in London, round Robin cast in his mind how to set the Maydens wittes a worke in Westminster, which he effected as occasion was offred in this sort.

Margaret and Gillian comming often by the shop, cast many a sheepes eye to spye out their beloved friend, and after they had many times mist him from his busines, they thought either that he was growne love-sick or lazie: but knowing him a man to be mightily addicted to the getting of money, judged that it was not idlenes, that withdrew him from his busines, but rather that he was gone a wooing to one pretty wench or other, for loving hearts have ever suspicious heades and jealousie is copartner with affection: whereupon Margaret entred into these speeches with round Robin.

I muse much (quoth Meg) where your Master layes his knife a boord now adayes, for seldome or never can I see him in his shop: trust me, I doubt, he is become thriftles, and will prove but a bad husband in the end: tell me Robin (said she) I pray thee say where doth the Cocke crow now?

> *Not so* (said Robin) *my Master will not that allow,*
> *I must not shew his secrets to one or other:*
> *Therefore you shall not know it though you were my mother,*
> *Yet thus much by thy speech I plainly do see,*
> *Thou thinkst not so well of him as he thinks on thee.*

Margaret, hearing round Robin rime to so good purpose, asked if hee knew his Masters minde so much? Truly (quoth shee) if I wist he bore any spark of love toward me, it should neither goe unregarded nor unrewarded, therefore sweet Robin let me know whereupon thou speakest; feare not my secrecie, for I will rather loose my life then bewray his love.

Heereupon Robin said, that his Master was very well affected towards her, and that if it were not that Gillian of the George did cast searching eyes into his actions, he would long ere this have uttred his mind: but (quoth Robin) he is so haunted by that female spirit, that he can take no rest in no place for her, and therefore the more to quiet his mind, he hath left his shop to my charg, and betaken himselfe to wander the Woods so wild.

These words uttered by Robin made Margarets heart leape in her belly: wherefore taking gently her leave of him, she thus began to meditate on the matter: Now doe I well see that the tongue of a wise man is in his heart, but the heart of a foole is in his tongue: and Richard (quoth she) hast thou borne me such secret good will and would never let me know it? Iwis, iwis, soone would thy sorrow be asswaged if thou soughtest remedie at my hand: well though the fire be long supprest, at length it will burst into a flame, and Richards secret good will, at last will shew it selfe, till when I will rest my selfe contented, thinking it sufficient that I know he loves me: and seeing it is so, I will make him sue and serve, and daunce attendance after me: when he is most curteous, I will be most coy, and as it were scorning his proffers, and shunning his presence, I will make him the more earnest to intreat my favour: when he sayes he loves me, I will laugh at him, and say he can faine and flatter well: if he affirme he be grieved through my disdaine, and that the lacke of my good wil hath been his greatest sorrow, I will say alas good soule, how long have you been love-sick? Pluck out thy heart man and be of good cheere, there is more maids then Malkin: though I doe lightly esteeme thee, there are some that perhaps will better regard both thy griefe, and thy good will: and therefore good Dicke trouble me no more.

Thus must maides dissemble least they be counted too curteous and shewing themselus overfond, become the lesse favoured, for a womans love being hardly obtained, is esteemed most sweet, therefore we must give our lovers an hundred denials for fashion sake, though at the first we could find in our hearts to accept their proffered pleasures.

Thus in a jolly humor Margaret jetted home, flattering herselfe in her happy fortune, in which delight we will leave her, and make some rehearsall of Gillians joy: who, comming in the like manner to Robin, asking for his Master, was certified by him, that for her sake onely he lived in such sorrow, that he could not stay in his shop, and therfore was faine to drive away melancholy by marching abroad.

O Gillian (quoth he) had it not bin for two causes, he would long ere this have uttered his mind unto thee, for he loves thee above measure.

Yfaith (quoth Gillian) is it true (Robin) that thou dost tell me?

Doubt not of that (quoth he) doe you think that I will tell you a lye? I should gaine nothing by that I am sure: if then you will beleeve me you may; if not, chuse, I meane not to intreat you thereto.

Nay good Robin (quoth she) be not angry, though I credit thy speeches, yet blame me not to aske a question.

Aske what you will (quoth Robin) I respect it not, and I may chuse whether I will answere you or no: Swounds, now I have opened my masters secret, you were best blab it through all the towne.

Nay good Robin that is not my mind (quoth Gillian) but I beseech the, let me know those two causes that keepes thy Master from uttering his mind.

Nay soft, there lay a straw for feare of stumbling (quoth Robin). Hold your peace Gillian, it is not good to eate too much hony, nor to gorge you with too much gladnes: let it suffice that you know what you know.

Nay good sweet Robin (quoth she) I pray the make it not dainty now to tell me all, seeing you have begun: the day may come that I may requite thy curtesie to the full.

Say you so, Gillian? (quoth hee). Now by good Crispianus soule I sweare, were it not that I am in hope you will prove kind to my Master, and be a good Mistresse to us when you are married, I would not utter one word more, no not halfe a word, nor one sillable.

Well Robin (quoth she) if ever I come to command in thy masters house, and to carry the keys of his Cubberts gingling at my sides, thou shalt see I will not keepe a niggards Table, to have bare platters brought from the boord, but you shall have meate and drinke plenty, and be used as men ought to be used in all reasonable manner. And whereas you seeme to make doubt of my kindnesse toward thy Master, ha Robin, I would thou knewest my heart.

Robin hearing this, told her this tale, that his master loved her intyrely, and would long since have uttered his mind, but for two reasons: the first was, that he could never find fit oportunity to doe it, because of Long Meg, whose love to him was more then he could wish, and such as he would gladly remove if he might: for (saith Robin) though my Master do not care a straw for her, yet she casts such a vigilant eye upon him, that if he do but speake, or looke upon any, she by and by poutes and lowres, and many times inveyes against the parties with disgracefull termes, which is to my Master such a griefe, that he is faine to keepe silent, what otherwise should be shown: and the second reason is this, that because he is not so wealthy as he could wish himselfe, you would disdaine his sute, and make no account of his good will.

Who I? (quoth Gillian). Now by these ten bones it was never my mind to say him nay. I tell thee Robin I doe more respect his kindnes then his goods: he is a proper youth and well conditioned, and it is far better to have a man without money, then money without a man.

Why then good Gillian (quoth Robin) harken hither three dayes hence, and you shall heare more, but in the meane space looke you play mum-budget, and speake not a word of this matter to any creature.

I warrant thee Robin (quoth she) and so away she went being as glad of this tydings as her Master was of a good Term.

Now when his Master came home, his man Robin asked him how he sped in his suit?

Verily (quoth he) even as Cookes doe in baking of their pies, sometimes well, sometimes ill. London Maids are wily wenches: on Sunday my sweet-heart was halfe won, but now I doubt she is wholy lost. Now she is in one mind, by and by in another, and to be briefe never stedfast in any thing.

Tush Master (quoth Robin) stoop not too much to a thistle, but take this comfort, that what one will not, another will. I tel you Master, Crabs yeeldes nothing but verjuice, a sower sauce good for digestion but bad to the taste, and these nice minions are so full of curiosity, that they are cleane without curtesie: Yet well fare the gallant girles of Westminster, that will doe more for a man then he will doe for himselfe.

What is that? (said his Master).

Mary (quoth he) get him a wife ere he is aware, and give two kisses before he calles for one.

That indeed is extraordinary kindnes (quoth Richard) but their loves are like braided wares, which are often showne, but hardly sold.

Well Master (quoth Robin) you know your two old friends, Meg and Gillian.

I, what of them? (quoth Richard).

In troth (quoth he) I have made them both so proud, that they prance through the streets like the Kings great horses: for I have made them both beleeue that you love them out of all cry.

And I beshroe thy heart for that (quoth Richard) for therein thou dost both deceive them, and discredit mee: I assure thee I like not such jesting.

> *Now gip* (quoth Robin) *are you griev'd at my talke?*
> *And if you be angry I pray you goe walke.*
> *Thus you doe never esteeme of a man,*
> *Let him doe for you the best that he can.*

Richard hearing his man so hot, pacified him with many cold and gentle speeches, wishing, if he had begun any jest, that he should finish it with such discretion, that no reproach might grow thereby unto him, and then he would be content: whereupon Robin proceeded in this sort.

Upon a time Margaret according to her wonted manner came thither, whom Robin perswaded that his Master was newly gone into Tuttle field, and that he left word if she came she should doe so much as to meet him there: but (quoth he) take heed in any case least Gillian of the George spie you, and so follow to the place where my Master attends your comming, who I dare sweare would not for all the Shooes in his shop it should be so: and therefore good Margaret if you chance to see her, goe not forward in any case, but rather lead her a contrary way, or make some queint excuse, that she may leave your company, and not suspect your pretence.

Tush (quoth Margaret) let me alone for that, if she follow me she were better no, for, Ifaith, I will lead her a dance shall make her weary before she have done, and yet shall she goe home as very a foole as she came forth, for any goodnesse she gets at my hand: and therefore farewell, Robin (quoth she) for I will trudge into Tuttle fields as fast as I may.

But looke (quoth Robin) *you loose not your Maiden-head by the way.*

Robin presently thereupon runnes unto Gillian, saying what cheere Gillian, how goes the world with all the pretty wenches here? It is a long while since I have seene you.

Ifaith, Robin (quoth they) we rub out with the rest, but what is the news with thee?

> *Small news* (quoth Robin) *yet somewhat I have to say,*
> *All Maides that cannot get husbands must presently marry,*
> *They that cannot stay,*
> *But heare you Gillian a word by the way.*

And with that (rounding her in the eare) he told her that incontinent it was his Masters mind that she should meet him in Tuttle fields, charging her if she met Margaret of the Spread Eagle, that she should in no case goe forward, but turne her steps some other way, for (quoth he) my Master cannot abide that great rounsefull should come in his company.

For that let me alone (quoth Gillian) but trust me Robin, it could not have come in a worse time this twelve moneth, for this day have we a mighty deale of worke to doe, beside a great bucke that is to be washt.

Why then let it rest till another time (quoth Robin)

Nay (quoth she) hap what hap will, I will goe to him, sith so kindly he sent for me; and thereupon making her selfe quickly ready, into Tuttle fields she got, where at last she espied Margaret with a hand-basket in her hand, who as sodainly had got a sight of her, and therefore made a shew as if she gathered hearbs in the field. I wis that craft shall not serve your turne (quoth Gillian) I will gather hearbs as fast as you, though I have as little need of them as your selfe.

But in the mean time Robin got him home, and hartily laught to see what paines these wenches tooke for a husband. O (quoth he) what a merry world is this, when Maids runnes a madding for husbands, with hand-baskets in their hands? Now may I well sweare what I have seene.

> *Two Maides runne as fast as they can,*
> *A mile in the fields to meet with a man.*

Then how can men for shame say that Maidens are proud, disdainfull or coy, when we find them so gentle, that they will run to a man like a Falcon to the Lure, but alas poore soules, as good were they to seek for a needle in a bottle of hay, as to search for Richard of the Rose in Tuttle fields: but hereby doe I know their minds against another time, if my Master should chance to request their company.

Thus did round Robin deride them when he found their fondness to be such: but to leave him to his humor, we will returne to the Maids that were so busie in picking up hearbs in the fields: when Meg saw that Gillian would not away at last she came unto her, asking what she made there?

Nay what doe you here? (quoth she). For my owne part I was sent for to seeke Harts-ease, but I can find nothing but sorrel.

Alack good soule (quoth Meg) and I come to gather thrift, but can light on nothing but thistles, and therefore I will get my waies home as fast as I can.

In doing so you shall doe well (quoth Gillian) but I mean to get some Harts-ease ere I goe away.

Nay Gillian (quoth she) I am sure I shall find thrift as soone as you shall find Harts-ease, but I promise you I am out of hope to find any to day.

I pray you get you gone then (quoth she).

What would you so faine be rid of my company? (quoth Meg). For that word I meane not to be gone yet: Ifaith Gill I smell a rat.

Then (quoth she) you have as good a nose as our gray Cat: but what rat do you smell, tell me? I doubt I doubt if there be any rat in the field, you would faine catch him in your trap, if you knew how; but Ifaith Meg, you shall be deceived as cunning as you are.

Then belike (quoth Meg) you would not have the rat taste no cheese but your owne.

All is one for that (said Gillian) but wheresoever he run I would have him creep into no corner of yours.

Your wordes are mysticall (quoth Meg) but if thou art a good wench, let us goe home together.

Not so (said Gillian) as I came not with you, so I meane not to goe with you.

No? (quoth Meg). Before God I sweare I will stay as long as thou for thy life.

In troth (quoth she) I will make you stay till midnight then.

Yea? (quoth Meg). Now, as sure as I live I will try that.

And in this humor sometimes they sat them downe, and sometimes they stalkt round about the field, till it was darke night, and so late, that at last the watch met with them, who contrary to Gillians mind, tooke paines to bring them both home together: at what time they gave one another such privie flouts, that the watchmen tooke no little delight to heare it: but their Mistresses that had so long mist them from home though they were very angry with their long absence, yet were glad they were come againe. And asking where they had been so long, the watchmen answered, that the one had beene to seek Harts-ease, and the other to gather thrift and therefore they should not blame them for staying so long to get such good commodities. Verily (quoth their Mistresses) we will not, for no marvell if they stayed out till midnight about such matters, seeing we have sought it this seven yeares and could never find it: and in this sort this jest ended.

Within a while after this, Richard through his long woing, had gotten the good will of his sweet-heart, and therefore making all things ready for his marriage, the matter being known through Westrninster, Margaret and Gillian had tydings thereof with the soonest, who comming unto Richard, said he was the most false and unconstant man in the world.

Have I (quoth Meg) set my whole mind upon thee to be thus served?

Nay (quoth Gillian) have I loved thee so deerly, and indured such sorrow for thy sake, to be thus unkindly cast off?

And I (quoth Meg) that never thought any thing too much for thee, that loved thee better then my life, that was at all times ready at thy call, and ready to run or goe at thy commandement to be so undeservedly forsaken, grieves not my heart a little.

Nay (quoth Gillian) could you make me leave my worke to waite upon the in Tuttle-fields?

Nay did I waite there halfe a day together (quoth Meg) at thy request to be thus mockt at thy hand? Now I wish it from my heart, if thou marriest any but me, that thy wife may make thee as errant a Cuckold as Jack Coomes.

So you are very charitable (quoth Richard) to wish me no worse then you meane to make your husband: but when did I request thee to come into Tuttle-fields?

What have you so weake a memory? (quoth she). I pray you aske your man round Robin whether it were so or no.

Well (quoth Robin) how then? Wherefore did you not speake with him at that present?

You know it comes in an houre, comes not in seven yeare,
Had you met him at that instant you had married him cleare.

A vengeance take her (quoth Meg) I could not meete him for Gillian.

And I could not meet him for Margaret, a morin take her (quoth Gillian).

Richard perceiving by their speech there was a pad lying in the straw, made this reply. It is a strange thing to see how you will blame me of discourtesie, when the whole fault lyes in your selves: had you come at the appointed time, it is likely I had marryed one of you, seeing my minde was as well addicted to the one as to the other.

Why may it not be yet (quoth they) if it please you?

Not so (said Richard) you speake too late, Men gather no grapes in January, my wine is already provided, and my wife prepared: therefore I thanke you both of your good wills, though I be constrained of force to forsake you.

The maidens being herewith struck into their dumps, with water in their eyes, and griefe in their hearts went home, to whom Robin carryed two Willow garlands, saying

> *You pretty soules that forsaken be,*
> *Take here the branches of the Willow tree,*
> *And sing loves farewell joyntly with me.*

Meg being merily inclined, shooke off sorrow in this sort, and gently taking the willow Garland, said: wherefore is griefe good? Can it recall folly past? No. Can it helpe a matter remedilesse? No. Can it restore losses, or draw us out of danger? No. What then? Can griefe make unkind men curteous? No. Can it bring long life? No, for it doth rather hasten our death. What then can it do? Can it call our friends out of their graves? No. Can it restore virginity if we chance to lose our maidenhead? No. Then wherefore should I grieve? Except I went to kill my selfe. Nay seeing it is so, hang sorrow, I will never care for them that care not for me, and therefore a Figge for the Cocke of Westminster: by this good day I am glad I have scapt him, for I doe now consider I should have never tooke rest after foure a clocke in the morning, and alas a young married wife would be loath to rise before eight or nine: beside that I should never have gone to bed before ten or eleven, or twelve a clocke at night by that meanes, what a deale of time should I have lost above other women: have him quoth you? Now God blesse me, I sweare by Venus, the faire goddesse of sweet love, in the minde I am in, I would not have him, if he had so much as would lie in Westminster Hall. And therefore Robin this Willow garland is to me right heartily welcome: and I will goe with thee to Gillian presently, and thou shalt see us weare them rather in triumph, then in timerous feare.

Well said, in good sadnes (quoth Robin) thou art the gallantest girle that ever I knew.

But when she came to Gillian, Robin staid for her at the staire foot: they found her sicke in her bed, fetching many sore sighes, to whom Margaret spake in this manner.

Why, how now, Gillian, what, sicke a bed? Now fie for shame, plucke up a good heart woman, let no man triumph so much over thee, to say thou gavest the Crow a pudding, because love would let thee live no longer: be content (quoth she) and take courage to thee, death is a sowre crabbed fellow.

Ah no (quoth Gillian) death is sweet to them that live in sorrow, and to none should he be better welcome then to me, who desires nothing more then death to end my miseries.

What now (quoth Margaret) whose Mare is dead? Art thou a young wench, faire and comely, and dost thou despaire of life? And all for love, and all for love. O fond foole worthy to weare a coate with foure elbowes, this were enough if there were no more men in the world but one, but if there were two, why shouldst thou languish, much lesse knowing there is so many to be had.

O (quoth Gillian) what is all the men in the world to me now I have lost Richard, whose love was my life.

I pray the rise (quoth Meg) and let us go drinke a quart of Sacke to wash sorrow from our hearts.

O (quoth shee) I cannot rise if you would give me a hundred pound, nor will I rise for any mans pleasure.

What (quoth Meg) if your father sent for you, would you not goe to him?

No (quoth she).

Would you not goe to your mother?

No.

But what if your brethren requested you to rise?

Yfaith I would not (quoth she).

Say that some of the Kings Gentlemen intreated your company?

Never prate, I would not goe to the best Lord in the Land (quoth Gillian) nor to no man els in the world.

No (quoth Meg) I am sure you would.

(Quoth she) if I doe, say I am an errant queane, and count me the veriest drab that ever trod on two shooes.

Nay (quoth Meg) seeing you say so, I have done, I was about to tell you of a matter, but I see it is to small purpose, and therefore Ile keep my breath to coole my pottage.

A matter? (said Gillian). What matter is it sweet Meg tell me?

No, no (quoth she) it is in vaine, I would wish you to cover your selfe close, and keepe your selfe warme, least you catch an ague, and so good night Gillian.

Nay, but Meg (quoth she) good Meg if ever thou didst love me, let me know what this matter is that you speake of, for I shall not be in quiet till I know it.

Tush tis but a trifle, a trifle (quoth Meg) not worth the talke: your sweet heart Richard, hath sent his man Robin for you, and, as he tels me he hath a token to deliver you.

What (quoth Gill) is that true? Where is Robin? Why comes he not up?

Truly (quoth Meg) he counts it more then manners to presse into a Maides chamber: beside he would be loath to give any cause of suspition to any of your fellowes, to thinke Ill of him or you, for now a dayes the world is growne to such a passe, that if a Maide doe but looke merrily upon a young man, they will say straight, that either she shall be his wife, or that she is his harlot: but if they see a man come into a womans chamber, they will not sticke to sweare that they have been naught together; for which cause Robin intreated me to come unto you, and to certifie you that hee stayed at the three-Tunnes for your comming: but seeing you are a bed I am sorry I have troubled you so much, and therefore farewell good Gillian.

O stay a little good Meg (quoth she) and I will goe along with you: and with that on she slipt her petticoate, and made such hast in dressing her selfe, that she would not stay the plucking on of her stockings nor the drawing on of her shooes.

Why, how now Gillian (quoth Meg) have you forgot your selfe? Remember you are Ill and sicke a bed.

Tush (quoth she) I am well enough now.

But if you goe foorth to night you are an arrant drab, and a very queane (quoth Meg).

Tush tis no matter for that (said Gillian). Griefe hath two tongues, to say, and to unsay, and therefore I respect not what you prate, and therewithall she ran downe the stayres after Margaret, who got Robin to goe before to the three-Tunnes, where when Gillian came, she asked him how his Master did, and what his errand was to her.

> *Soft: First let us drinke* (quoth Robin) *and then let us talke,*
> *That we cannot pay for, shall be set up in chalke.*

You speak merrily (quoth Margaret) whatsoever you meane, but I would I could see the wine come once, that I may drink a hearty draught; for sorrow they say is dry, and I find it to be true.

> *Then drinke hard* (quoth Robin) *and bid sorrow adue.*

Thus when they had whipt off two or three quarts of wine, Gillian began to grow as pleasant as the best, and would needs know of Robin, what it was he had to say to her.

Nothing (quoth he) but to doe my Masters commendation, and to deliver you his token.

This token? (quoth Gillian). What, a Willow garland? Is the matter so plaine? Is this the best reward he can give me for all my good will; had he no body to flout but mee?

Yes by my faith (quoth Meg) it was his minde that I should beare you company, therefore, looke what he sent to you, he did the like to mee, and that thou maiest the better believe me, see where it is.

O intollerable injury (quoth Gillian) did I take paines to rise and come out of my warme bed for this? O how unfortunate have I beene above all other in the world? Well, seeing I cannot recall what is past, I will take this as a just penance for my too much folly; and if Margaret will agree, we will weare these disdainfull branches on his marriage day to his great disgrace, though to our continuall sorrow.

Content (quoth Meg) all is one to mee, looke what thou wilt allow, I will not dislike, and so paying the shot, away they went.

At length, when the marriage day was come, and that the Bride, in the middest of her friends was set downe to dinner, Margaret and Gillian, attyred in red Stammell petticoats, with white linnen sleeves, and fine Holland Aprons, having their Willow garlands on their head, entred into the Hall singing this song:

> *When fancie first fram'd our likings in love,*
>   *sing all of greene Willow:*
> *And faithfull affection such motion did move,*
>   *for Willow, Willow, Willow.*
> *Where pleasure was plenty we chanced to be,*
>   *sing all of greene Willow:*
> *There were we enthral'd of our liberty,*
>   *and forced to carrie the Willow garland.*
>
> *This young man we liked and loved full deere,*
>   *sing all of greene Willow:*
> *And in our hearts-closset we kept him full neere,*
>   *sing Willow, Willow, Willow.*
> *He was our hearts-pleasure and all our delight,*
>   *sing all of greene Willow:*
> *We judg'd him the sweetest of all men in sight,*
>   *Who gives us unkindly the Willow garland.*
>
> *No cost we accounted too much for his sake,*
>   *sing all of greene Willow:*
> *Fine bands and handkerchers for him we did make,*
>   *sing Willow, Willow, Willow.*
> *And yet for our good will, our travell and paine,*
>   *sing all of greene Willow:*
> *We have gotten nothing but scorne and disdaine;*
>   *as plainly is prov'd by this Willow garland.*
> *Then pardon our boldnesse, thou gentle faire Bride,*
>   *sing all of greene Willow:*
> *We speake by experience of that we have tride,*
>   *sing Willow, Willow, Willow.*
> *Our over much courtesie bred all our woe,*

sing all of greene Willow:
But never hereafter we meane so to doe,
For this onely brought us the Willow garland.

Their song being thus ended, the Bride said she was heartily sorry for their hard fortune in love, greatly blaming the Bridegroom for his unkindnes.

Nay, do not so (quoth Meg) for you shal find him kind enough soon at night: but seeing he hath disappointed me in this sort, it shall go hard, but I will make shift to lose my maiden-head as soone as you shall lose yours, and you shall make good haste, but I wil be before you. O God (quoth she) have I been so chary to keep my honesty, and so dainty of my maiden-head that I could spare it no man for the love I bore to hard-hearted Richard, and hath he serv'd me thus? Well Gillian (quoth she) let us go, never wil I be so tide in affection to one man again while I live; what a deale of time have I lost and spent to no purpose since I came to London? And how many kinde offers have I forsaken, and disdainfully refused of many brave Gentlemen, that would have bin glad of my good will? I thinke I was accurst to come into his company: Well, I say little, but henceforward hang me if I refuse reason when I am reasonably intreated; trust me, I would not for a good thing, that my friends in the country should know that one of my ripe age, bone and bignesse hath all this while liv'd in London idly, like an unprofitable member of the common-wealth; but if I live, they shall heare that I will be better imploy'd, and so adue good Gillian.

Thus Margaret in a melancholy humor went her waies, and in short time after she forsooke Westminster, and attended on the Kings army to Bullen, and while the siege lasted, became a landresse to the Camp, and never after did she set store by her selfe, but became common to the call of every man, till such time as all youthfull delights was banished by old age, and in the end she left her life in Islington, being very penitent for all her former offences.

Gillian in the end was well married, and became a very good house-keeper, living in honest name and fame till her dying day.

CHAPTER IV

How round Robin and his fellowes sung before the King.

The Kings Majesty having royally won the strong town of Bullen, victoriously he returned and came into England, and according to his accustomed manner, lying at his Palace of Whitehall, divers of the Nobility, passing up and down Westminster, did many times heare the Shoomakers journymen singing; whose sweet voyces and pleasant songs was so pleasing in the eares of the hearers, that it caused them to stay about the doore to hearken thereunto: Robin above the rest, declared such cunning in his song, that he ever obtained the chiefest praise; and no marvell, for his skill in pricksong was more then ordinary, for which cause the Singing men of the Abbey did often call him into the Quire.

Now you shall understand, that by their often singing in the Shop, the journeymen of that house were noted above all the men in Westminster, and the report of their singing went far and neer, in so much that at the last, the Kings Majesty had knowledge thereof, who hearing them so greatly commended, caused them to be sent for to the Court. Whereupon round Robin and his foure fellows made themselves ready, and their Master being of a good mind, against the day that they should goe before our King, he suted them all at his owne proper cost, in doublets and hose of crimson Taffety, with black Velvet caps on their heads, and white feathers; on their legs they had fine yellow stockings, pumps and pantofles on their feet: by their sides each of them wore a faire sword; and in this sort being brought before his Majesty, upon their knees they craved pardon for presuming to come into his royall presence.

The King, seeing them to be such proper men, and attyred in such Gentleman-like manner, bad them stand up: Why my Lords (quoth he) be these the merry minded Shoomakers you spake of?

They are most dread Soveraigne (said they).

Certainly (said our King) you are welcome every one, but who among you is round Robin?

> *My Liege* (quoth Robin) *that man am I,*
> *Which in your Graces service will live and die:*
> *And these be my fellowes every one,*
> *Ready to waite your royall Grace upon.*

How now Robin (said our King). What, canst thou rime?

A little my Liege (quoth he) *as I see place and time.*

His Grace laughing heartily at this pleasant companion, told him that he heard say he could sing well.

> *Trust me* (quoth Robin) *at your Graces request,*
> *You shall well perceive we will doe our best.*

Hereupon the King sate him downe, where many great Lords and Ladies of high estate attended on his Highnesse. And being in the Christmas time, after the master of merry disports had performed all his appointed pastimes, Robin, with his fellowes had liberty to declare their cunning before our King, but the Majesty of his Princely presence did so amate them, that they were quite dash'd out of countenance, which his Grace perceiving, gave them many gracious words of encouragement, whereupon they began in this sort, singing a song of the winning of Bullen.

The Song of the winning of Bullen sung before the King by round Robin and his fellowes.

In the moneth of October
Our King he would to Dover:
          By leave of Father and the Sonne:
A great armie of men,
Well appointed there was then,
          Before our noble King to come.

The valiant Lord Admirall,
He was captaine Generall,
          Of all the royall Navie sent by Sea:
The sight was worthie to behold,
To see the ships with shining gold,
          And Flag and Streamers sailing all the way.

At Bullen then arriving,
With wisdome well contriving:
          The armed men were set in battle ray;
And Bullen was besieged round,
Our men with Drum and Trumpets sound,
          Before it marchd couragious that day.

Then marke how all things chanced,
Before them was advanced
          The royall Standard in the bloodie field;
The Frenchmen standing on the walls,
To them our English Heralds calls,
          Wishing in time their Citie for to yeeld.

Our King hath sent to prove you,
Because that he doth love you,
          He profferd mercy, if you will imbrace:
If you deny his kinde request,
And in your obstinacie rest,
          Behold you bring your selves in wofull case.

(Quoth they) wee doe deny you,
And flatly we defie you,
          Faire Bullen is a famous Maiden towne:
For all the deeds that hath beene done,
By conquest never was she won,
          She is a Lady of most high renowne.

When they so unadvised,
His proffer had despised,
          Our Ordinance began to shoote amaine;
Continuing eight houres and more,
For why our King most deeply swore,
          Her Maiden-head that he would obtaine.

When thus his Grace had spoken,
Hee sent her many a token,
          Firie balls, and burning brazen rings:
Faire broad arrowes sharpe and swift,
Which came among them with a drift,
          Well garnish'd with the gray goose wings.

This Maiden towne that lately
Did shew herselfe so stately,
          In seeking favour, many teares she shed:
Upon her knees then fell she downe,
Saying, O King of high renowne,
          Save now my life, and take my maiden-head.

Lo, thus her selfe she ventred,
And streight her streets wee entred,
          And to the market place we marched free:
Never a French-man durst withstand,
To hold a wepon in his hand,
          For all the gold that ever he did see.

Their song being ended, our King cast them a purse with fifty faire angells
for a reward, commending both their skill and good voyces, and after much
pleasant communication, they had liberty to depart; and when they came
home, they told to their Master, all their merriment before the King, and what
reward his Grace had bestowed on them; and powring the gold downe upon
the Table, the same being truly told by their Master, every mans share came
just to five pound a piece. Which, when round Robin saw, he swore he would

bestow a supper upon his Master and Mistresse that night, though it cost him two angels; which his fellowes hearing, and seeing Robins liberall heart to be such, said, they would joyne with him, and laying their money together, would have all the Shoomakers in Westminster to beare them company.

> *Content* (quoth Robin) *with all my heart,*
> *And twenty shillings I will spend for my part:*
> *And as I am true man, and sung before our King,*
> *As much shall each of you spend before our parting.*
> *So shall we have musicke and gallant cheere,*
> *Secke and Sugar, Claret wine, strong ale and Beare.*

This being concluded, they met all together at the signe of the Bell, where they were so merry as might be, at what time Robin began to blame his Master, that had not in three yeeres space gotten his Mistresse with childe.

Hold thy peace (quoth he) all this while I have but jested, but when I fall once in earnest, thou shalt see her belly will rise like a Tun of new Ale: thou knowst I am the Cocke of Westminster.

> *I* (quoth Robin) *you had that name,*
> *More for your rising, than your goodnesse in Venus game.*

The company at this laugh'd heartily, but seven yeeres afte this jest was remembred; for in all that space had not his wife any child: Wherefore Robin would often say, that either his Master was no perfect man, or else his Mistresse was in her in fancy nourished with the milk of a Mule, which bred such barrennesse in her; for till her dying day she never had child.

And after they had lived together, many yeeres, at last, Richard Casteler dyed, and at his death he did divers good and godly deeds: among many other things he gave to the City of Westminster a worthy gift to the cherishing of the poore inhabitants for ever. He also gave toward the reliefe of the poore fatherlesse children of Christs Hospitall in London. to the value of forty pound land by the yeere; and in the whole course of his life he was a very bountifull man to all the decayed housekeepers of that place, leaving behind him a worthy example for other men to follow.

CHAPTER V

The pleasant Story of Peachey the famous Shoomaker of Fleet-street in London.

Much about this time, there lived in London a rich Shoomaker, and a gallant housekeeper; who being a brave man of person, bore a mind agreeable thereunto, and was therefore of most men called lusty Peachey: he kept all the yeere forty tall men on worke, beside Prentises, and every one he clothed in tawny coats, which he gave as his livery to them, all with black caps and yellow feathers; and every Sunday and holiday, when this gentleman-like Citizen went to Church in his black gown garded with Velvet, it was his order to have all his men in their liveries to wait upon him, with every man his sword and buckler, ready at any time, if need required.

It came to passe upon Saint Georges day, that this jolly Shoomaker (being servant to the Duke of Suffolk) went to the Court with all his men after him, to give attendance upon his noble Master, which some yong Gentlemen, more wanton than wise, beholding and envying his gallant mind, devised how they might picke some quarrell, thereby to have occasion to try his manhood.

(Quoth they) Did you ever know a shoomaker, a sowter, a cobling companion, brave it so with the best, as this fellow doth? See with what a train of hardie squires he goes, wat squaring lads they be: they look as if they would fight with Gargantua, and make a fray with the great Turk, and yet I durst lay my life they dare scantly kill a Hedgehog: mark him I pray, I warrant you there is never a Knight in this countrey that goes with so great a train.

Swounes (quoth one) it were a good sport to draw, and try what they can do.

My Masters be advised (quoth another) and attempt nothing rashly: I tell you this fellow is a hardy Coine, he is currant mettle yfaith, and whensoever you try him, Ile warrant you shall finde he will not flie a foot.

With that comes by lusty Tom Stuteley and Strangwidge, two gallant Sea Captaines, who were attired all in Crimson Velvet, in Marriners wide slops that reacht to the foot, in watched silk thrumb hats and white feathers, having Pages attending with their weapons, who seeing a cluster of Gentlemen in hard communication at the Court gate, askt what was the matter?

Marry Captaine (quoth they) we are all beholding to yonder lusty Gallant, that hath so many waiting on him with Tawny Coats.

Sblood, what is he? (quoth Stuteley).

He seemes to be a gallant man (said Strangwidge) whatsoever

he be: and were it not I see him in the Duke of Suffolks liverie, I should have taken him by his train to be some Lord at the least.

Nay (quoth Stuteley) he is some Knight of good living.

Gentlemen (quoth they) how your judgements deceive you: it is certaine he is as good a Shooemaker as any is in Fleetstreet.

What? Is he but a Shooemaker? (quoth Stuteley). O how that word makes me scratch my elbo: Can a Shooemaker come to the Court with more Servingmen at his heeles then Captaine Stuteley? See how it makes my blood rise: O the passion of my heart, how the villaine squares it out? See, see, what a company of handsome fellowes follow him, it is twenty pound to a penny but they were better borne then their Master.

Not so (quoth the Gentlemen) but I think their birth and bringing up was much alike, for they be all Shooemakers and his stoole companions.

Now, by this iron and steell (quoth Stuteley) were it not that he is attendant on the good Duke, I would have him by the eares presently. I will lay an hundred pound, and stake it downe straight, that Captaine Strangwidge and I will beat him and all his forty men.

The Gentlemen being ready to set this match forward, greatly commended the Captaines high courage: notwithstanding they would not hazard their money on such a desperate match.

Well Gentlemen (quoth they) you say he dwels in Fleetstreet,

and that he is a Shoomaker, never trust us more if we become not his customers, but the crossest customers shall he finde us that ever came to his shop for shooes.

Nay (quoth Stuteley) we will bespeak Boots of him, and thus we will raise our quarrell: when they are made, if they come not on easie, and sit on our legs neatly, we will make them pluck them off againe, and presently we will beat them in peeces about his pate, which if he seeme to take in dudgin, and with his men follow us into the street for revenge, if we make them not leap before us like Monkies, and force them run away like sheep-biters, let us lose our credits and Captainships for ever.

But what if you should chance to kill any of them? (said the Gentlemen).

Swounes (quoth they) what care we, we are bound to sea on a gallant voyage, wherein the King hath no small venture, and without us it cannot go forward, so that it is not the death of twenty men can stay us at home, and therefore when they should be seeking of us in Fleetstreet, we would be seeking out the Coast of Florida.

You say well Captaines (quoth they) and no doubt if you do any such thing we shall heare of it: for the report thereof will be famous through London.

Within a while after Stuteley and Strangwidge, having thus determined, came into Fleetstreet, and making inquiry for Peachies shop, they were by every man directed to the house: where, when they were come, they called for the good man of the house: the foreman of the shop demanded what their will was?

Why knave (quoth they) what carest thou, let us speak with thy Master.

Gentlemen (quoth he) if you lack any such commodity as we make, you shall finde me sufficient to serve you, for to that end hath my Master set me in the shop.

Why, Jack-sauce (quoth Stuteley) you whorson peasant, know you to whom you speak?

The fellow being very cholerick, and somewhat displeased at these disdainfull speeches, made him this round answer: ask you to whom I speak? (quoth he).

I, goodman flat-cap (said Strangwidge) we ask to whom you speak?

Sir (quoth he) I speak to a Velvet foole, a silken slave that knowes not how to governe his tongue.

With that Stuteley swore like a madman and presently drew out a dudgin haft dagger that he had by his side, and began to lay at the fellow, which one of his fellowes seeing, flung a Last at his head and feld him to the ground: Strangwidge thereupon drew his sword, but by that time the fellow had took downe his sword and buckler, which hung in the shop hard at hand, and therewith so well defended himselfe, that Strangwidge could do him no hurt: and by that time Stuteley recovering crald up againe.

But Peachie hearing a great hurly burly in the shop, came forth and demanded the cause of the quarrell? His servants told him that those Gentlemen had given the Journeymen very ill words.

How can they chuse but speak ill (quoth Peachie) for it may be they never learn'd to speak well: whereupon he went unto them saying; how now, Captaines, how grew this quarrell twixt you and my men?

Thy men? (quoth Stuteley). Thy Roags, and thy selfe is no better that brings them up.

Sir (quoth Peachie) you wrong me too much, and get you quickly from my doore, or, by this sunne that shines, Ile set you packing, and therefore never think to outface me with great looks, for I tell thee Stuteley and Strangwidge both, did you look as big as the Devill I feare you not. And you forgot your maners too much to give me such base tearms, for I would you well knew I keepe forty good fellowes in my house, that in respect of their manhood may seeme to be your equals.

O intollerable Comparison (quoth Stuteley) flesh and blood cannot beare such abuse. Ile tell the what (quoth he) if we two beat not thee and thy forty men, I durst be hangd up at thy doore.

Fie, fie, tis too much oddes (quoth Peachy) dare you two take ten? Nay dare you fight with five?

Take that and try (quoth Strangwidge) and therewithall gave him a sound blow on the eare.

Nay this is too much (quoth Peachy) put up this and put up all. Stuteley and Strangwidge (quoth he) if you be men, meet me in Lincolnes-Inne-fields presently.

Content (quoth they) and thereupon went their wayes.

Peachie fetching straight his sword and buckler, call'd his man John Abridges to go with him, charging all the rest not to stir out of doores, and so into the fields they went, where immediately they met with these lusty Caveliers. The Captaines seeing him come only with one man, askt if that were all the helpe he had?

I will request no more (quoth Peachie) to swinge you both out of the fields.

Brag is a good Dog (quoth Stuteley) but tell us, hast thou made thy Will, and set thy house in order?

What if I have not (quoth Peachie)?

Why then (quoth Strangwidge) for thy wife and childrens sake go home againe and do it, or else get more aide about thee to preserve thy life.

Why how now Master (quoth John Abridges) come you into the field to fight with women? Why these be two disguised butter whores Ile lay my life, that have more skill in scoulding then in fighting: but heare you (quoth he) if you be men, leave your foule words, and draw your faire weapons, and because I will spare your middle peece, if I strike a stroke below the girdle, call me Cut.

Sblood shall we be thus out-braved? (quoth Stuteley). And therewith drawing their weapons, they fell to it lustily, where Peachie and his man laid so bravely about them, that they beat both the Captaines out of breath, in which fray, Stuteley was wounded in the head, and Strangwidge in the sword arme, but at last they were parted by many Gentlemen that came in good time to prevent further mischiefe.

The Captaines got them straight to the Surgion, and Peachie with his man went directly home: and while they were a dressing, Peachie hearing how they were hurt, sent to Stuteley a kerchiefe by one of his men, and by another a scarffe to Strangwidge, by the third he sent them a silver bottle of Aqua vitae, wishing them to be of good cheare, for hee intended to be better acquainted with them ere long. The Captaines finding these favours to be but flouts, were more grieved thereat, then at their hurt, and therefore with many disdainfull speeches, they refused his proffer'd curtesie.

And you shall understand that afterward Peachies men by two and two at a time, did often meet and fight with them, and so narrowly would they watch for them, that they could be in no place in peace, insomuch that the Captaines found fighting work enough, and a great deale more then willingly they would, whereby they received many scarres and wounds in the body, so that lightly they were never out of Surgions hands. Upon a time it chanced that, being upon the point of their voyage, and shortly to go to sea: Stuteley and Strangwidge having beene at the Court, and newly come from my Lord-Admirals lodging, before they came to Charing-crosse, they were encountred by a couple of Peachies men, who presently drew upon them, and laid so freely about, that the two Captaines were glad at length to house themselves for their refuge.

Now a plague on them (quoth Stuteley) shall we never be in quiet for these quoystrels? Never were we so ferrited before, swownes we can no sooner look into the streets, but these shoomakers have us by the eares: a pox on it that ever we medled with the rascals: sblood they be as unluckie to be met, as a Hare on a jorney, or a sergeant on a Sunday morning, for ever one mischiefe or other followes it. Captaine Strangwidge (quoth he) there is no other shift but to seek their friendship, otherwise we are in danger every houre to be maimed, therefore to keep our lims sound against we go to Sea, tis best to finde meanes to quiet this grudge.

Then (said Strangwidge) it were good to do so, if a man knew how: but you may be sure they will not easily be intreated, seeing we have so mightily abused them in speech.

Thus they cast in their mindes divers times by what meanes they might be reconciled: and albeit they sent divers of their friends unto Master Peachie and his men, yet they would not yeeld, nor give consent to be appeased, nor to put up such wrong as they had received without further revenge: so that the Captaines were at length constrained to make sute to the Duke of Suffolk to take up the matter: who most honorably performed their request: and so the grudge ended betwixt them, to the great credit of Master Peachie, and all his men.

CHAPTER VI

How Harrie Nevell, and Tom Drum came to serve Peachey of Fleet-street.

The fame of Peachey, running through England by meanes of the frayes which he and his men had with Stuteley and Strangwidge, it made many of that occupation desirous to come and dwell with him, for beside that he was a tall man of his hands, he was also an excellent good workman, and therewithall a bountifull house keeper. Among many other that was desirous of his service, there was one called Tom Drum, that had a great minde to be his man, a very odde fellow, and one that was sore infected with the sin of cogging: this boasting companion, sitting on a time sadly at work in his Masters shop at Petworth, and seeing the Sun shine very faire, made no more to doe but suddenly shrowded up S. Hughes bones, and taking downe his pike-staffe, clapt his pack at his back, and called for his Master, who comming into the shop, and seeing his man prepared to be prauncing abroad, demanded what the matter was that he followed not his businesse.

O Master (quoth he) see you not how sweetly the Sun shines, and how trimly the trees are deckt with green leaves?

Well and how then? (quoth his Master).

Marry sir (quoth he) having a great mind to heare the small birds sing, and seeing the weather fitter to walk then to work, I called you forth to take my leave and to bid you farewell, I hope sir, I have no wager in your hand.

Why no (quoth his Master) thou wilt be sure to take an order for that, and therefore seeing thou wilt be gone, adue.

God be with you good master (quoth he) and farewell all good fellowes of the gentle craft, and therewith he departed.

The journeymen of the Towne hearing that Tom Drum went away, according to their ancient custome they gathered themselves together to drink with him, and to bring him out of town: and to this intent, up they go with him to the signe of the Crowne, where they parted not till they had drunk a Stand of Ale drie.

Which being done, they bring him a mile on his way, carrying a gallon of beere with them: and lastly there once againe they drink to his good health, and to Crispianus soule: and to all the good fellowes of Kerbfoord: which being done, they all shook him by the hand, and with hollowing and whooping, so long as they can see him, they bid him a hundred times farewell.

So soone as he was gone out of their whooping, the sweat reeking in his hand, and the Ale in his head, he trips so light in the highway, that he feeles not the ground he goes on: and therefore, being in a merry vaine, and desirous to drive out the weary way, as he walks he begins thus pleasantly to sing:

> *The Primrose in the greene Forrest,*
> *the Violets they be gay:*
> *The double Dazies and the rest,*
> *that trimly decks the way,*
> *Doth move the spirits to brave delights,*
> *where beauties Darlings be:*
> *With hey tricksie, trim goe tricksie,*
> *under the greenewood tree.*

The singing of this song awaked a young Gentleman whom sorrow had laid asleepe on a greene bank by the high wayes side. Who having unadvisedly displeased his Parents, in a cholerick humour departed from them, betaking himselfe to travell, thereby to try how fortune would favour him abroad: but having now spent all his money, he was in a wofull taking, not knowing what to do, for never had he beene brought up to any trade, whereby he might be able to get a penny at his need. Wherefore being in this distresse, he was fully purposed to go to London, and there to learne some occupation, whereby he might keep himself a true man, and not to be driven to seek succour of his friends.

Now therefore when he heard Tom Drum so trimly tune it on the way, raising himselfe from the sad ground, he awaited his comming, at whose sudden sight Tom Drum started like one that had spied an Adder: and seeing him provided with a good sword and buckler, supposed he had beene one that waited for a fat purse: for which cause he began thus to enter parly with him.

Good fellow (quoth he) God give you good morrow, but ill speed.

Why saist thou so? (quoth Harrie).

Because (said Tom) by the good light of the day thou maist see to passe beside me, and that by thy speeding ill, I may speed the better.

What hast thou such store of money (quoth Harrie) that thou art loath to lose it?

No by my faith (quoth he) I have so little that I cannot spare it: for I assure thee all my store is but one poore pennie, and that thou maist see here under my little finger.

Why then (quoth Harrie) if I were minded to assault thee, it should be more to rob the of thy manhood then thy money: but tell me what pack is that thou bearest at thy back?

Marry they be Saint Hughes bones.

Saint Hughes bones (quoth Harrie) what is that?

A kind of commodity (said Tom) which I cannot misse, for they be my working tooles.

I pray thee (said Harrie) what occupation art thou?

Sir (quoth he) I am a Goldsmith that makes rings for womens heeles.

What meanest thou by that? (said Harrie).

I am (quoth Tom) of the Gentle Craft, vulgarly called a Shoomaker.

The happier art thou (quoth Harrie) that thou hast a trade to live by, for by that means thou carriest credit with the in every place: but tell me good friend, what is thy name, and how far dost thou travell this way?

Sir (quoth he) I travell to the next towne, but my jorney is to London, and as for my name, I am not ashamed to shew it: For my name is a Nowne substantive that may be felt, heard, and understood, and to speak the truth I am called: whoe there, I trust sir you ask for no hurt, you are no Bayliffe nor Bayliffs man, are ye?

No not I (said Harrie).

Gods blessing on you (quoth he) I love you the better: for I was never so fraid lest my Hostesse of the George in Petworth had sent you to arrest me, for I think I owe her some ten Groats on the score, set up in very faire Chalk, as one of the principals of her house is able to testifie: but I pray God send her meat, for I verely think I shall never send her monie.

But yet (quoth Harrie) I know not how to call your name.

Verily (said he) I am called Thomas Drum or Tom Drum, chuse you whether.

Well Thomas (quoth Harrie) I perceive thou art a man and a good fellow, therefore I will not be strange to open my need unto thee. I have beene unto my parents untoward, and more then that, not knowing when I was well, wilfully I came from them: and now that I have spent all my money and worne my selfe out of credit, I have utterly undone my selfe, for I am not worth a groat, nor no man will trust me for two pence.

Why then (quoth Tom) thou art not worth so much as goodman Luters lame nagge, for my Lord of Northumberlands huntsman would have given halfe a Crowne for him to have fedde his dogges: notwithstanding be of good cheere, if thou wilt goe to London with me, I will beare thy charges, and, Ifaith, at the next towne we will be merry and have good cheere.

Alas (quoth Harry) how can that be, seeing you have but one penny?

Ile tell the what (quoth Tom) wert thou a Shoomaker as I am, thou mightst goe with a single penny under thy finger, and travell all England over, and at every good towne, have both meate, drinke and lodging of the best, and yet have thy penny still in store, as when we come to Gilford you shall soone see.

Beleeve me (quoth Harry) that is more then any tradesmen in England els can doe.

Tush (quoth Tom). Shoomakers will not see one another lacke, for it is our use if wee know of a good fellow that comes to towne, wanting either meate or money, and that he make himselfe knowne, he shall neede to take no further care, for he shall be sure that the jorneymen of that place will not onely give him kinde welcome, but also provide him all things necessary of free cost: And if he be disposed to worke among them, he shall have a Master provided by their meanes, without any sute made by himselfe at all.

Verily (quoth Harry) thou dost ravish me with the good report of thy passing kind and curteous trade, and I would spend part of my gentle bloud, to be of the gentle Craft: and for thy curtesie if thou wouldst teach it mee, I would annoint thee a gentleman for ever.

Wilt thou say and hold? (quoth Tom).

Or els hang me (said Harry).

Then (said he) annoint me a Gentleman, and I will shape thee for a Shoomaker straight.

Thereupon Harry tooke his knife, and cutting his finger, all besmeared Tom-Drums face with his bloud, that he made him looke like the Image of Bred-streete corner, or rather like the Sarazines-head without New-gate.

Tom Drum, seeing him doe so, said he might by that means as well annoint him a Joyner, as a Gentleman.

Nay (said Harry) I do not deceive thee I warrant thee, seeing this blood did spring from a Gentleman, if thou wilt not beleeve me, aske all the men in the towne-Malin, and they will say the like.

Well, Ile take thy word (quoth Tom). And therefore looke that presently thou strip thy selfe, for I will cast the in a Shoomakers mould by and by.

Harry perceiving his meaning did what he willed, and so he was suted in Toms attire, and Tom in his; so that Harry bore the pike staffe and Saint Hughes bones: and Tom swaggered with his sword and buckler; and comming in this sort to Gilford, they were both taken for shoomakers, and very hartely welcomed by the jorneymen of that place, especially Harry, because they never saw him before: And at their meeting they askt him and if he could sing, or sound the Trumpet, or play on the Flute, or recon up his tooles in rime, or manfully handle his pike staffe, or fight with sword and buckler?

Beleeve me (quoth Harry) I can neither sound the Trumpet, nor play on the Flute: and beshroe his nose that made me a shoomaker. For he never taught me to recon up my tooles in rime nor in prose.

Tom hearing him say so: told them that he made of an old serving man a new shoomaker.

When was that? (quoth they).

Marry (saith he) when I was annointed a Gentleman, I thinke this face can shew, that I have a gentle blood about me.

Why then (quoth they) thou art but a painted Gentleman, but we must account this young man wise, that to avoid misery betakes himselfe to follow mistery, for cunning continueth when fortune fleeteth, but it will be hard for such as never were brought up to the bodily labour to frame their fine fingers to any course faculty.

Not a whit (quoth Harry) for labour by custome becommeth easie.

This saist true (said Tom). I durst lay a good wager I have made more shoes in one day then all the jorneymen here have done in a month.

With that one of the jorney-men began to chafe, saying, how many a paire of shooes hast though made in a day?

I made, quoth Tom, when the daies were at longest, eight score paire of shoes in one day.

O monstrous detestable lye (quoth they) and thereupon one ran into the chimney and cried, come again Clement, come againe.

Whom calst thou? (quoth Tom).

I call Clement Carry Lye, that runnes Poste betwixt the Turke, and the Devill; that he may take his full loading ere he goe, for the best jorneyman that ever I knew, never made above ten paire in a day in his life: and I will lay my whole yeeres wages with thee, that thou canst not make twenty paire in a day as they ought to be: I should be ashamed but to doe as much as another, and I never saw him yet that could out worke me, yet dare not I take upon me to make a doozen paire of shooes in a day: but tis an old saying, they brag most that can doe least.

Why thou Puppie (quoth Tom) thou house Dove, thou Cricket, that never crept further then the chimney corner, tell me what Countries hast thou travelled?

Far enough (quoth he) to prove as good a work-man as thou art.

I deny that (quoth Tom) for I have been where I have seene men headed like Dogs, and women of the same shape, where if thou hadst offered them a kisse, they would have beene ready to have snapt off thy nose: othersome I have seen, that one of their legs hath been as good as a penthouse to cover their whole bodies, and yet I have made them shooes to serve their feet, which I am sure thou couldest never do: nay if thou wilt go with me, if thou seest me not make an hundred paire of shooes from sunrising to sunsetting, count me worse then a stinking Mackrell.

Now verily thy talke stinkes too much (quoth they) and if thou canst do so, never make further jorney, but try the matter heere.

I tell you (quoth Tom) I cannot try it in England, nor yet in France, Spaine, or Italy, nor in any part of the lowe countries, nor in high Germany, Sweathland, or Polonia.

We think no lesse (quoth they) nor in any part of the world beside.

Yes (quoth Tom) I can do it as we travell to Russia, for there every day is five and fiftie of our dayes in length: nay Ile tell you further, quoth Tom, in some parts of the world where I have been, it is day for halfe a yeare together, and the other halfe yeare is continually night: and goe no further, quoth he, but into the further part of Scotland, and you shall find one day there (in the month of June) to be foure and twenty houres long, and therefore my Masters while you live, take heed how you contrary a traveller, for therein you shall but bewray your owne ignorance, and make your selves mocking stockes to men of knowledge.

And travellers (quoth they) uncontrouled, have liberty to utter what lies they list.

Masters tell me (quoth Tom) were you not borne in Arcadia?

No (quoth they) but why aske you?

Because (said Tom) that countrey doth most abound in plenty of Asses, where they swarme as thicke as Bees in Cicily.

We have cause to give you much thanks (quoth they) for calling us Asses so kindly.

Not so (said Tom) I did but aske a question; but seeing you are so cunning, tell mee what Countrey breeds the best Hides, and Leather, and from whence have we the best Corke?

Our best Corke comes from Portugall (quoth they) but the best Leather grows in our owne land.

I deny it (quoth Tom) there is I confesse good Corke in Portugall, but the best grows in Sparta; but for Hides and Lether there is none comparable to that in Siciona: where I have made a man a paire of shooes that hath lasted him a twelve month to toyle in every day. O tis a gallant Countrey, for Ile tell you what, there is never a shoomaker in England that kept so many men as I did at that time.

Then said the rest, thou speakest thou knowest not what: Master Peachy of Fleet-streete keeps continually forty men a work, and the green-King of Saint-Martins hath at this time little lesse then three-score journey men.

This is pretty well (quoth Tom) but what say you to him that for halfe a yeere together, kept waiting on him above a hundred men that never did him stitch of work? This was a shoomaker of some account.

But who was that? (quoth they).

Marry (quoth Tom) simple though I stand here, it was my selfe, and yet I never made brags of it.

O what a shamelesse lyer art thou (quoth they) we never knew thee able to keep one man.

Now, by this bread (said Tom) you do me mighty wrong, and were it not that you be all of the gentle Craft, which science I doe so greatly love and reverence, this Iron and steele should make it good upon your flesh, for I tell you once againe, I have beene Master of an hundred men, and put six-score to the hundred.

I pray you tell us (quoth they) what men were they?

What men were they (quoth Tom) they were vermin.

In troth (quoth they) we thought as much, and we commend you for telling truth, and we suppose if you were well searcht we should find twenty vermin waiting on you still. But tell us Tom, art thou minded to be Master Peachies man?

I am (quoth he) except he will make me his fellow.

By the Masse (quoth they) then wert thou best to have thy wards ready, and thy hilts sure, for he receives no servant before he tries his man-hood.

So much the better (quoth Tom) and for that purpose I poste up to London.

Thus having had at Gilford very good cheere, the journey-men of the towne paid for all, and beside gave them money in their purses to spend by the way, and so toward London they went with all speed.

CHAPTER VII

How the wilde Knight Sir John Rainsford for burying a Massing Priest alive, was faine to leave his Lady, and forsake his house, till he had obtained his pardon of the King: who meeting with Harry Nevell, and Tom Drum, went with them to serve Peachy of Fleet street, where for a while he became a Shoomaker.

You shall understand that at this time there lived a gallant Knight called Sir John Rainsford, who was for his courage and valiant heart inferiour to few men living: he kept a bountifull house, and a brave company of tall men to waite upon him. To all the poore round about where he dwelt, he was very charitable, releeving them daily both with money and meate; he was a famous Courtier, and in great favour with the King, and the onely thing that disgraced his vertues, was this, that he was something wild in behaviour, and wilfull in his attempts, often repenting sadly what he committed rashly.

It came to passe upon a time, that as this couragious Knight was riding home to his own house, there was at a certaine village, a corps carried to be buried, the deceased father of five small children and the late husband of a wofull Widow, whose poverty was such, that she had no money to pay for his buriall: which thing Sir John the parish Priest doubting, would not by any meanes doe his duty to the dead man, except he might first have his money.

The Widdow and her children, with many teares intreated him to do his office, but he would not be perswaded, saying: What you beggers, would you have me open my sacred lips to invocate and call upon the King of Heaven, to receive thy husbands soule, and to perswade our great Grandmother the earth to wrap his cold body in her warme bosome, for nothing? I tel thee no: first shall his soule frie in the flames of purgatory, till it be as thin as a pancake, and his body remaine above ground till the Crowes have pickt his carrion carkasse to the bare bones: and therefore leave your puling, and prate no more, least you make me as chollericke as a quaile.

And therewithall, as he was going away, the poore Widdow falling on her knees, pluckt him by the gowne, saying: good Sir John, for sweet Saint Charity, say one Ave Maria, or one Pater noster, and let my poore husbands corps be covered, though it be but with one handfull of holy ground.

Nay dame (quoth he) do you remember at the last shrift how you served me? You would not, no forsooth you would not: and now good Mistris I will not: no penny, no Pater noster, that is flat: I pray you now see if your honesty be sufficient to keepe your husband from the Crowes. I thought a time would come at length to cry quittance for your coynes: and with that word away he went.

The poore Widdow seeing his obstinacy, with a heavy heart turned to the high wayes side, which was hard adjoyning to the Church-yard, and there she and her children wofully begged of the passers by, some money to bury their fathers dead body.

At the last Sir John came riding with all his men, of whom the poor Widdow in this manner began to aske his almes: good Sir (quoth she) if ever womans misery mooved your heart to pitty, give me one penny for Gods sake, toward the burying of my poore husband: in like manner the children cried, saying, one penny for Christ his sake good Master, good Master one penny.

Sir John, hearing their lamentable cry, and seeing the dead corps lying there, askt why the Priest did not bury it?

O Sir Knight (quoth she) I have no money to pay for the buriall; and therefore the Priest will not doe it.

No? (quoth Sir John). By Gods blessed mother I sweare, Ile make him bury the dead or Ile bury him alive: whereupon he willed one of his men presently to goe to the Parsonage for the Priest, and to bring him thither immediately. His man did so, and foorth came Sir John, in his gowne and corner cap, roughly demanding who would speake with him?

That would I (quoth Sir John Rainesford): therefore tell me, how comes it to passe, that according to order you put not this dead corps into the pit?

Sir (quoth he) because according to order they will not pay me for my paines.

Above all men (quoth Sir John) Priestes should respect the poore, and charitably regard the state of the needy, because they themselves doe teach charity to the people, and perswade men unto works of mercy: and therefore Sir Iohn, seeing good deeds are meritorious, doe you win heaven by this good work, and let the dead possesse their due.

I, so they shall (said the Priest) so I may not loose my due: for I tell you further, I count it little better then folly, to fill my soule with pleasure by emptying my purse with coine.

Wilt thou not bury him? (said the Knight).

No, not without money (said the Priest).

I pray thee (said the Knight) let me intreat the for this time to doe it, because the woman is poor.

Then let me intreat you to pay me (quoth the Priest) because you are rich.

Sir John Rainsford seeing him stand so peremptory on his points, swore a deep oath, that it were best for him to bury him, or (quoth he) Ile bury thee.

Bury me? (said the Priest). A fig for you, and bury blind bayard when he is dead, or the dogs that your Hawks will not eate.

The Knight at these words being marvelous angry commanded his men to take him up and cast him into the grave: his men made no more to do, but presently upon their Masters word tooke up the Priest, and wrapping him round in his gowne, put him quicke into the grave, and the rest cast earth upon him as fast as they could, at what time the Priest cried out, hold, hold, for Gods sake, let me rise and I will bury him.

Nay soft (quoth the Knight) thou art not like to rise, no rising here before the generall resurrection, that thou shalt rise to judgement.

And therefore quicke as he was they buried him, which being done, he commanded the Sexton to make another grave for the dead man, and sending for another Priest, he askt him if he wold bury the dead without money, who, making twenty legs, shivering and shaking with feare, answered: I forsooth with all my heart for they are knaves and no Christians that will not doe it.

Now when the dead man was buried, the Knight gave the poore Widdow an angell in gold to comfort her and her children, and so rode his way.

When he came home, he told to his Lady what he had done, who greatly grieving thereat, wisht he had paid for twenty burials, rather then he had made that one buriall.

Tis done now (said the Knight) and undone it cannot be againe, though with griefe I should kill my selfe.

Now you shall understand that the Deane of the Dioces, having word hereof, rode up presently to London, and made a great complaint thereof unto the King, which when his grace had considered, he was very wroth thereat, and therefore sent down pursevants to apprehend the Knight, but he before had forsaken his house, and wandred in disguise up and downe the Countrey. His Lady in the meane space made great suite for his pardon, being therein assisted by divers grave Counsellors, and Noble Lords, who much lamented the Knights case: notwithstanding they could hardly forbeare laughing many times when they thought upon this mad pranke.

But as Sir John disguisedly wandred, he chanced twixt Gilford and London to light in the company with Harry Nevell and Tom Drum: But Harry vewing him well in the face, discried by his countenance what he was, and marvelling much to see him in such distresse, made himselfe not known, but sounded him in this sort.

Sir (quoth he) whither do you wander this way, or to what place travell you?

Gentle youth (quoth he) fitly dost thou aske me whither I wander, seeing indeed we doe all but wander in this vale of misery: dost thou demand whither I travell? nay rather aske wherefore I trauell, or wherewith I travell? and then could I soone answer thee.

Sbones (quoth Tom) I durst lay a haporth of Ale, that the Peasant is in labour with love.

Nay (quoth Sir John) hadst thou said I had travelled with griefe, and that I was in labour with sorrow, then hadst thou said right, for I may say to thee, I have had a sore labour continuing this month in paine, and yet is not the time of my deliverance come, wherein I should be freed from this untoward child of care: thou didst thinke I was in love, O would to God it were so, for while I was in love, my dayes ran foorth in plesant houres, but I am cast off like a lumpe of earth from the gardiners spade: I love, but I am not beloved, but rather hated and despised.

Tush (quoth Tom) bridle these foolish passions, for Ile tell the what, hunger asswageth love, and so doth time, but if thou be not able to doe any of these, then to take an halter, which if thou doest use as it ought, if ever thou complaine more, of sorrow or care, never trust my word for a cupple of blacke puddings.

Belike (said Sir John) thou hast been some hangman that thou art so cunning in the nature of an halter: but howsoever thou accountest it good, yet it is an Ill word foure times a yeer at Newgate, and as small comfort is it to me to heare it rehearst at this time.

Indeed (said Harry) these are unsavory tearmes to be spoken to a sorrowfull man: neither have any of us great cause to be merry at this meeting, considering the hard cases wee are in, that are both masterlesse, and moneylesse, which if God doe not soone send us, will cause our sodaine misery.

With that the Knight turning his head, pluckt his hat to his eyes to hide the teares that trickled down his face, saying, O my masters, want of money cannot make a man miserable, if he have health and liberty, to worke for his living, but indeed the frownes of a good Master, the displeasure of a good Master, the hate of a good Master, may easily make a servant miserable, as by mine own experience I have seen, and to my grief but lately felt.

What man, be blith (said Tom) and never grieve so much for the Ill will of a Master. God keepe me from being of thy mind, for if I should have grieved at the Ill will of every Master that I have served, I verely thinke I should have had kild a proper man long ere this; for I am sure I have had as many Masters, as there are Market townes in England.

And yet perhaps (quoth Harry) none so good a Master as his was.

Never did man speake truer word, said the Knight, for he was to me good, kind and liberall, but howsoever he hath banisht me his house, yet shall my heart serve him while I live: now doth it come in my mind, how happy they are that live in his favour: how blessed they be that enjoy his presence; O were my head once againe shadowed under his faire roofe, it would expell all unquiet thoughts, which like milstones presseth downe my hearts comfort.

What, would you goe dwell with him againe? (quoth Tom). Fie, what a base mind doe you beare; were it to me, by this flesh and bloud, I would rather run as far as Jerusalem to seeke a Master.

Tom, Tom (said the Knight) I know this, wealth makes men lofty, but want makes men lowly, and commonly gentle. Masters have proud servants, but had I beene as wise, as I was wilfull, I might have led a happy life, but if teares might satisfie for mine offence, I would quickly recover his favour.

Hereupon the wofull Knight would have parted their company, but Harry, secretly conferring with him had knowledge how his griefe grew, and making themselves known the one to the other, agreed to goe to London together, and there to try what fortune would befall them.

The Knight tooke great comfort by this conference, and having good store of gold about him, made them great cheere at Kingstone, and in the end was content to take their counsaile: and comming into Fleet-streete, Tom Drum brought them to Peachies house, where such meanes was made, that at last upon the tryall of their manhood, they were all entertained; and so well did Peachy like of Sir John that he vowed he should not be his man, but his fellow.

Within short time after the French-men had landed in the Ile of Wight, about two thousand men of warre, who burned and spoyled the Country very sore, for which cause the King had made ready an army of men to goe thither. Peachy at his owne proper cost, set forth thirty of his owne servants, well armed at all essayes, and himselfe as Captaine over them mustred before the King: who liked so well of them, that he chose out seaven of that company for his owne Guard; at what time Sir John, in disguised manner shewed there such good service, that thereby he won his Majesties high favour, and was by him most graciously pardoned. Peachy was hereupon made the King's Shoomaker, who lived long after in great favour and estimation, both with his Majesty and all the honourable Lords of the Court.

CHAPTER VIII

Of Tom Drums vants, and his rare intertainment at Mistris Farmers house, the faire Widdow of Fleet-street.

There lived in Fleet-streete at this time a faire Widdow, who was as famous for her beauty, as she was esteemed for her wealth; she was beloved of many

Gentlemen, and sued unto by divers Cittizens, but so deepe was the memory of her late husband ingraven in her heart, that she utterly refused marriage leading a sober and solemne life.

Harry Nevell having his heart fired with the bright beames of this blazing Comet, sought all meanes possible to quench the heate thereof with the floudes of her favourable curtesie: and lacking meanes to bring himselfe acquainted with so curious a peece, bewrayed by his outward sighs, his inward sorrows: which upon a time, Tom Drum perceiving, demanded the cause of his late conceived griefe, saying, How now Hal, what wind blowes so bleake on your chekes now? Tell me mad wag, hath Cupid and you had a combate lately? Why lookest thou so sad? Hath the blind slave given thee a bloody nose, or a broken head?

Oh, no Tom (quoth he) that little tyrant aimes at no other part but the heart, therefore tis my heart, and not my head that bleeds.

With whom Hal, with whom art thou in love, tell me man? It may be I may pleasure thee more in that matter then my Lord Mayor: therefore, Ifaith Harry say who is it? Never be afraid man to unbuckle your Budget of close counsell to me, for if I bewray your secrets call me dogs-nose, and spit in my face like a young kitling. I tell thee Harry, I am held in greater account among women then you are aware, and they will more willingly shew their secrets to me then to their ghostly father.

But art thou so in favour with fine wenches? (quoth Harry).

Ifaith Sir I (quoth Tom) for I tro I have not lived thus long, but I know how to make a woman love me, by a cunning tricke that I have: I durst lay my life, I will make a dozen maids runne after me twenty miles for one nights lodging, striving among themselves who should first bestow her maiden-head upon me.

That tricke surpasses of all the trickes that ever I heard (quoth Harry).

Nay (quoth Tom) Ile tell thee once what a merry pranke I plaid, God forgive me for it: upon a time, on a Saterday in the evening, I went into East-cheape of purpose to spie what pretty wenches came to Market, where I saw a great many as fresh as flowers in May, tripping up and down the streets with handbaskets in their hands, in red stammell petticoates, cleane neckerchers and fine holland aprons as white as a Lilly: I did no more but carry the right leg of a Turtle under my left arme, and immediately the wenches were so inamoured with my sight that they forsooke the butchers shops, and inticed me into a Taverne, where they spent all the money they should have laid out at Market, onely to make me merry: and never had I so much to doe, as to be rid of their company, where they were ready to fall together by the eares, for the kisses they would have bestowed on me.

But it may be (quoth Harry) your art would faile you now, to help your friend at a dead lift.

Not so (said Tom) and therefore if there be any in this street that thou hast a mind unto, thou shalt carry but the head of a dead crow about thee, and it shall be of force to bring her to thy bed, were it fine Mistres Farmer herself.

But art thou acquainted with her (quoth Harry) or dost thou thinke thou couldst prefer a friend to her speech?

I (quoth Tom). Why I tell the I am more familiar with her then with Doll our kitchen drudge: why man she will doe anything at my request, nay, I can command her in some sort, for I tell thee she will not scant be seene in the street, though some would give her twenty pound for every step, and I did but slightly request her to walke into the fields with me, and straight she went, and I never come into her house, but I have such entertainment as no man hath the like: for as soone as ever she sees me set footing on her checkquerd pavement, presently with a smiling looke, she meetes me halfe way, saying, what my friend Tom-Drum? Honest Thomas, by my Christian soule, hartily welcome: then straight a chair and a cushion is fetcht for me, and the best cheere in the house set on the table, and then sitting downe by my side in her silken gowne, she shakes me by the hand and bids me welcome, and so laying meate on my trencher with a silver forke, she wishes me frolicke, at what time all the secrets of her heart she imparts unto me, craving my opinion in the premises.

I assure thee (said Harry) these are high favours, well bewraying the great friendship that she beares thee, and I much marvell that thou, being a young man, wilt not seeke a wife that is so wealthy, and so make thy selfe famous, by marrying Mistris Farmer, for it is likely she could will a way to make him her husband, to whom she opens her hearts secrets.

Tis true (quoth Tom) and I know that if I spoke but halfe a word she would never deny me: nay she would spend ten of her twelve silver Apostles, on condition I would vouchsafe to be her husband. But wot you what Harry, it is well known though Lillies be faire in shew, they be foule in smell, and women as they are beautifull so are they deceitfull: beside, Mistris Farmer is too old for me.

Too old? (quoth Harry). Why man she is not so old as Charing Crosse for her gate is not crooked, nor her face withered: but were she an hundred yeare old, having so strong a body and so faire a face, she were not in my opinion much to be mislikt; yet in my conscience I thinke, since first her faire eyes beheld the bright sunne, she never tasted the fruites of twenty flourishing Somers: nor scant felt the nipping frostes of nineteene cold winters, and therefore her age need be no hurt to her marriage.

Ile tell thee my mind (quoth Tom) after a woman is past sixteene yeeres old, I will not give fifteene blew buttons for her: but tell me Harry, dost thou like her? If thou dost, say so, and I will warrant her thy owne.

Gentle Tom Drum (quoth Harry) the true figure of unfained friendship, and the assured Map of manhood, doe but prefer me to her acquaintance, and I will request no greater curtesie.

Here is my hand (quoth Tom) it shall be done, and on Thursday at night next we will goe thither, and then thou shalt see whether Tom Drum can command anything in Mistresse Farmers house or no.

The day being thus set downe, Harry had prepared himselfe a faire sute of apparell against the time, and beside had bought certaine giftes to bestow on the faire Widdow: Tom Drum in like sort had drest himselfe in the best manner he might, still bearing Harry in hand that none in the world should be better welcome then he to the Widdow: which God wot was nothing so, for she never respected him but onely for the shooes he brought her: but you shall see how it fell out.

The day being come, Tom taking Harry by the hand, and comming to the Widdows doore, took hold of the Bell and rung thereat so lustily, as if he had beene bound seaven yeares Prentise to a Sexton: whereupon one of the Prentises came straight to the doore, saying, who is there?

Sirra (quoth Tom Drum) tis I, open the doore.

The fellow seeing it to be Tom Drum, with a frown askt him what he would have, who answered, he would speake with his Mistris.

My Mistris is busie (quoth the fellow) cannot I doe your errand?

No marry can you not (quoth Tom) I must speak with her my selfe.

Then stay a little (said the boy) and I will tell her. And with that in he went, leaving Tom still at the doore, where they sate till their feet waxt cold before the boy returned.

By the Masse (quoth Harry) whatsoever your credit with the Mistris is I know not, but the curtesie is small that is shewen you by her man.

Tush (quoth Tom) what will you have of a rude unmannerly boy? If any of the Maids had come to the doore, we had beene long ere this brought to their Mistris presence: therefore once againe I will use the help of the Bell-rope.

At his second ringing, out comes one of the Maids, saying with a shrill voyce: who the Divell is at the doore, that keepes such a ringing?

Why you queane (quoth he) tis I.

What Tom Drum (quoth shee) what would you have?

I would speak with your mistresse (quoth he).

Trust me (said the maid) you cannot speake with her now, for she is at supper with two or three that are sutors; Master Doctor Burket is one, and Master Alderman Jarvice the other.

Tut (quoth Tom) tell me not of sutors, but tell her that I am here, and then good enough.

Well, I will (quoth shee) and with that, claps to the dore againe, and keepes them still without.

This geare workes but ill-favouredly yet (said Harry) and you are little beholding either to the men or the maids, for ought that see, that will not shew you so much favour to stay within dores.

Tis no matter, Harry (quoth he) but if their Mistresse should know this, she would swinge their coats lustely for it.

And with that, one of the boyes opening the doore, told Tom that his mistresse wold have him send up his errand.

Sblood (quoth he) is she so stately that she will not come downe? I have seene the day when she would have bin glad to have spoken with me.

I (quoth the fellow) it may be so, when you have brought her a new paire of shoes, that hath pincht her at the toes.

Come Harry (said Tom) I will take paines for this once to goe up to her.

By my faith but you shall not (said the fellow): and therefore keepe backe, for you come not in here.

Tom Drum, seeing himselfe thus disgrac'd before his fellow Harry, became very angry and askt if this was the best entertainment that they could affoord their Mistresses Friends? And therewithall began to struggle with them: which their mistresse hearing, started from the table, and suddenly came to see what the matter was, who being certified of Tom Drums sawcinesse, began thus sharpely to check him:

Why, fellow (quoth she) art thou mad, that thus uncivilly thou behavest thy self? What hast thou to say to me, that thou art thus importunate?

No hurt (quoth he) but that this gentleman and I would have bestowed a galland of wine to have had three or foure houres talke with you.

I tell thee (said she) I am not now at leasure, and therefore good honesty trouble me no more: neither is it my wont to be won with wine at any time.

Gods Lord (quoth he) are you grown so coy? If you and I were alone I know I should finde you more milde: what must no man but Doctor Burket cast your water? Is his Phisicke in most request? Well I meane to be better entertained ere I goe, for there is never a Flemming of them all shall out ace me, by the morrow Masse I sweare.

Mistris Farmer seeing him so furious, answered he should have present entertainment according to his desert; whereupon she made no more to doe, but quietly went to her servants, and willed them to thrust him out by the head and shoulders: which presently they performed. But Harry was by her very modestly answered, that if he had occasion of any speech with her, the next day he should come and be patiently heard and gently answered: with which words after she had drunke to him in a gobblet of Claret wine, he departed, and going home he told Tom Drum he was highly beholding to him for his curtesie in preferring his sute to Mistris Farmer.

Surely (quoth he) you are in very high favour with the faire woman, and so it seemed by your great entertainment: I pray thee Tom tell me how tasted the meat which she set on thy trencher with her silver forke: and what secret was that which she told in thy eare? Trust me, thou art precious in her eyes, for she was as glad to see thee, as if one had given her a rush, for when after many hot wordes she heard thee draw thy breath so short, she for very pitty tumbled thee out into the street to take more ayre.

Well (quoth Tom) floute on, but I am well enough served, Ile lay my life had I not brought thee with me, never a man should have had more welcome then I: and now I consider with my selfe that it did anger her to the heart when she saw I was purposed to make another co-partner of her presence: but it shall teach me wit while I live, for I remember an old saying, love and Lordship brookes no fellowship.

But when this matter was made known to the rest of the jorney-men, Tom-Drums entertainment was spoke of in every place, insomuch that it is to this day a proverb amongst us, that where it is supposed a man shall not be welcomed, they will say he is like to have Tom Drums entertainment. And to avoid the flouts that were daily given him, poore Tom Drum forsooke Fleet-street, and at last went into Scotland, being prest for a Drummer at Muskelborough field, where the noble Duke of Sommerset and the Earle of Warwick were sent with a noble army: where the Englishmen and Scots meeting, there was fought a cruell battle, the victory whereof fell to the Englishmen: at what time there was slaine of the Scots to the number of foureteene thousand, and fifteene hundred taken prisoners, where we will leave Tom Drum till his returne, making mention how Harry Nevill behaved himselfe in the meane space in London.

CHAPTER IX

How Harry Nevell wooed Mistris Farmer and deceived Doctor Burket: and how they were both beguiled by a Prentice that dwelt in the house, who in the end married her.

Mistris Farmer fiering the hearts of many with her faire beauty, was wondrously wooed by Doctor Burket, who would give unto her divers rich gifts, the which though they were faire and costly, yet Mistris Farmer would hardly accept them, but even what he in a manner by perforce constrained her to take, least by his cunning he should insert therein some matter more then ordinary, that might moove any motion of love, contrary to her naturall inclination.

Upon a time Harry Nevell comming thether, and finding the Doctor very diligent to breed the Widdows content, whereby he greatly hindred his proceedings, cast in his mind how he might disburden the house of the Doctor and get opportunity to prefer his owne sute. At last lighting on a device fit for the purpose, in this sort he delt with the Doctor.

There was an Egyptian woman that at Black-wall was in travell with child, and had such hard labour, that she was much lamented among all the wives that dwelt thereabout. Harry Nevell comming that way, and hearing thereof, thought it a fit matter to imploy Doctor Burket about, while in the meane space he might the better bewray his affection to the Widow.

Whereupon he sent one to him attyred like a serving man, booted and spurd, who comming to the Widdows house all in a sweate, laid load on the doore demanding for Master Doctor.

What would you with him? (quoth one of the Maids).

Marry (quoth he) my Lady Swinborne hath sent for him in all post hast, and therefore I pray you let me speake with him.

I will presently doe your errand (said the maid) whereupon running up she told him that my Lady Sunborne had sent a messenger in great hast to speake with him. Doctor Burket hearing that, and being well acquainted with the Lady Sunborne took leave of the Widdow and went to the messenger, saying how now good fellow, what would my good Lady have with me

Sir (said the messenger) she would desire you if ever you did tender the life of a Lady, to make no delay, but presently to put your selfe a horse-back and come to her, for she is wondrous sick.

I am sorry for that (said the Doctor), and surely I will make all the speed possible to come to her: whereuon the Doctor tooke horse and immediately went with the servingman.

Harry hearing of his departure, came unto the Widdow with a smiling countenance, and thus merily began to wooe her.

Now Mistris Farmer, happy it is that a yong man once in a moneth may find a moment of time to talk with you: truth it is that your good graces have greatly bound me in affection to you so that onely above all the women in the world I have settled my delight in your love, and if it please you to requite my good will with the like kindnesse, I shall account my birthday blessed, and remaine your faithfull friend for ever.

Gentle man (quoth she) for your good will, I thank you, but I would have you understand, that the lessee you love me, the better I shall like you, for your delights and mine are not alike, I have setled my fancy on a single life, being a Widdow unmeete to marry, and unapt to love; once indeed I had learned that lesson, but my schole master being untimely dead that taught me, I grew forgetfull of all those principles and then swore never to follow that study more: wherefore if you will become a faithfull friend to me, let me be assured thereof by this, that from henceforth you will not any more trouble me with this matter, and thereby you shall bind me to think the better of you while I know you: and doe not think I speak this of any affection proceeding from myself to any other, or for the desire of any benefit proferred by any other to me.

Faire Mistris (quoth Harry) I know it is the custome of women to make their denials unto their lovers, and strictly to stand on nice points, because they will not be accounted easily won, or soone entreated: alack deere Dame, consider nature did not adorne your face with such incomparable beauty, and framed every other part so full of excellency, to wound men with woe, but to worke their content. Wherefore now in the Aprill of your yeares, and the sweet summer of your dayes, banish not the pleasures incident to bright beauty, but honour London streets with the faire fruite of your womb and make me blessed by being father to the issue of your delicate body; and though your beauty as the spring doth yet yearely grow, yet in the black winter of old age it will not be so, and we see by daily experience, that flowers not gathered in time rot and consume themselves: wherfore in my opinion you should doe the world intollerable wrong to live like a fruitlesse figtree.

Nay then Sir (quoth she) I perceive you will grow troublesome, and shew your selfe no such man as you professe your selfe: and seeing among many I request but one thing at your hands, and you refuse to doe it for my sake, I may say your frindship is more in words then in works; wherefore I perceive I must be constrained to call my Maid for a cup of voyding beere ere you will depart.

Nay Mistris (quoth he) I will save you that labour, seeing your love commands me, and I pray God grant you a more favourable mind at our next meeting, and with these words he departed.

Now you shall understand, that this gallant Widdow had in her house a very proper youth which was one of her aprentices, who had a long time borne his Mistris great good will: whereupon he became so diligent and carefull about all things committed to his charge, that thereby he won much commendations among all the neighbors, and was for the same highly esteemed of his Mistris: who after he had long concealed his grief at last unburdened himselfe of some sorrow, by making a friend privy to his passions, who comforted him in this sort.

Tush man (quoth he) what though she be thy Mistris, and thou her prentise, be not ashamed to shew thy affection to her: she is a woman wise and modest, and one that however she answers thy demand, will not think worse of the for thy good will: therefore try her, thou knowest not how fortune may favour thy sute, and the worst is she can but say the nay.

O (quoth he) if I were out of my years, I could have some heart to wooe her, but having yet three quarters of a yeere to serve, it may be some hindrance to my freedome if she should prove froward.

Tush stand not on those tearms (said his friend Francis) she will never requite kindnes with such discurtesie, and therefore William prove not a foole by being too fearefull.

O my deare friend Francis (quoth he) how can I suppose I should speed well, seeing she disdains Doctor Burket, and refuses Master Alderman, and will shew no countenance to gallant Master Nevell.

What a bad reason is this (quoth Francis) some cannot abide to eate of a Pig: some to taste of an Eele, othersome are sicke if they see but a Crab, and divers cannot away with cheese: yet none of them all but doe live by their victuals, every man hath his fancy, and every woman will follow her own mind, and therefore though she find not an Alderman or a Doctor for her diet yet she may think William her man a fit morsell for her own tooth.

I wis (quoth William) thy reasons are good, and I have advantage above all other suters to follow my sute, being in the house daily with her, and every evening when they are away: beside she hath appointed me this after noone to come to her Closet, that I may shew her my reckoning and accounts and in what sort her state standeth: wherefore seeing I have such occasion, I will no longer trifle out the time: but so soon as that businesse is ended, put my selfe to the hazard of my happy fortune: wherefore good Francis farewell till I see the againe, and how I speed, at our next meeting thou shalt know.

The time at last being come that Mistris Farmer had appointed to have her books cast over, getting into her closet she whistled for her Maid, and bad her call up William; (quoth she) let him bring his books of account with him.

The maid did as her Mistris commanded, and up comes William with his books under his armes: and after he had very reverently don his duty to his Mistris, she bad him sit downe saying, now William let me see these reckonings justly cast up, for it is long since I have cast an eye into mine estate.

Mistris (quoth he) doubt not but your estate is good, and your accounts justly kept for I have had as great regard thereto as the goods had been my owne.

Therein (quoth she) I am the more beholding to thee, neither shal thy true service goe unrewarded if I live; or if I dye thou shalt not be altogether forgotten.

These kind speeches greatly comforted Williams heart, whereupon he fell to his reckonings roundly, till his mind running too much on his Mistris beauty, sometimes he would misse and count three-score, and foure-score, nine-score.

Nay there you faile (quoth his Mistris) and over-tell forty, for three and foure is but seaven.

Tis true indeed Mistris (said he) and three times seaven is just five and twenty.

I tell the (quoth she) tis but one and twenty; what fellow, begin you to dote in your yong yeares?

O my deere Mistris (said he) blame me not if I doe so, seeing your sweet presence hath made farre wiser then my self to dote: O my good Mistris pardon my presumption, for being thus bold to unburden my hearts griefe unto you, my hearty love to your sweet selfe is so great, that except you vouchsafe favourably to censure, and kindly to judge thereof, that the sorrowes of my mind will wound my very soule, and make my life loathsome unto me.

Wherefore my good Mistris, despise not your poore servant, but yeeld unto him such succour, as may prolong his dayes with many blessed houres.

His Mistris obscuring her beauty with lowring browes, (like foggy vapours that blot the sky) made him this answer: How now Sirra? Hath my too much mildnesse made you thus sawcy? Can you set your love at no lower a pitch, but you must mount to be Master of your Mistris?

No Mistris (quoth he) no master, but your servant for ever.

Goe to, leave your prating (quoth she) or I will breake thy head I sweare, have I refused as thou seest, a grave and wealthy Alderman that might make me a Mistris of worship and dignity, and denied master Doctor of his request, who as thou knowest is at this day esteemed the cunningest Physition in London, and diverse other honest and well landed Gentlemen, and among the rest young Master Nevell, who as some say is descended of a noble house, and whose love I dare sweare is to me most firmely devoted, so that in my heart I am perswaded he loves the ground the better that I tread on: and should I (I say) forsake all these to make my foot my head, and my servant my superiour, to marry the which art a Prentice boy?

Nay Sir (quoth she) seeing you are grown so lusty, tis time to tame you and looke to your steps: therefore I charge you leave the shop and get you into the kitchin to help the Maid to washe the dishes and scowre the Kettles; and whereas since my husbands decease I have given foure nobles a yeare to a water bearer, I will make the save me that charges, for it is well seene, that too long the water Tankard hath beene kept from thy lazy shoulders, and if thou scornest to doe this, get where thou wilt; but if thou wilt remaine with me, so long as thou hast a day to serve, thou shalt be thus imployed.

Hereupon she called up her man Richard to supplie his place, and to be fore-man of the shop, gracing him with the keyes of the counting house: which William seeing, sadly went out of her sight, wofully to himselfe bewayling his hard fortune, but yet such was his love to his Mistris, that he rather chose to be drudge in her kitchin, then to change her service for any other. All the servants in the house much mused at this alteration: but to no creature did his Mistris tell the cause thereof, but kept it secret to her selfe: toward the evening, foorth he must needs goe for water, at what time he wanted no flouts of all his fellows, nor of many of the neighbors servants: where meeting with his friend Francis, discoursed to him the whole cause of his disgrace: he greatly chafing thereat, perswaded him never to endure such base drudgery, but rather to seeke preferment in some other place. Notwithstanding William would not follow his counsell, but rather chose patiently to abide all brunts.

Night being come, and supper ended, William was set to performe his penance for his presumption in love, that is to say, to scrape the trenchers, scowre the kettles and spits, and to wash up the dishes: which he went about with such good will, that it seemed to him rather a pleasure then a paine.

His Mistris closset joyning to the kitchin, had a secret place therein to look into the kitchin, where closely sitting, she earnestly beheld her man how he bestirred himselfe in his busines: Where- upon she entered into this consideration with her selfe. Now fie for shame, how ill doth it beseeme me to set so handsome a youth to such drudgery? If he bore a mans mind he would never indure it, but being of a base and servile condition, he doth easily indure the yoake of servitude, and yet I am to blame so to thinke, for if he had stubbornly disobeyed my commandement, how could I otherwise judge, but that in pride and disdaine he thought himselfe too good to be at any direction: some servants would in such a case have given me many foule words, and rather malepartly set me at nought, and forsake my service, then to have indured the tearms of disgrace that he hath done by this means: but heereby it is evident that love thinks nothing too much. Well Will (quoth she) the vertue of thy mind shall breed better thoughts in thy Mistris, which shall make her reward thy good will in a large measure: see, see, how neately he goes through his work, how handsomely he handles everything: and surely well may I suppose that he which is so faithfull a servant, would certainly prove a kind husband, for this hath beene no slender triall of his constant heart.

With that, hearing the Maid and some other of the servants talke with him, she lending a heedfull eare to their speech, heard them speake to this purpose.

Good Lord William (quoth one) I marvell much that you, being of so good parents and having so little a while to serve, will be thus used at her hands? It were too much if you were but this day bound prentice, to be set to such slavery.

I sweare (quoth another) I have three times longer to serve then you and if she should bid me doe as thou dost, I would bid her doe it herselfe with a morin.

Ile tell you what (quoth the third) Ile be plaine and use but few words, but I would see my faire Mistris with the black Devill before I would doe it.

Well well my masters (quoth William) you are mad merry wags but I take it as great favour done me by my Mistris thus to imploy me, that thereby I might have knowledge how to decke up a kitchen that meeting with a bad huswife to my wife, I know how to instruct her in houshold affaires.

I care for no such favour (said he).

Their Mistris hearing all, said nothing, but determined to try them all what they would doe ere it were long wherefore being now greatly affectioned to her man, covered her love with such discretion, that none could perceive it: For Master Doctor being newly returned, came thither puffing and blowing, saying he was never so served since he was borne; (quoth he) since I was here, I have at least ridden an hundred miles with an arrant knave that carried me I knew not whether: he rode with me out of Bishops-gate foorth right as far as Ware, and then compassing all Suffolke and Norfolke, he brought me backe againe through Essex, and so conducted me to Black-wall in Middlesex to seeke out my Lady Swinborne, my good Lady and Mistris: at last I saw it was no such matter, but the villaine being disposed to mocke me, brought me to a woman Egiptian, as blacke as the great Divell, who lay in child-bed and was but delivered of a child of her owne colour: to the which in despite of my beard they made me be God-father, where it cost me three crownes, and I was glad I so escaped, and who was the author of all this deceipt but Master Nevell? But if ever I come to give him Phisicke, if I make him not have the squirt for five dayes, count me the veriest dunce that ever wore velvet cap.

Master Doctor (quoth she) I am very sorie you were so used, notwithstanding to make Master Nevell and you friends I will bestow breakefast upon you to morrow, if it please you to accept my offer.

Faire Widdow (quoth he) never a one in the world would have vrged me to be friends with him but your selfe, and I am contented for your sake to doe it: and thus till next morning he took his leave.

Next day as soone as she was up she called up one of her men saying, Sirra run quickly, take a basket and fetch me a bushel of oysters from Billinsgate.

The fellow frowning said, I pray you send another, for I am busie in the shop.

Why knave (quoth she) Ile have thee goe.

(Quoth he) make a drudge of some other and not of me, for to be plaine I will not goe.

No? (quoth she). Call me John hither.

When he came, she desired him very gently to fetch her a bushel of oysters.

Why Mistresse (quoth he) my friends set me not here to be a Porter to fetch Oisters from Billingsgate. I tell you true, I scorne you should require any such matter of me.

Is it true? (quoth she). Very well, I will remember this when you forget it.

Thus when she had tried them all, she called her man William: saying: sirra goodman scullian take the great close basket, and fetch me a bushell of oysters from Billinsgate, and look you tarry not.

I will forsooth Mistris (quoth he) and presently away he went with such good will as none could go with better, being marvellous glad that she would request anything at his hands.

When he was come againe, with a smiling countenance she said, what Wilkin art thou come already? It is well done, I pray thee bring some of them up into my Closset, that I may taste how good they be.

Yes forsooth (quoth William) and after her he went, the Maide likewise carried up a couple of white manchets, and with a Diaper napkin covered the table.

Now Maid (quoth she) fetch me a pint of the best red wine.

I will forsooth (said the Maid).

Mistris (said William) if it please you, I will open your Oysters for you.

I pray you do (quoth she).

Then taking a towell on his arme, and a knife in his hand, being glad he had gotten so good an office, shewed himselfe so feat and expert in his occupation, that he opened as fast as his Mistresse could eat.

Beleeve me William (quoth she) you are nimble at an oyster, and quick in carving up shellfish, though dull in casting up accounts, I pray the tell me how many shels are in three and thirtie oysters?

Threescore and six (said William).

You are a witty youth (quoth she) if thy speech be true it must then needs follow that I have eaten three and thirty oysters, have also devoured threescore and six shels, which is too much lor one womans breakfast in a cold morning in conscience, and therefore I had need quickly to give over, least I break my belly with oyster shels: whereupon she cald her maid, saying: come hither Joane, and bring me a goblet of wine that I may wash Williams shels from my stomack.

Indeed Mistris (quoth he) if you take my words so, I spoke without book.

It is true (quoth she) for they are alwayes without that are never within, and either thy knowledge is small, or thy blindnesse great, or oyster shels very soft, that I should eat so many and I never feele one: for surely, if there be threescore and six oystershels in three and thirty oysters, there must needs be as many more in three and thirty oysters: and to affirme my words true, behold here the shels that were out of the oysters, now shew me those that were within the oysters.

William, seeing his Mistris thus pleasant, began to gather some courage to himselfe, and therefore thus uttered his mind: Deare Mistris, needs must I prove both blinde in sight, and dull in conceipt, while your faire eyes that gives light to the Sunne obscure themselves, and dark the glory of their shine, when I seek to receive comfort thereby: and the want of your good will makes my wits so weak, that like a barren tree it yeelds no fruit at all.

True (quoth she): three times seven is just five and twenty: but tell me what is the cause that moves thee to desire my favour, and to request my good will?

Good Mistris pardon me (quoth he) and I will tell you.

Whereupon she replied, saying, trust me William, my pardon is easier to be gotten then the Popes, and therefore be not afraid to proceed.

Why then my deare Mistris, seeing you have so graciously granted liberty to my hearts advocate, to pleade at the bar of your beauty, and to open the bill of my complaint: know this, that hope against hope perswaded me to labour for your love, that gaining the same I might be called a blessed man by winning such a wife.

What Will (quoth she) art thou not ashamed, that such a youth as thy selfe, a lad, a stripling, a prentice boy, should in the ignorance of his age, cumber himselfe with the cares of the world, and wantonly take a wife, that knowes not how to guide himselfe? I tell the fellow, first learne to thrive, and then wive.

O my deare Mistris (said William) let not pleasant youth which is the glory of many be a disgrace to me: neither without triall deere Mistris disable not my manhood, which now I take to be in his chiefe prime.

Nay (quoth she) if thou wilt have thy manhood tried, prepare thy selfe for the warres, and purchase honour by beating down our countries foes, and so shalt thou weare the golden wreath of honour for ever.

In troth Mistris (quoth he) I had rather have my manhood tried in another place.

By my troth (said he) in your soft bed, which is far better then the hard field.

Why thou bold knave (quoth she) it were a good deed to make you a bird of Bridewell for your saucinesse.

Beleeve me Mistris (quoth he) I am sorie you should be offended, rather will I get me into a corner and die through disdaine, then stay in your sight and grieve you: and with that away he went.

She seeing him so hastily depart, called him againe saying: William come hither, turne againe you faint hearted coward, what, art thou afraid of Bridewell? Use thy selfe well, and I will be thy friend.

The young man that with these words was revived like a sick man out of a dead sound, turning merrily to his Mistris, gave her a kisse, saying: on that condition I give you this.

How now sir (quoth she) I called you not back to be so bold: in good sadnesse do so againe, and I will give you on the eare.

Nay, Mistris (quoth he) if that be all the danger, take then another, and lay me on the eare (so I may lay you on the lips) and spare not.

Nay, then (said his Mistris) I see my too much softnesse makes thee saucy, therefore for feare thou shouldest catch a surfet, I charge the on paine of loves displeasure, to get you downe about your businesse, and see that all things be in readinesse against my friends come: why goe you not? What stand you in a maze? Pack I say and be gone.

And thus my deare Mistris (quoth he) parts my soule out of Paradise, and my heart from heavens joy: notwithstanding you command and I consent and alwayes let me finde favour, as I am forward to follow your precepts, and therewithall away he went.

He was no sooner gone, but she having determined what to do, sent for her friends, at what time the Alderman comming thither, and Master Doctor, she had also invited Master Peachie and his Wife, and with them came gallant young Nevill.

When they were all set at the table, after they had well tasted of the delicates there prepared: Mistris Farmer told them for two causes she had requested their companie that day to breakfast: the one was, that master Doctor and young Nevill might be made friends: and the other that in their sight she might make her selfe sure to her husband, that they might be witnes of their vowes.

The companie said, they should be very glad to see so good a work performed: whereupon she calling up all her men servants, spake to this purpose. My good friends and kinde neighbours, because I will have none ignorant of that which is to be effected, I have presumed to bring my servants into your presence, that they also may beare record of the reconciliation betwixt Master Doctor and Master Nevill, and therefore my Masters, if your hearts consent to an unitie, declare it by shaking hands, that it may not bee said, that my house was the breeder of brawles, and on that condition I drink to you both: the Gentlemen both pledged her, and according to her request ended the quarrell.

When this was done, she merrily told them, that among her men she had chosen her Master: albeit quoth she, this matter may seeme strange in your sight, and my fancie too much ruled by follie, yet this my determination I purpose by Gods grace to follow, hoping it shall breed no offence to any in the companie, in such a chance to make mine own choice.

Her man Richard, and the rest that supposed themselves most graced by her favours, began at this speech to look something peart, and all the companie held opinion that she bore the best minde to the foreman of her Shop: for first of all turning her speech to him, she said: Richard come hither, thou hast greatly to praise God for making thee so proper a man, thou art a neat fellow, and hast excellent qualities, for thou art not proud, nor high minded, but hast a care to thy businesse, and to keepe the Shop: and because I have committed great matters into thy hands, I pray thee go downe and look to thy charge, for I have nothing more to say to thee at this time.

The fellow at these words lookt as blew under the eyes, as a stale Codshead under the gill: and going downe the staires shook his head like one that had a flea in his eare.

Now come hither John (quoth she) I must needs say thou art come of good parents, and thou knowst they bound thee not Prentice to fetch oysters from Billinsgate like a Porter, nor to have thy daintie fingers set to drudgerie, therefore good John get you downe after your fellow, for here is nothing for you to doe at this time.

Her man William, that all this while was playing the scullion in the kitchin was then sent for, who comming before the companie with his face all begrim'd, and his cloathes all greasie, his Mistris spake in this manner. What a slovenlie knave comes here? Were not this a fit man think ye to be Master of this house and Lord of my love?

Now by my troth (said Mistris Peachie) I never saw a more unhandsome fellow in my life: fie how he stinkes of kitchin stuffe: what a face and neck hath he? A bodie might set Leekes in the very durt of his lips. I thinke in my conscience three pound of Sope, and a barrell of Water is little enough to scowre him cleane: the like flowts used all the rest at poore William, to which his Mistris made this answer.

Good Lord my masters, how much do your sights deceive you? In my sight he looks the loveliest of them all, having a pleasant countenance, and a good grace, and so pleasing is he in every part my sight, that surely if he will accept of mee for his wife, I will not refuse him for my husband: her friends looking one upon another, and marvelling at her speech, thought verily she had but jested, till such time she took him by the hand, and gave him a kisse.

Whereupon William spake thus unto her: faire Mistris, seeing it hath pleased you, beyond my desert, and contrarie to my expectation, to make me so gracious an offer, worthie I were to live a beggar, if I should refuse such a treasure: and thereupon I give you my heart and my hand.

And I receive it (quoth she) for it is thy vertue and true humilitie that hath conquered my former conceipts, for few men would have wonne a wife as thou didst.

No, how did he win you? (said Harrie Nevill).

By fetching oysters from Billingsgate (quoth she) which I know you would not have done, seeing all the rest of my servants scorn'd to do it at my request.

Sblood (quoth Harrie) by feching of oysters: I would have fetcht oysters, and mustles, and cockles too, to have got so good a bargaine.

The Alderman and the Doctor lookt strangely at this matter: neverthelesse seeing it was not to be helpt, they commended her choice, saying it was better for a man in such a case, to be favourable in a womans eyes, then to have much gold in his coffers.

Then did she set her black man by her white side, and calling the rest of her servants (in the sight of her friends) she made them do reverence unto him, whom they for his drudgerie scorned so much before: so the breakfast ended, she wild them all next morning, to beare him companie to Church, against which time, William was so daintily trickt up, that all those which beheld him, confest he was a most comely, trim, and proper man, and after they were married, they lived long together in joy and prosperous estate.

Harrie Nevill became so grieved hereat, that soone after he went from Master Peachie, and dwelt with a Goldsmith, and when he had beene a while there, committing a fault with his Masters daughter, he departed thence and became a Barber-Surgion: but there his Mistris and he were so familiar, that it nothing pleased his Master, so that in halfe a yeare he sought a new service and became a Cook: and then a Comfetmaker dwelling with master Baltazar, where after he grew something cunning, having done some shrewd turne in that place, he forsooke that service, and became a Smith, where their maide Judeth fell so highly in love with him that he for pure good will which he bore her, shewed his Master a faire paire of heeles: and then practised to be a Joyner, where he continued till hee heard his Father was sick, who for his abominable swearing had cast him from his favour, but after he had long mist him, and that he could heare no tidings of his untoward and wilde wanton Sonne, hee sent into divers places to enquire for him, and at last one of his servants lighted where he was, by which meanes he came to his father againe: who in a few yeares after, leaving his life, this sonne Harrie became Lord of all his lands: and comming upon a day to London with his men waiting upon him, he caused a great dinner to be prepared, and sent for all those that had been his masters and mistresses: who being come, he thus began to commune with them. My good friends, I understand that a certaine kinsman of mine was sometimes your servant, and as I take it, his name was Harrie Nevell: who as I heare, used himselfe but homely toward you, being a very wilde and ungracious fellow, the report whereof hath beene some griefe to me, being one that alwayes wisht him well: wherefore look what damage he hath done you I pray you tell me, and I am content with reason to see you satisfied, so that he may have your favours to be made a freeman.

Surely sir (said Peachie) for mine own part I can say little, save only that he was so full of love, that he would seldome follow his businesse at his occupation: but that matter I freely forgive and will not be his hindrance in any thing.

Marry sir (said the Goldsmith) I cannot say so: for truly sir he plaid the theefe in my house, robbing my daughter of her maiden- head, which he nor you is ever able to recompence, though you gave me a thousand pound, yet I thank God she is married and doth well.

I am the glader of that (said the Gentleman) and for that fault I will give toward her maintenance forty pound.

The Barber hearing him say so, told him that hee had injured him as much, and had beene more bold a great deale then became him, whereby (quoth he) I was made a scorne among my neighbours.

Tush you speake of ill will (said the Gentleman) if your wife will say so I will beleeve it.

To which words the woman made this answer. Good sir, will you beleeve me there was never so much matter, the youth was an honest faire conditioned young man, but my husband bearing a naughty jealous minde, grew suspicious without cause, onely because he saw that his servant was kinde and gentle unto me, and would have done any thing that I requested: notwithstanding I have had many a fowle word for his sake, and carried some bitter blowes too, but all is one, I am not the first woman that hath suffered injury without cause.

Alas good soule (said the Gentleman) I am right sorry for thy griefe, and to make the amends, I will bestow on thee twentie Angels, so your husband will not take it in dudgin.

The woman with a low cursie gave him thanks, saying: truly sir I am highly beholding to you, and truly I shall love you the better because you are so like him.

The smith likewise for his maide said all that he might, to whose marriage the Gentleman gave twentie pound.

Thus after he had fully ended with them all, hee made himselfe knowne unto them, at what time they all rejoyced greatly, and then after he had bestowed on them a sumptuous dinner, they all departed. And ever after, this Gentleman kept men of all these occupations in his own house, himself being as good a workman as any of them all.

CHAPTER X

Of the greene king of S. Martins and his merry feats.

There dwelt in S. Martins a jollie Shooemaker, hee was commonly called the Greene king, for that upon a time he shewed himselfe before King Henry, with all his men cloathed in greene, he himselfe being suted all in greene Satten. He was a man very humorous, of small stature, but most couragious, and continually he used the Fencing-schoole. When he went abroad, he carried alwayes a two handed sword on his shoulder, or under his arme: he kept continually thirtie or fortie servants, and kept in his house most bountifull fare: you shall understand that in his young yeares, his father dying, left him a good portion, so that he was in great credit and estimation among his neighbours, and that which made him more happie, was this, that God blest him with the gift of a good wife, who was a very comely young woman, and therewithall very carefull for his commoditie: but he whose minde was altogether of merriment, little respected his profit in regard of his pleasure: insomuch that through his wastefull expence he brought povertie upon himselfe ere he was aware, so that he could not do as he was accustomed: which when his daily companions perceived, they by little and little shund his company, and if at any time he passed by them, perhaps they would lend him a nod, or give him a good morrow and make no more a doe.

And is it true (quoth the Greene king) doth want of money part good company, or is my countenance chaunged, that they do not know me? I have seene the day when never a knave of them all, but would have made much of my dog for my sake, and have given me twenty salutations on a Sunday morning, for one poore pint of Muskadine: and what, hath a thred bare cloake scarde all good fellowship? Why though I have not my wonted habites, I have still the same heart: and though my money be gone, my mind is not altred: why then what Jacks are they, to reject mee? I, I, now I finde my wives tale true, for then she was wont to say, Husband, husband, refraine these trencher flies, these smooth faced flatterers, that like drones live upon the hony of your labour and sucke away the sweetnes of your substance. I wis, I wis, if once you should come in want, there is not the best of them all, that would trust you for ten groates: by which saying Ile lay my life she is a witch, for it is come as just to pas as Marlins prophesie. Fie, I would the other day but have borrowed 12 d. and I tride 13 frinds, and went without it: it being so, let them go hang themselves, for I wil into Flanders, that is flat, and leave these slaves to their servill conditions, where I will try if a firkin barrell of butter bee worth a pot of strong beere, and a loade of Holland chese, better then a gallon of Charnico: and if it be, by the crosse of this sword I will never staine my credit with such a base commodity againe.

With that he went to his wife, saying: woman dost thou heare? I pray thee looke well to thy busines till I come againe: for why? To drive away melancholy, I am minded to walke a mile or twaine.

But husband (quoth she) were you there where you layd your plate to pawne? I pray you is it not misused? And is it safe?

Woman (quoth he) I was there, and it is safe I warrant thee, for ever comming into thy hands againe, thou knowest I borrowed but twentie marke on it, and they have sold it for twentie pound: tis gone wife, tis gone.

O husband (quoth she) what hard fortune have we to be so ill delt withall? And therewithall she wept.

Fie (quoth he) leave thy weeping, hang it up, let it goe, the best is, it never cost us groate: were our friends living that gave us that, they would give us more: but in vaine it is to mourn for a matter that cannot be helpt, farewell wife, looke to thy house, and let the boyes plie their worke.

The greene king having thus taken his leave, went toward Billingsgate, of purpose to take Barge: where by the way he met with Anthony now now, the firkin Fidler of Finchlane.

What master (quoth he) well met, I pray whither are you walking? And how doe all our friends in saint Martins? Will you not have a crash ere you goe?

Yfaith, Anthony (quoth he) thou knowest I am a good fellow, and one that hath not been a niggard to the at any time, therefore if thou wilt bestow any musick on me, doe; and if it please God that I return safely from Flanders againe, I will pay thee well for thy paines; but now I have no money for musick.

Gods-nigs (quoth Anthony) whether you have money or no, you shall have musick, I doe not allwayes request coyne of my friends for my cunning: what, you are not every body, and seeing you are going beyond sea, I will bestow a pinte of wine on you at the Salutation.

Saist thou so Anthony (quoth he) in good sooth I will not refuse thy curtesie, and with that they stept into the Tavern, where Anthony cald for wine: and drawing forth his Fiddle began to play, and after he had scrapte halfe a score lessons he began to sing.

> *When should a man shew himselfe gentle and kinde,*
> *When should a man comfort the sorrowfull minde?*
> > *O Anthony now, now, now.*
> > *O Anthony now, now, now.*
> *When is the best time to drinke with a friend?*
> *When is it meetest my money to spend?*
> > *O Anthony now, now, now.*
> > *O Anthony now, now, now.*
> *When goes the King of good fellowes away?*
> *That so much delighted in dauncing and play?*
> > *O Anthony now, now, now.*
> > *O Anthony now, now, now.*
> *And when should I bid my Master farewell?*
> *Whose bountie and curtesie so did excell?*
> > *O Anthony now, now, now.*
> > *O Anthony now, now, now.*

Loe ye now Master (quoth he) this song have I made for your sake, and by the grace of God when you are gone I will sing it every Sunday morning under your wives window, that she may know we dranke together ere you parted.

I pray thee do so (said the Greene king) and do my commendations unto her, and tell her at my returne I hope to make merry.

Thus after they had made an end of their wine, and paid for the shot, Anthony putting up his Fiddle departed, seeking to change musicke for money: while the Greene king of Saint Martins sailed in Gravesend Barge. But Anthony in his absence sung this song so often in Saint Martins, that thereby he purshast a name which he never lost till his dying day, for ever after men called him nothing but Anthony now now.

But it is to be remembred that the Green kings wife became so carefull in her businesse, and governed her selfe with such wisdome in all her affaires, that during her husbands absence she did not onely pay many of his debts, but also got into her house everything that was necessary to be had, the which her diligence won such commendations, that her credit in all places was verie good, lo and her gaines (through Gods blessing) came so flowing in, that before her husband came home, she was had in good reputation with her neighbours: and having no need of any of their favours, every one was ready to proffer her curtesie, saying good neighbour if you want any thing tell us, and looke what friendship we may doe you, be sure you shall find it.

I neighbour (quoth she) I know your kindnesse, and may speake thereof by experience: well may I compare you to him that would never bid any man to dinner, but at two of the clocke in the after noone, when he was assured they had fild their bellies before, and that they would not touch his meate, except for manners sake: wherefore for my part I will give you thankes, when I take benefit of your proffer.

Why neighbour we speake for good will (quoth they).

Tis true (quoth shee) and so say they that call for a fresh quart to bestow on a drunken man, when they know it would doe him as much good in his bootes as in his belly.

Well neighbour (quoth they) God be thanked that you have no cause to use friends.

Mary Amen (quoth shee) for if I had I think I should finde few here.

These and the like greetings were often betwixt her and her neighbors; til at last her husband came home, and to his great comfort found his estate so good, that he had great cause to praise God for the same, for a warme purse is the best medicine for a cold heart that may be. The greene king therefore bearing himselfe as brave as ever he did, having sworne himselfe a faithfull companion to his two-hand sworde, would never goe without it.

Now when his auncient acquaintance saw him again so gallant every one was ready to curry favour with him, and many would proffer him the wine. And where before they were wont scornefully to thrust him next the kennell, and nothing to respect his poverty, they gave him now the upper hand in every place, saluting him with cap and knee: but he remembring how sleightly they set by him in his neede, did now as sleightly esteeme their flattery, saying: I cry you mercy, me thinkes I have seene your face, but I never knew you for my friend.

No (quoth one) I dwell at Aldersgate, and am your neere neighbor.

And so much the worse (said the Greene king).

Wherefore? (quoth the other).

Because (said he) I thinke the place meete for an honester man.

I trust sir (said his neighbour) you know no hurt by me.

Nor any goodnes (quoth the greene king) but I remember you are he, or one of them of whom once I would have borrowed fortie pence, yet could not get it, if thereby I might have saved fifty lives: therefore goodman hog, goodman cog, or goodman dog, chuse you which, scrape no acquaintance of me, nor come any more in my company, I would advise you, least with my long sword I crop your cowards legs, and make you stand like Saint Martins begger upon two stilts.

The fellow hearing him say so, went his wayes, and never durst speake to him afterward.

CHAPTER XI

How the Greene King went a walking with his wife, and got Anthony now to play before them, in which sort he went with her to Bristow.

The Green king being a man that was much given to goe abroad, his wife upon a time, thus made her mone to him: good Lord, husband (quoth she) I thinke you are the unkindest man alive, for as often as you walke abroad, you were never the man that would take me in your company: it is no small griefe to me, while I sit doating at home, every Sunday and Holy-day, to see how kindely other men walke with their wives, and lovingly beare them company into the fields, that thereby they may have some recreation after their weekes weary toyle: this pleasure have they for their paines, but I poore soule could never get such curtesie at you hands: either it must needs be that you love me but little, or else you are ashamed of my company, and I tell you true you have no reason either for the one or the other.

Certainly wife (said hee) I should be sorrie to drive any such conceit into thy head, but seeing you find your selfe grieved in this kinde, let me intreate thee to be content, and then thou shalt perceive that my love is not small toward thee, nor my liking so bad to be ashamed to have thee goe by my side. Thursday next is Saint James day, against which time prepare thy selfe to goe with me to the faire, where, by the grace of God, Ile bestow a fat Pig upon thee, and there I meane to be merry: and doubt not but I will walke with the till thou art weary of walking.

Nay (quoth shee) I should never be weary of your company, though I went with you to the Worlds end.

God a mercy for that wife, quoth hee, but so doing I doubt I should trie you a very good foote-woman, or a bad flatterer.

Thus it past till Thursday came, in the meane season meeting with two or three other shoomakers, he asked them if they would walke with him and his wife to Saint James faire.

That wee will with all our hearts.

But will you not like flinchers flie from your words? (quoth he).

To that (they said) if they did they would forfeit a gallon of wine.

Tush (said the greene king) talke not to me of a gallon of wine, but will you bee bound in twenty pound a peece to performe it?

Why what needs bands for such a matter? (quoth they). We trust you will take our wordes for more then that.

My masters (said the greene king) the world is growne to that passe, that words are counted but wind, and I will trust you as little on your word as Long Meg on her honesty: therefore if you will not be bound, chuse, I will make no account of your company.

The men hearing him say so, knowing him to be a man of a merry mind, after their wits were all washt with wine, to the Scriveners they went, and bound themselves in twenty pound according to his request. They had no sooner made an end of this merry match, but as they stumbled into another Taverne, who should they meet but Anthony now now: who as soon as he spide the green King smiling with a wrie mouth, he joyfully imbrac't him with both his hands, saying: what my good master well met, when came you from the other side the water? By my troth you are welcome with all my heart.

God a mercy good Anthony (quoth he) but how chance you come no more into Saint Martins?

O Master (quoth he) you know what a dainty commoditie I made at your parting to Gravesendbarge?

Yes mary (said the greene king) what of that?

Why (quoth he) by singing it under your window, all the merry shoomakers in Saint Martins tooke it by the toe: and now they have made it even as common as a printed Ballad, and I have gotten such a name by it, that now I am called nothing but Anthony now now.

Why Master Ile tell you, it hath made me as well acquainted in Cheapeside, as the cat in the creame-pan: for as soone as the Goldesmiths wives spie mee, and as I passe along by the Marchants daughters, the apes will laugh at me as passes: beside that all the little boyes in the streets will run after mee like a sort of Emits. Anthony now now, sayes one: Anthony now now, another: good

Lord, good Lord, you never knew the like: heare ye master? I am sure that song hath gotten mee since you went, more pence then your wife hath pins: and seeing you are come againe, I will make the second part very shortly.

But hearest thou, Anthony? (said he). If thou wilt come to me on Saint James his day in the Morning, thou shalt walke with us to the faire, for I meane to make merry with my wife that day.

Master (quoth he) by cock and pie, I will not misse you. And thus after they had made Anthony drinke, he departed.

Saint James his day at last being come, he cal'd up his wife betimes, and bad her make ready, if she would to the faire: who very willingly did so: and in the meane space her husband went to his cubbert, and tooke thereout forty faire soveraignes, and going secretly to one of his servants, he willed him to take good heed of his house, and to see that his fellowes plide their businesse: for (quoth he) I goe with my wife to Saint James faire, and perhaps you shall not see us againe this sennight.

Well Master said the fellow, I will have regard to your busines I warrant you.

Wherewith he cal'd his wife, saying: come wife will you walke?

With a good will husband (quoth she) I am ready.

With that Anthony now now, began to scrape on his treable viall, and playing a huntsup, said good morrow master good morrow, foure a clocke and a faire morning.

Well said, Anthony (quoth he) we be ready for thy company therefore along before, and let us heare what musicke you can make.

Fie husband (quoth she) take not the Fidler with you, for shame.

Tush be content (quoth he) Musicke makes a sad mind merrie.

So away they went, and at Saint Giles in the fields he met the rest of his company. Well found, my masters (quoth he) I perceive you have a care of your bonds.

So away they went with the Fidler before them, and the Greene king with his two-hand sworde marching like a master of Fence going to play his prize: when they came to the high way turning downe to Westminster, his wife said: yfaith husband we shall come to the faire too soone, for Gods sake let us walke a little further.

Content wife (quoth he) whereupon they went to Kensington, where they brake their fast, and had good sport by tumbling on the greene grasse, where Anthony brake his Fiddle, for which cause the Greene king gave him ten shillings, and willed him to goe back and buy a new one.

And now my friends (quoth he) if you will walke with mee to Brainford I will bestow your dinner upon you, because I have a minde to walke with my wife.

They were content, but by that time they came there, the woman began to wax somewhat wearie, and because the day was farre spent before they had dined, they lay there all night: where he told his friends that the next morning he would bring his wife to see the George in Colebrook, and then would turne home: but to be briefe, when he came there, he told them flatly he meant to goe to Saint James his faire at Bristow: for (quoth he) my wife hath longed to walke with me. and I meane to give her walking worke enough.

But sir (quoth they) we meane not to goe thither.

Before God but you shall (quoth hee) or forfeit your band.

The men seeing no remedy, went along to Bristow on foote, whereby the poore woman became so weary, that an hundred times she wisht she had not come foorth of doores: but from that time till she died, she never intreated her husband to walke with her againe.

An hundred merry feates more did he, which in this place is too much to be set downe. For afterward Tom Drum comming from the winning of Mustleborow, came to dwell with them, where he discoursed all his adventures in the wars: and according to his old cogging humor, attributed other mens deeds to himselfe, for (quoth he) it was I that killed the first Scot in the battell, yet I was content to give the honour thereof to Sir Michaell Musgrave, notwithstanding (quoth he) all men knowes that this hand of mine kild Tom Trotter, that terrible traytor, which in despite of us, kept the Castell so long, and at last as he cowardly forsooke it, and secretly sought to flye, with this blade of mine I broacht him like a roasting pigge. Moreover, Parson Ribble had never made himselfe so famous but by my meanes. These were his daily vaunts, till his lies were so manifest that hee could no longer stand in them.

But after the Greene king had long lived a gallant housekeeper,
at last being aged and blinde, he dyed, after he had
done many good deedes to divers
poore men.

FINIS

Appendix

[The two chapters that follow are reproduced from the version of the first part of *The Gentle Craft* held in the Biblioteka Gadańska and discussed in 'A Note on the Text' (see above p. xxix). Chapter XI below would follow Chapter X in the substantive text of Part I above, causing the subsequent chapters to be renumbered. The erroneously numbered 'Chapter XVIII' below, actually the seventeenth rather than the eighteenth chapter of the Gdansk copy, would come after Chapter XV of Part I above, thus forming a new overall ending to the first part of *The Gentle Craft*. 'A new love Sonnet' does not appear in this version. Although uncertainty remains, a good case can be made for the Gdansk version predating the seventeenth-century ones upon which this edition is based. If the 1599 date is genuine, then later printers may have adjusted the text in the absence of the promised third part and as a mark of respect to its late author. For these additions I have retained the spelling of the originals but have made editorial interventions similar to those applied in the main text. Ed.]

CHAPTER XI

The dreame of Symon the shoemaker, and how he bought all the goods in the great Argosie of Candy, through his wives pollicie.

Now wife I wil tel thee what a dreame I had the other night. Me thought in my sleepe, that a strange man comming by my stall, brought mee a blacke swan, and willed me to take her and get her drest, and make merry among my friends. I giving him thanks, took in the swan, and presently gave her unto thee to be made ready. Now when you had dressed her, and baked her in a Pie, me thought shee was set on the table, and we fell closely to eating, and still me thought the more we eate, the bigger the pie grew: which I heedily beholding, thought my selfe there was growen a great house of squared stone in the midst of the pie, which by litle and litle crept into the street where stretching out in length it winded round about and stood fouresquare, wherby there became a great and mighty yard or court in the midst therof, and by and by me thought all the yard was fild with cowhides, and backs of tand leather, which I seeing, went in and bought much of it, and so came home againe: and therewithall I awaked. I promise thee wife I never had such a dreame before in all my life, and I hope it bodes me good.

I hope so to (said his wife) and I doubt not but we shall have good lucke, for there was a spider this morning that came from the seeling of the Hall, drawing downe her thrid into my lap as I sate at worke, and my gossip Crothorne sitting by me, did see it, and said it was a token that we should receive good store of money.

God graunt it woman (quoth he) and with that he cald John Frenchman saying, hee had that evening spoken to an Alderman that would deale with the Grecian for all his goods, if he would let him have a reasonable penniworth in it: but (quoth Simon) I heare say that of late there came much of such marchandice out of flaunders, which hath even cloid the Citie, and that they looke shortly for a great many more of other ships to come from Hambrough with the like commodities, which will make this mans market to bee the worse: therefore it is best for this Grecian to put of his goods as soone as he can.

I will goe to him in the morning (said John) and if you will take the paines to goe along with mee, you shall heare what he will say.

I care not greatly if I doe (said his master) though I get nothing by it. I would be glad to pleasure the man what I could, and the rather for that hee is so farre a stranger borne. Soone after, bed time insuing, they went to take their rest: but Symons wife tooke little sleepe, her minde ran so much on the good bargaine they hoped for.

Nowe when the skies had cast off her cloudy darke mantle, so soone as the cheerful sunne began to shew his face, up rose the good wife, and about she went, seeking to borrow apparell for her husband: and the whilst Symon and his man John, went to the Merchants lodging, who declared unto him what his master before had said, telling that one of the chiefe Aldermen in the Citie would buy all his goods, if so he would afford a reasonable bargaine, otherwise there was no hope to make a sale thereof in this land. Wherefore to make short, they concluded, and Symon gave him halfe a dosen angels in earnest, wishing John the Frenchman to tell him that the Alderman should come to him in the afternoone himselfe, and fetching his note of goods, should deliver him his bill to bee paid at a moneths end: and therefore did wish that they might be brought downe the river with the first winde. And therewithall delivering a note of his name, hee with his man departed for that time, and home came Symon with a merrie minde, telling his wife that they were agreed: which she hearing, for very joy, tooke him about the necke, giving him for recompence xx kisses.

The afternoone being come, shee attired her husband in manner aforesayde, who according to promise went to the merchant which attended him to come at his lodging: and when he gave him his bill of loading, he found the summe thereof to amount to five thousand pound. Nowe you shall understand that the shippe was no sooner come within sight of the Citie, but twentie Merchants of London were ready by and by to goe aboard to knowe what her loading was: and finding it to be the onely commoditie that the land did lacke, every one was greedie to buy part therof, and for that purpose diligently sought out the Merchant that ought it: who perceiving by them that they came about his Merchandize, showed them presently the bill of sale thereof was to one Symon Eier dwelling in Tower street, who had made bargaine for the whole fraught. They which knewe no such Merchant to live in London, wondred who that should be that was of so great abilitie to make payment of such a bargaine. At length by search it was Symon the shoemaker, whereby they were driven into further admiration, who comming to him as he stood at his cutting boord, saluted him in this sort.

Sir, God speed your worke: You are heartily welcome said Symon. I pray you come neere, for here be as good shoes though I say it, as any be in this Citie.

We thinke no lesse (quoth they) but we come not about any such matter at this time. Neverthelesse hereafter we will bee your continuall customers. And therewithall putting off their caps they said:

Sir it is so, that we understand you have bought all the merchandize in the great Argosie called the blacke Swanne of Candy, and wee would gladly bargaine with you for some part thereof: you shall have ready money of us.

In troth gentleman (said Symon) it is true I have bought a poore commoditie there, and looke what you like you shal have, if we can agree on the price. Hard by the Tower is my warehouse, and when the ship is unloaded, come there and take your choice of any thing I have.

We heartily thanke you sir [quoth they] and so departed. This matter being noised round about the Citie, the Aldermen sent their servants to request Master Eier to come unto them (for that title had he now won among them all) he answered, he was at their worships commaundement. They were no sooner gone, but the Lord Maior of London sent to him one of his foure Esquires, and with him his ring, who did his message in this sort.

Master Eier, my Lord Mayor hath his most harty commendations unto you, and hath sent you here his lordships ring earnestly requesting you would doe him that favour, to come you and your wife to supper soone at night.

I most humbly thanke his Lordship (quoth Symon), we will waite upon him: his honour shall finde bould guests of us I warrant you.

Good Master Eier you shall be most heartily welcome (said his Esquier) and so with great reverence departed. Then Symon going in unto his wife said:

Jesu Jesu woman, what a coile is here, now that I have bought these goods.

Why, what is the matter? (quoth she).

Trust me woman, I thinke here hath beene twentie Merchants of the Citie with me this day, and divers Aldermen have sent unto me, intreating that they may buy some of my goods. Good Master Eier (quoth one:) I pray you Master Eier (quoth another) let us be better acquainted.

Why, Symon, did they call thee Master Eier? That was somewhat yet: but if once I might see thee that they might come and say: Good morrowe master Alderman, or els, doth Alderman Eier dwell here? O it would doe my heart good.

O wife, but it would please you a great deale better (quoth he) to heare gentle-women come in and say thus to you: God morrow my Lady Maiores, how doe you good Madam? I am glad to see your Ladyship in good health. But gods lady, deere wife, what had I forgot: Nowe by the masse thou and I are both sent for to my Lord Mayor soone at night. And that thou mayest beleeve me the better, see here, he hath sent me his ring that wee should not faile to come to his Lordship.

But I tro husband (quoth she) you have not promised to go.

Yes in good faith woman (quoth Symon).

What (quoth she) and that I should come too?

I, verely, (said her husband) for so my Lord requested.

Now by my troth, you have made a faire hand to promise that I should come; and I have never a cleane nekercher ready, nor never a raile to pinne about my necke, and so we shall utterly shame our selves.

Why wife (quoth he) the matter is not great and if thou do stay at home I will excuse thee to my Lord in some reasonable maner.

Nay by the masse husband (quoth she) you shall not cosen me of a good supper so, nor of the company of such good gentle women as will bee there. I will goe wash me a neckercher and a raile presently, and brush up my best gowne. And seeing it was my Lord Mayors minde, I shoulde come, I will not stay behinde that is flatte. But in troth husband, I cannot forget this: did my good Lord send for us to supper?

Certainely wife he did (said Symon) and sent no worse man to bid us, then one of the foure Esquires.

Well husband, thus you may see how quickely wealth will bring a man in credit, for which you may thanke my wit. And yet men will not sticke to say: Woemen, alas, what are they but clogs of care? necessary evils, good for nothing but to prittle prattle, and tell a gossips tale. And, poore soules, they must not speake in their husbands presence, or if they doe, then straight saies their husbands, you may see many women, many words, holde your tongues you fooles, or harken how like simple asses they talke. But I cannot tell, were it not for your wives counsailes, some of you would doe ill favoured enough sometimes.

I, wife, now thou hitst me home.

I mary but when will you hit me home? (quoth she). And therewithall away she went, and to washing shee goes, being so diligent in the matter, that before it was night, shee had all things so fit and necessary as possibly might be devised.

CHAPTER XVIII

The Historie of M. Richard Castler: otherwise called the Cock of Westminster.

There was a very comely young man dwelling in Westminster, (named Richard Castler) who having served vij years as an apprentice with his Maister: and being at length come out of his time, undertooke on a marvellous small stock, to try what he could do in the worlde. And being fully resolved hereon, departing away honestly from his maister, he set up shop in Kings street in Westminster. But by that time that he had bought him tooles, and made up his windowes, his stock was all gone, and having then but one groat left, and not an inch of Leather, he was quite out of conceit with himselfe, wishing he had not so hastily left his master, or that his money had bin more.

I have (quoth he) but one poor groat in my purse, and never a but of bread in my Belly, nor a jot of Leather in my shoppe: and to make my need known amongst my companions, it would rather breede my reproach, then profit me a peny. For what would they say but this? That my wit and my wealth did well agree, being as well stored of the one as of the other. What a shame were it for me having taken a shop, and made it fit for my purpose, and shoulde now be faine to leave it for lack of a litle leather? And likewise when any of my acqaintance shall passe by, what will they say? See, here is the shop, but where be the shoes? I would to God (quoth he) that I had never taken it in hand, or bin better provided. But repentance doth ever follow that foule falt of Rashnes. Alas, what shal I do? My Belly cries out as sore for victuals, as my shop doth for shoes. But fond foole that I am, why do I keep this groat and starve myselfe? Seeing that by the same, I may make three meales, but not one shoe, yet better it were to go upon Credit for meat, then to be quite without money. And there-upon setting a merry countenance on a sad matter, shutting up his dore, he stept into the next Cookes house, where having acquaintance, he got credit for a dinner.

When he had somthing refresht himselfe, he purposed speadily to go towards the Tanners, and by a groates earnest, to binde a bargain of a crowns worth of Leather. But as he past over the fieldes to S. Giles, it was his chaunce to meet with a fine little Dog stragling in the way, which (as it seemed) was by misfortune lost from some greate Gentle-woman. The young man taking him up, carried the Dog under his arme to the Tanners, and knocking at the doore, foorth came the good wife, who in her Apparell was very brave and fine, her husband being one of the wealthiest Tanners in that dwelt neere London, who no sooner glaunst her curious Eye on the man, but straight she spide the Puppie.

Jesus Richard (quoth shee) where got you this fine Dog?

Faire Mistris (quoth he) it was my good fortune to find him in the fieldes comming hither, and truly I meane to bestow him upon an Honorable Ladie.

Sweet Dick (quoth shee) give him to me, and if I requit not thy curtesie, never trust woman for my sake: and though I be not so honorable, yet perhaps I may be as beneficiall as any Lady can be unto thee.

Certainly (said Richard) I know that the guift of this poore Dog to my Lady of Leicester, would be no lesse worth to me then 4 golden Aungels in my hand: for (quoth he) she is a woman of a most Noble nature, as bountiful as she is beautiful: and truly such a guift would be my making, especially at this time being newly set up for my selfe, and quite without money.

Tush [quoth the Tanners wife] what if thou lackest Coyne, thou maist have credit. I know my husband wil not stick to trust thee for two or three backes of Leather: and therefore come to me, and thou shalt soone see what may be done. So along they went to the good man, to whom she spoke in this sort.

Husband, heere is a new Customer come unto you, (Richard Castler) who is now new set up for himself, and he woulde request you to credit him for a back or two of Leather. Trust me husband it were a good deed for to set him forward in the world. Hard beginnings make a good end, and no doubt he will prove a good husband.

Richarde indeed (quoth the Tanner) is an honest fellow. Notwithstanding wife, men are mortall, I would not stick to trust him of half a dozen backs of Leather, so I might have security for my own, for if he should dye, before the debt be due, then how should I come by my money?

Go too sweet heart (quoth she): in faith you shal trust him, what he is a young man, and likely to live many a yeere: and for his honest dealing with you, I wil pawn my word and credit, so good an oppinion do I conceive of the young man.

Your credit (quoth he), what is your credite worth? I thinke about some couple of Chips, or of as great value as a Ring of a Rush.

Gods lord (quoth shee) tis happy you can set me so light now, but ifaith, ifaith, the day hath bin, when you would have beene glad to have taken my word for more then a dicker of Leather. My word? I, sir you would have bin right glad if I would have spoke but half a word to you in such a case: then I might have commaunded that which now I cannot get by intreatie. I think you cannot say that ever I troubled you before, nor would not now but for this honest yong man. And do not you think thogh you carry so hard a conceit toward him, but he may have credit inough in other places: but this the young man hath got for his good will, in comming to offer his custome unto you. But come hither Dick (quoth she), I will send thee where thou shalt have Leather inough and never be beholding to him. And therewithall plucking a gold Ring from her finger she said:

Go thy waies Dick to my brother King (you know that man well inough I am sure) he dwels at Knightsbridg, and tell him I woulde request him to deliver unto thee three backs of Leather, or what thou wilt have thyself, by this token, and tell him I will see him paid.

I thanke you good mistres Martin (quoth he) and for the great good will and favour which I see you beare towards me, I wil bestow my little Dog upon you.

Now god a mercy gentle Richard (quoth she) and therwithall stepping in, she went to her Chest and fetcht him foorth a couple of Spur-royals, saying: Heere Dick, take this in requitall of thy kindnes, and if it ly in my lot to do thee any pleasure, I pray thee make daintie to demaund it. And so farewell good Richard.

God keepe you in health good mistris Mattin (quoth he) and so departed away.

Then went Richard merrily towards Knightsbridg, as fast as he could, and by that token which he carried, he got great store of lether. And thus going foorth with one groat, he returned home with leather on his back and gold in his purse, accounting this both a happie chance and a blessed beginning. Then fel he close to his busines and plied his worke so hard, that in a short space he got much money, and gayned great commendations through the Cittie by his good husbandrie. For he was up every morning by iiij. of the Clock, and wrought hard al day till viij. or ix. at night, and in this sort continued so long, that he was called the Cock of Westminster, of whose pleasant life and love, and also of his great riches, and charitable deeds, mencion shall be throghly made in the second part of this booke, wherein also shall be shewed the lives and most notable deedes of Pechey of Fleetstreet, who with twenty of his own men mustred before King Henry the 8, being al set out at his own propper cost and charges. Likewise there shall be shown unto you the pleasant humors of the greene king of saint Martins, so named by our gracious soveraigne, King Henry of famous memory. Also the great hospitallitie and worthy actions of Nightingale of Redding, Spickernell or Spickemell of Salisbury, and Squier of Lewes,
who for their bountifull housekeeping, and divers
and sundry other Honorable and vertuous
qualities, are woorthy to be had
in continuall remem-
brance.

FINIS

Explanatory Notes

Sources. There are three stories in *The Gentle Craft* Part I: the legend of Hugh and Winifred; the romance of Crispine and Crispianus; and the 'history' of Simon Eyre. Deloney could have read the story of Winifred in Jacobus de Voragine's *Legenda Aurea* (c. 1470), but also, as the *Life of St. Ursula* and the *Life of St. Winifred*, in William Caxton's *Golden Legend*, from which he derived the story of Crispine, Crispianus and Ursula. These fifteenth-century versions of the story were republished many times throughout the sixteenth century. The figure of St Hugh would have been influenced by Deloney's reading of such romances of knight errantry as *Guy of Warwick* and *Bevis of Hampton*, although in his edition of *The Gentle Craft* (see bibliography), F.O. Mann also reminds his readers that Shakespeare's *Romeo and Juliet* was presented in 1596. There are similarities between the circumstances of Crispine and Ursula and Shakespeare's lovers, although Mann notes that 'Deloney […] avoids the tragic issues so alien to the spirit of his domestic romanticism' (p. 523). The story of Simon Eyre comes from London tradition. Eyre was Sheriff of London in 1434 and Mayor in 1445. He died in 1458. Eyre's story was also told in John Stowe's *A Survey of London* (1598).

There are three stories in *The Gentle Craft* Part II: the story of Richard Casteler; the story of Master Peachey and his household; the story of the Green King. Deloney could read of Richard Casteler (or Casteller, or Castell) in Raphael Holinshed's *Chronicles of England, Scotland and Ireland*. The 1587 version of this text (first printed 1577) was that used by Shakespeare and his contemporaries. He had also read *Long Meg of Westminster*, a popular jest-book of 1582, but Mann warns that 'Deloney's use of printed sources must not be over-emphasized. Richard Casteler was probably well known to London tradition as a recent benefactor. He died in 1599. Long Meg is a byword in contemporary literature' (p. 531) although she is a far more sympathetic figure in *The Gentle Craft* than in the sources. Gillian of the George seems to have been a product purely of Deloney's imagination.

The story of Peachey was probably traditional but Deloney seems to have peopled it with figures whose names are derived from Holinshed and Stowe, as well as from real historical figures from the area around Newbury, Berkshire that he knew so well. The two sea Captains Stukely and Strangewidge were based on real figures, celebrated in many ballads and plays (see introduction, note 18). A number of sources compete as the basis of the character Sir John Rainsford but little is certain. The story seems to have been more of a Reformation rural myth. As far as Tom Drum is concerned, critics have drawn a parallel with Shakespeare's Falstaff. Dr Burket was a well-known physician, mentioned in Henry Chettle's *Kind Hart's Dream* of 1593, the text that contained a apology for the attack made by Robert Greene in *A Groatsworth of Wit* which Chettle had edited the year before. Chettle's book also mentions Anthony Now-now, a ballad singer of considerable celebrity in Elizabethan London.

References are to page numbers.

Part I

4   The places and people in Deloney's note to his readers come from Humphrey Llwyd's *The Breuiary of Britaine* (1573) and the 1587 edition of Raphael Holinshed's *Chronicles of England, Scotland and Ireland.*

7   **tongelesse like a Stork:** an expression from Thomas Johnson's *Cornucopiae* (1595).

8   **as unprofitable as snow in harvest:** the phrase is reminiscent of the First Murderer's bleak comment to Clarence about his brother in Shakespeare's *Richard III*:

Clarence: O do not slander him, for he is kind.
First Murderer: As snow in harvest. Come, you do deceive
                          yourself.
            Tis he that sends us to destroy you here.
                          (Act I, scene iv, 236-8)

9   **from whence he went into Italy:** like many early-modern writers, Deloney regards Italy with considerable suspicion as a place of decadence, immorality and, of course, of Catholicism. Yet it was also common for such disdain to be mixed with a high degree of fascination.

13   **Elephant with stiffe joynts:** see Shakespeare's *Troilus and Cressida*: 'the elephant hath joints, but none for courtesy: his legs are legs for necessity, not for flexure' (Act II, scene iii, 114-6).

16   *stain*: disdain.

18 **shadowed with a sheet of pure Lawn:** lawn is a pure linen and 'shadowed' means veiled, so Winifred is seen as a Rose, but made pale in colour.

18 **with thy gore blood fully gorged:** 'gore' means thick, and the line finishes as it started, with rather exaggerated alliteration

20 **Runnet:** curdled milk used in the production of cheese.

20 **Mother Bumby:** in John Lyly's *Mother Bombie*, first performed in 1594, she is a 'cunning woman"; but it may have been a proverbial term for a witch.

20 **sort of shoomakers:** a group of shoemakers, but with an implied common purpose.

21 **as Saint George doth of his horse:** since Saint George is never seen without his horse, the shoemakers will equally attach themselves to the poem.

21 **Posie:** the short motto inscribed in a ring, but possibly 'poesy', as in the whole poem.

22 **Logria:** Deloney sees Logria as Kent, probably following Humphrey Llwyd's geography, although Edmund Spenser and others saw Logris as the whole country. See *The Faerie Queene*, II, x, 14.

25 **Rochester Castle:** some editions have 'Colchester' (Essex) but Rochester (Kent) would seem to fit better with the geography of the story.

29 **Christ-church:** the Cathedral Church of Canterbury.

30 **Saint Gregories Chappell:** St Gregory's Priory, Canterbury.

32 *she gives him brawn and sowse*: brawn is the pickled meat of a boar or pig and 'sowse' is usually pickled fish.

35 **biggins:** children's caps.

35 **crosse-cloths:** bands of cloth wound around the heads of babies and infants.

35   **tailclouts:** swaddling clothes.

35   **crickets, and beside that a standing-stole, and a posnet to make the child pap:** a 'cricket' is a foot-stool and a 'standing-stole' a stool used to help an infant learning to walk. A posnet is a little cup (from the French 'poçonet') and 'pap' is food especially softened for children using milk or water.

35   **By Cock and Pie, I swear:** an oath, with 'Cock' meaning 'God', and 'Pie' referring to the Roman Catholic regulations for the recognition of religious ceremonies.

36   **Wagtaile:** 'harlot'.

37   **the time of her travell:** the time of her labour, as in 'travail'.

37   **Rutupium, Aruvagus, Doris, Duur:** all these refer to Dover, as the fifth man says: Dubris was the Roman town upon which Dover was build, and Rutupium was another name for the town in the time of 'Aruiragus, King of the Britaines', according to Llwyd. Durr refers to the River Dour.

39   **as fortunate as Policrates:** Polycrates. Lawlis (see bibliography) notes that despite his reputation for piracy in the Aegean basin in the sixth century before Christ, Deloney seems to think highly of him, noting 'perhaps he has in mind Polycrates' numerous public works and patonage of the arts (Anacreon lived at his court). But in 515 B.C. he died by crucifixion at the hands of his enemies (p. 367)'.

40   **three days before the Feast of Simon and Jude:** October 25th.

42   **sent to the Conduit for water:** the fetching of water from London's numerous spring-fed sources of water was one of the tasks of the apprentices. Such 'conduits' were also places of general assembly and therefore sources of gossip.

43   **This man was the first … or as you see a cock carry his hinder feathers:** Stow notes in *A Survey of London* that 'there were in those Times three sorts of Shoes worn … one of these three sorts covered the Legs, or at least some part of the Leg, as others were for the Feet. And those perhaps for the Legs were the Huseaus, somewhat like it may be to the Buskin, or perhaps rather to the High

Shoes, which Countrymen wear in some dirty, miry Countries … the shoes, Goloshes &c. were with the Toes of an extraordinary length, and sharp … The People, especially the better Sort so affected the wearing them, that an Act was fain to be made to restrain the Length of these Pykes to a certaine Measure (Book V, p. 213)', quoted by Mann, p. 528.

47   **furred round about the skirts with the finest foynes:** 'foynes' are decorative fur trimmings, usually made from weasel fur.

49   **going betweene the two Chains:** possibly the chains that surrounded St. Paul's Churchyard.

53   **beat as a stockfish:** dried fish, beaten to make them tender.

56   **Shrivaltie:** the duties pertaining to the jurisdiction of the Sheriff of London.

61   **the Abbey of Grace on Tower Hill:** the Abbey was just to the east of Tower Hill and as it had been demolished by Deloney's time, the reference shows his knowledge of fifteenth-century London.

61   **slampam:** to give a slampam is to play a trick.

61   **bore him through the nose with a cushin:** to bore someone through the nose is to cheat them, in this case, by means of a 'cushin', or a drink.

61   **parbreaking:** vomiting.

62   **Postern Gate:** the gate to the north of the Tower where the Constable and his men were stationed.

65   **Pancake Bell:** while there is no evidence that the ringing of the bell for an apprentices' Shrove Tuesday holiday was Sir Simon Eyre's innovation, the tradition was established. Mann points out that the pancake bell was rung as late as 1795 in Newcastle.

65   **A new love Sonnet:** it is unclear whether or not the ballad verses that complete of Part I here are by Deloney. They were added to later versions and certainly do not appear in the edition dated 1599 (see Appendix).

Part II

72   **promised in the first part:** seems to support a case for the authenticity of the 1599 version which makes this kind of promise. See the 'Note on the Text', page 2 of the main text, and the Appendix.

73   **Tom Drums entertainment:** a proverbial saying which Holinshed notes is 'to bale a man in by the head, and to thrust him out by the shoulders' so that 'entertainment' is used ironically to show the treatment given an unwelcome guest. Shakespeare mentions Drum and the manner of his entertainment in *All's Well that Ends Well*.

76   **Master Cornelius of the Guard:** Mann suggests that this was a real historical figure, one Cornelius van Dun, a Yeoman of the Guard under Henry, Edward, Mary and Elizabeth Tudor.

78   **Posset:** a drink made of milk mixed with ale or wine and with added spices. It was a remedy for fever but also a nightcap (see Shakespeare's *Macbeth*, Act II, scene ii, 6).

79   **Graves-end Barge:** a reference to the daily barge service from London to Gravesend in Kent.

79   **thou shalt find me no Crinkler:** a 'crinkler' is a trickster, or one who goes back on their word

81   **he keeps all his gownes for Gillian:** implies gowns made green by love-making in the grass.

81   **Tallow cake:** congealed fat (with reference to Gillian).

83   **foule stammell:** 'stammel' is red petticoat but also a slang term for a young woman.

84   *Hippocras*: a drink of wine and herbs named after the Greek physician Hippocrates.

84   *turn it over my naile*: from a drinking ritual imported from France and mentioned by Thomas Nashe in *Pierce Penniless His Supplication to the Devil* (1592). The idea is to drink the draught in one go, leaving only a single drop that can be captured on the thumb-nail.

85   *stampe the crab*: to press the juice from crabapples, but here with a sexual connotation, as with many phrases in this story.

86   **come in my office:** the servants' area of a house, in this case the Spread Eagle Inn.

87   **pottle of wine:** half a gallon.

87   **pay tribute to Ajax:** a traditional joke based on 'jakes', a privy.

90   **Margaret jetted home:** to jet is to swagger or strut.

91   **play mum-budget:** to keep secret.

91   **a good Term:** either a reference to the legal Term or to the day that a landlord would collect rent; either way, a profitable period.

92   **braided wares:** soiled goods.

93   **a needle in a bottle of hay:** 'bottle' is from Old French 'botel', a bundle, so that this phrase is like 'a needle in a haystack'.

94   **to seeke Harts-ease, but I can find nothing but sorrel:** a nice double pun. Heartsease means a wall flower or pansy, whilst sorrel was a bitter plant used in medicines.

95   **a Cuckold as Jack Coomes:** Deloney's readers would no doubt have recognized this figure, but he is lost to history.

96   **wherefore is griefe good?:** a parody of Falstaff's soliloquy in honour in 1 Henry IV (Act V, scene i, 133-42).

100   **town of Bullen:** Henry VII captured Boulogne in 1544.

101   **pricksong:** sight-singing from the dots used in notation.

101   **pumps and pantofles:** pumps are low slippers, and pantofles high-heeled shoes.

102   **The Song of the winning of Bullen:** this might be compared to Shakespeare's account of the seige of Harfleur in *Henry V*. Henry calls upon the citizens thus:

The gates of mercy shall be all shut up,
And the fleshed soldier, rough and hard of heart,
In liberty of bloody hand shall range

With conscience wide as hell, mowing like grass
Your fresh fair virgins and your flow'ring infants.

(Act III, scene iii, 93-7)

105   **sowter:** from the Latin 'sutor', a shoemaker.

105   **watched silk thrumb hats:** 'watched' means light blue, and 'thrumbed' refers to tufts of coarse cloth.

107   **goodman flat-cap:** Stangwidge sneers at someone still wearing a once fashionable but now outdated flat cap.

107   **dudgin haft dagger:** a dagger with a boxwood hilt.

109   **quoystrels:** originally a groom, but later a generic term for a base person.

110   **Petworth:** a small town in Sussex, about fifteen miles south of Guildford.

113   **the Sarazines-head without New-gate:** a popular and large tavern.

113   **towne-Malin:** Malling, near Maidstone.

114   **Clement Carry Lye:** Deloney seems to have made up this ironic name.

115   **vermin:** see Falstaff's joke at the expense of Francis Feeble in 2 *Henry IV*, Act III, scene ii.

116   **Sir John the parish Priest:** 'Sir John' is a contemptuous generic name for a priest.

118   **blind bayard:** a blind horse, and therfore a reckless one.

120   **Kingstone:** the route taken from Petworth is through Guildford and Kingston and into London.

120   **French-men had landed in the Ile of Wight:** Holinshed records the attack on the Isle of Wight in 1545 and the fact that forces were raised in London to aid Henry VIII in his French wars.

122   **twelve silver Apostles:** spoons, with the head of each one an apostle, often given to children at baptisms.

124   **what must no man but Doctor Burket cast your water?:** a well-known procedure in Elizabethan medicine.

133   **Bridewell:** according to Stowe, this had, by 1553, become a workhouse for the poor and idle of the city.

136   **master Baltazar:** Lawlis notes that in 'using this name Deloney may be trying once again to account for a first occurrence; he seems to have a genuine historical mind, attempting always to find information about the beginnings of an industry in England or the first use of a phrase. Mann points out (p. 545) that Deloney's master Baltazar may be the Spaniard, Balthaser, perhaps the first confectioner in England' (Lawlis, p. 377).

138   **Marlins prophesie:** a reference to the magician Merlin and his accurate prophesying.

139   **the firkin Fidler of Finchlane:** 'firkin' here means 'dancing around', the word supplying a nice alliteration.

139   **the Salutation:** a tavern on the south side of Newgate Street.

142   **Worlds end:** a possible pun on the World's End tavern in Spring Gardens, Knightsbridge.

142   **Saint James faire:** the point of the joke is that there were two Saint James fairs on July 25th, one in Westminster and the other in Bristol.

143   **a huntsup:** a song or tune to wake people up in the morning.

143   **Brainford:** Brentford, about eight miles west of London and a popular place of resort for Elizabethan Londoners.

Selected Bibliography

Archer, I., *The Pursuit of Stability: Social Relations in Elizabethan London* (Cambridge: Cambridge University Press, 1991).

Baker, E., *A History of the English Novel: the Elizabethan Age and After* (London: Witherby, 1929).

Barker, S.A., "Allarme to England!": Gender and Militarism in Early Modern England' in J. Munns and P. Richards, *Gender, Power and Privilege in Early Modern England* (Edinburgh and London: Pearson, 2003), pp. 140–158.

Breight, C., *Surveillance, Militarism and Drama in the Elizabethan Era*, (Houndmill and London: Macmillan, 1996).

Chandler, W.K., 'The Sources of the Characters in *The Shoemaker's Holiday'*, *Modern Philology* 27 (1929), pp. 175–82.

Davies, W., *Idea and Act in Elizabethan Fiction* (Princeton: Princeton University Press, 1969).

Hamilton, A.C., 'Elizabethan Romance: the Example of Prose Fiction', *English Literary History* 49 (1982).

Haslasz, A., *The Marketplace of Print: Pamphlets and the Public Sphere in Early Modern England* (Cambridge: Cambridge University Press, 1997).

Hock, R.F., 'Simon the Shoemaker as an Ideal Cynic', *Greek, Roman and Byzantine Studies* 17 (1976), pp. 41–53.

Holinshed, R., *The Chronicles of England, Scotland and Ireland* (1577, enlarged 1587).

Hope, V., *My Lord Mayor: Eight Hundred Years of London's Mayoralty* (London: Weidenfeld & Nicolson, 1989).

Hutjens, L.A., *The Renaissance Cobbler: the Significance of Shoemaker and Cobbler Characters in Elizabethan Drama*, Ph.D thesis (Toronto: University of Toronto, 2004).

Jordan, C., 'The "Art of Clothing": Rôle-playing in Deloney's Fiction', *English Literary Renaissance* 11.2 (Spring 1981).

Kaplan, J.H., 'Virtue's Holiday: Thomas Dekker and Simon Eyre', *Renaissance Drama* ns 3 (1969), pp. 103–22.

Kuehn, G.W., 'Thomas Deloney: Two Notes', *Modern Language Notes* LII (1936).

Lawlis, M.E. (ed.), *Apology for the Middle Class: the Dramatic Novels of Thomas Deloney* (Bloomington, Indiana: Indian University Press, 1960).

Lawlis, M.E. (ed.), *The Novels of Thomas Deloney* (Connecticut, Westpoint Press, 1961) reprint of above.

Mann, F.O. (ed.), *The Works of Thomas Deloney* (Oxford, Oxford University Press, 1912).

McKeon, M., *Origins of the English Novel, 1600–1740* (Baltimore: Johns Hopkins University Press, 1987).

Morrow, D., 'The Entrepreneurial Spirit and "The Life of the Poore": Social Struggle in the Prose Fictions of Thomas Deloney' in *Textual Practice* 20.3 (Summer, 2006) pp. 395–418.

Novarr, D., 'Dekker's Gentle Craft and the Lord Mayor of London', *Modern Philology* 57 (1960), pp 233–39.

Pettegree, A., *Foreign Protestant Communities in Sixteenth-century London* (Oxford: Clarendon Press, 1986).

Rappaport, S., *Worlds within Worlds: Structures of Life in Sixteenth-century London* (Cambridge: Cambridge University Press, 1988).

Rich, B., *Allarme to England, foreshewing what perilles are procured when people live without regarde to Martiall Lawe* (London, 1578).

Riley, H.T. (ed. and trans), *Chronicles of the Mayors and Sheriffs of London A.D. 1188 to A.D. 1274* (London: Trübner, 1863).

Ruoff, J.E., *Macmillan's Handbook of Elizabethan and Stuart Literature* (London and Basingstoke: Macmillan, 1975).

Salzman, P., *English Prose Fiction 1558–1700* (Oxford: Oxford University Press, 1985).

Shepard, A. and Withington, P., *Communities in Early Modern England: Networks, Place, Rhetoric* (Manchester: Manchester University Press, 2000).

Simons, J., *Realistic Romance: the Prose Fiction of Thomas Deloney*, Contexts and Connections: Winchester Research Papers in the Humanities (Winchester: King Alfred's College, 1983).

Smallwood, R.L. and Wells, S. (eds), *The Shoemaker's Holiday* (Manchester, Manchester University Press, 1979).

Spufford, M., *Small Books and Pleasant Histories: Popular Fiction and its Readership in Seventeenth-century England* (London: Methuen, 1981).

Stevenson, L., *Praise and Paradox: Merchants and Craftsmen in Elizabethan Popular Literature* (Cambridge: Cambridge University Press, 1984).

Straznicky, M., 'The End(s) of Discord in *The Shoemaker's* Holiday', *Studies in English Literature 1500–1900,* 36.2 (1996), pp. 357–72.

Stowe, J., *The Chronicles of England* (1580) , reprinted as *The Annals of England* (1592).

Stowe, J., *A Survey of London* (1598), revised and enlarged in 1618 and in later editions by Anthony Munday and others.

Suzuki, M., 'The London Apprentice Riots of the 1590s and the Fiction of Thomas Deloney', *Criticism* XXXVIII: 2 (Spring, 1996), p. 181–217.

Swann, J., *Shoemaking* (Princes Risborough, Buckinghamshire: Shire, 1997).

Tazon, J.E., *The Life and Times of Thomas Stukely* (Burlington, Vermont: Ashgate, 2003).

Walter, J. and Wrightson, K., 'Death and the Social Order in Early Modern England', *Past and Present* 71 (May 1976), pp. 22–42.

Wright, L.B., *Middle-Class Culture in Elizabethan England* (Chapel Hill, North Carolina: University of North Carolina Press, 1935).

Wright, T., *The Romance of the Shoe* (London: Farncomb, 1922).

Index